P9-CPZ-735

# SMART GIRLS, GIFTED WOMEN

Barbara A. Kerr, Ph.D.

**Ohio Psychology Press**
**P.O. Box 90095**
**Dayton, Ohio 45490**

Published by Ohio Psychology Press
P.O. Box 90095, Dayton, Ohio 45490
Copyright ©1985.
Printed and bound in the United States of America.

Library of Congress Cataloging-in-Publication Data:

Kerr, Barbara A.
  Smart girls, gifted women

  Includes bibliography and index.
  1. Gifted girls—Psychology—Case studies.
  2. Gifted women—Psychology—Case studies.
  3. Achievement motivation—Case studies.
  4. Success—Case studies.    I. Title


Third Printing, 1990


BF723.G52K47  1985    155.3'33    85-29678
ISBN 0-910707-07-3

# CONTENTS

To my mother and father,
who knew a thing or two about smart girls.

Thanks to my St. Louis classmates in "Track I-A," whose personal experiences were the catalyst for this book; to my editors and publishers, Dr. James T. Webb and Henry Saeman for their confidence in and commitment to *Smart Girls, Gifted Women;* to Sherry Johnson and the team at the Word Processing Center for typing and proofing many revisions; to the staff members of the Guidance Laboratory for Gifted and Talented and the University of Nebraska-Lincoln (UN-L) Women's Resource Center who provided ideas and resources; and to my husband and colleague Chuck Claiborn for his support and interest.

# FOREWORD

It began as a simple attempt to understand why one small group of gifted girls did not fulfill the promise of their childhood. It grew into a research project, then a counseling program for gifted girls and women and now, finally, a book. Like my research, *Smart Girls, Gifted Women* begins with a class of girls identified as gifted soon after the launch of Sputnik in 1957 and uses my study of these girls — my classmates — as the starting point for exploring the lives of gifted women. The biographical studies of eminent women and scientific studies of gifted girls and women that follow shed light not only on what happened to those post-Sputnik bright girls, but also on processes that affect the development of all gifted girls and women in American society today. *Smart Girls, Gifted Women* tells of the barriers to achievement bright women encounter; and it tells how they can be helped to surmount these barriers.

Gifted girls make up one-half of what is probably the most misunderstood and neglected group in our schools today. In 1982, the award winning book, *Guiding the Gifted Child,* by James T. Webb, Ph.D., Betty Meckstroth and Stephanie Tolan created a new awareness of the plight of the gifted child. In that book, the sorry facts about our society's treatment of the gifted surfaced more clearly. Although thousands of federal dollars are spent annually on the learning disabled child, only pennies are earmarked for the gifted child. About one-half of all gifted children have never been identified. Many teachers and counselors resent gifted children, and some parents cannot cope with their precocious children's intellectual differences.

So what happens? Despite the myth that those children can make it on their own and need no special help, many become discipline problems at home and in school, suffer from depression, become underachievers and have difficulty relating to others. These problems can usually be traced to rejection by others, and the failure of schools to provide special classes, training and guidance for gifted children. Parents, too, often receive little, if any, guidance. Gifted individuals, throughout their school years, experience nagging feelings of dissatisfaction with themselves, alienation from others, and self doubt.

Gifted girls suffer from all the problems described by Dr. Webb and his coauthors as characteristic of gifted children. But there is more to their story — and that is what this book is about.

Giftedness has been defined in many ways and, in fact, has been plagued by controversy over definitions. Generally, though, gifted individuals are described as those who are in the upper 3 to 5 percent intellectually based on standardized intelligence (I.Q.) test scores. They generally predict school performance fairly well. But used alone, these I.Q. tests often fail to identify creatively gifted children and children with unusual talents; also, I.Q. tests do not seem to yield a fair measure of the abilities of children who are culturally disadvantaged or handicapped. Thus, tests for creativity and specific talents have been developed to help identify many gifted children who would otherwise remain undiscovered.

In my work with gifted children and adults, I have found test scores helpful but often unnecessary. My experience is that parents who suspect their child is gifted are correct 99 percent of the time.

The definition of giftedness in *Smart Girls, Gifted Women* is broad. It embraces exceptional academic ability and creative talent and includes a range from "high-potential" girls (the upper 25 percent on school achievement tests) to the near-genius Presidential Scholars.

Therefore, it includes almost all women who have the potential to graduate from college or whose abilities are at a similarly high level in other areas. I hope this book will be interesting to all bright women as well as to the men who care about them. And it should be helpful to all parents and grandparents of those smart girls with the potential for intellectual and creative achievement.

Traveling around the country lecturing about gifted women, I have been dismayed at the vast number of gifted women who are defensive about their lifestyles. To my surprise, the seemingly simple question, "Why don't gifted girls achieve more in their careers?" has often drawn hostile rejoinders. Occasionally, it has led to my being put in the hot seat, bombarded with angry questions. "So what's wrong with not having a career?" and "Homemaking *is* a career!" demand women who consider themselves traditional; "You're measuring women by masculine standards of achievement," and "Your value judgments about occupations are sexist," feminists cry out. I now realize that most women are feeling insecure and defensive about their lifestyle and their definitions, including me.

*Smart Girls, Gifted Women* offers a way out of this dilemma by suggesting new perspectives on achievement and careers. Research studies traditionally define achievement in terms of school grade-point averages, or occupational status and salary. Career is usually defined as income-producing employment, most often at a professional level. In describing such scientific studies in this book, traditional definitions used by previous authors are retained. But the reader will see that a different meaning for "achievement" and "career" evolves at the conclusion of *Smart Girls*. New definitions of these terms are needed, and can help gifted girls and women to understand and plan their lives more meaningfully and effectively.

By the end of *Smart Girls*, I have redefined "achievement" to mean the use of one's gifts and talents to the fullest. Achievement will come to mean being all that you can be — self-actualization, to use a popular psychology term. Achievement then is not tied to grades or salary, but to the woman's potential; not to a particular environment, because a women can operate at full tilt, and peak capacity in many settings; not to academic honors, titles, and offices, since these are by-products or signs of achievement, but are not equivalent to achievement.

In *Smart Girls,* "career" should be seen as a series of goal-directed activities that exercise a women's talents to their utmost and give meaning to her life. A career is not a job. It is a mission, a belief in fulfillment and an urge to use one's energies and talents. An important implication of this redefinition is that someone can take away your *job* — as a secretary or an attorney; but nobody can take away your *career* — whether it is the understanding of eighteenth-century literature, the search for a cure for Hodgkins disease, or advocacy for the rights of gifted children.

By understanding achievement and career in terms of maximum use of talents and self-fulfillment, women can stop defending their lifestyles against myriad criticisms and can search for those challenges that will permit fulfillment of potential.

*Smart Girls, Gifted Women* builds on theories and findings of research to create a portrait of gifted girls and women.

The first two chapters tell the story of a personally meaningful follow-up study I conducted with a group of gifted women. They were my classmates in a special program for gifted established in response to the Russian launch of Sputnik — a program designed to train the "Leaders of Tomorrow." Four patterns of development emerged in this small group: full-time homemaking, in which half of the women were employed; traditional female occupations, another quarter; dual career couples, only a few; and single professional career women, also just a few.

After exploring the reasons why these gifted women underachieved, the book takes a look into gifted women's successes. The lives of eminent women often expose more than formal research about the ways women can find fulfillment and surmount barriers to achievement.

The life stories of seven eminent women were chosen. From the experiences of Marie Curie, Eleanor Roosevelt, Georgia O'Keeffe, Margaret Mead, Gertrude Stein, Maya Angelou, and Beverly Sills, we can derive important principles for guiding gifted girls. Key among these are the importance of time alone, the effects of feeling "different" and the role of individualized instruction and childhood mentoring. Guidance and encouragement clearly are critical during difficult adolescence. Finally, the determined refusal to acknowledge limitations of gender, an ability to combine roles, a strong sense of one's personal identity, taking responsibility for oneself, and a mission in life characterize women who attain eminence in adulthood.

The next three chapters explore the major scientific studies on the girlhood, adolescence, and adult career development of gifted women. The famous long-range study on the lives of gifted individuals from childhood to old age by Lewis Terman yielded proportions of women in homemaking, traditional occupations, and professional careers surprisingly similar to proportions found in my study of my classmates. Not much difference was found in the patterns of women born in 1902 or in 1952.

Society's most highly gifted Presidential Scholars of 1964-68 were studied by Felice Kaufmann, confirming these women to be accomplished in their crafts but poorly paid. A third research project shows high-potential women lagging behind high-potential men in career achievement; marriage and childbirth prompt them to defer or drop their plans for careers. A combination of other studies highlights the problems of gifted women's lifestyles when a choice between career and marriage is forced. Two different research projects underscore that gifted women need both love and achievement; these can be integrated in a lifestyle combining family and career, but the task is neither easy nor the path self-evident.

Chapter 8 ranges beyond actual studies of gifted women. Many barriers to achievement have been described, but often have not been examined scientifically. Some barriers are external, established by societal traditions; others, often more subtle and difficult to recognize, are internal expectancies, beliefs and fears harbored by so many bright women. Several theories attempt to explain women's difficulties with achievement — the Fear of Success (or Horner Effect), the Cinderella Complex, the Imposter Phenomenon — and these are described. Paradoxically, gifted women may be at a disadvantage because they can cope so ably. Their adept coping may be more of a factor in their accepting lower status careers and salaries than any particular syndrome or complex.

*Smart Girls* would lack value if I failed to apply the lessons learned from scientific studies, observations, and the lives of eminent women. Practical programs for gifted girls are described that seem to have an impact on the problems of math anxiety, career aspirations, and self-concept barriers to success. Finally, there are specific suggestions for parents of gifted girls and gifted women themselves, including a set of guidelines for guiding gifted girls from preschool to professional school — or to wherever their sense of mission and meaning might take them.

As a psychologist, I have chosen the study of giftedness as my particular mission. My conviction is that people are happiest when they are pushing the limits of their personal potentials. Freud said the healthy individual is the one who is able to love and to work. In *Smart Girls, Gifted Women,* I want to show the limitless challenges and opportunities for bright women to work arduously, to love deeply, and to live fully.

# 1

# The Leaders of Tomorrow

I knew only two of the other girls who were to be my classmates; both had been a half-grade ahead of me at my old school. The taller (five feet at age ten) was Mary Barker, the other Gina Pasquale. I had often admired Mary on the playground because she was the best softball player in school. She also won all-city prizes in track. And *smart*! I'd seen her give accurate, instant answers to intricate math problems that other girls had spent hours huddled over in the bathroom trying desperately to solve before handing in their papers. Sometimes Mary would only help others with homework for money. She had a side that was unscrupulous and fearless, and her almost insatiable appetite for makeup and earrings required money despite her tender age. Nobody could believe her mother *allowed* her to use lipstick and wear earrings, but no one would deny that she looked good. The shirtwaist, her thick, long, blunt-cut auburn hair, the skeptical brown eyes all made her look mature and intimidatingly attractive.

Gina, standing with her, was so completely opposite in character and values that the two seemed destined to despise one another. A little overweight, heavy-featured, and curly-haired, Gina didn't care what she wore, so long as her clothes were neat. For her first day at "gifted school," her parents had given her a genuine leather briefcase in which to carry her prized books. Gina, in everybody's opinion, was some kind of genius. She did not have Mary's facile, smart-aleck intelligence. Rather, her intellect was deep, bottomless, almost weird. Information about *everything* just floated to the top of her brain whenever she needed it. She had taught herself algebra. She typed long, footnoted essays where a hand-written short composition would have sufficed. When she talked, she sounded forty years old. Mostly, Gina was reserved and distant, but quick to explode with biting comebacks. Ready to detect any insult, Gina instantly retaliated as though to protect herself from the cruelty so often showered upon homely children by their peers. She terrified me, and I looked away whenever her small, critical eyes examined me appraisingly.

Mary, always one to enjoy combat, stood with Gina that morning trying to engage her in conversation, inviting me to join in with a generous "Come on over here, Shrimp." Dutifully, as always, I obeyed Big Mary. I would rather have stayed back though, standing near another girl who had politely introduced herself as Linda Martin from Norton school.

Linda seemed nice; she talked easily to me about her poodle, Charlie. Her pixie haircut was darling — just like I wanted — and she wore a plaid jumper and new Hushpuppies, and carried a shiny red plaid satchel. Most enviable of all, she had a Barbie lunchbox, with containers and compartments for everything. That morning, she seemed to me the perfect girl — petite and neither ostentatious nor shy. She was probably really smart, but she didn't act it, and that, of course, was good. She was showing me the inside of her lunchbox when the bus came. By that time Mary and Gina were trading insults — "Jerk!" "Barbarian!" — and we all had to scramble to get aboard.

The fourth girl at the bus stop that day, I was small, anxious, and eager to please. Sometimes with others, if I knew them, I could show off a little; I could think up and write imaginative stories; I was reasonably good at school work. But looking around me on the bus that morning I felt terribly average — or even below average. As I admired

Mary's determined strength, Gina's uncanny brilliance, and Linda's neat perfection, I began to fear that the people who had scored my own entrance exams must have made an awful mistake. The bus took us out of our neighborhood, with its closely packed brick houses, into a lovely, spacious St. Louis Hills area. Our new school sat on the corner of a large park. It was a modern, one-story building with tinted windows and spotless entranceways — a far cry from the littered, gloomy schools from which we had come.

We took our seats in the fifth-grade classroom, where even our odd-looking desks were new. The teacher, Miss Mary O'Malley, was a small, square-shouldered woman with short, tightly curled red hair. I had already heard about her; the school principal had told my parents that Miss O'Malley was the best teacher in the district, and that's why she had the task of teaching the new class of gifted students. Even the teachers had to take intelligence tests, parents were told, and Miss O'Malley had scored very high.

Miss O'Malley introduced herself and then asked us to do the same. There were thirty of us, fifteen boys and fifteen girls. I was surprised to see how tall most of my classmates were. All were white except for one Japanese-American girl, and most wore new and stylish clothes. Several boys wore ties. We came from eight different elementary schools in St. Louis, and almost every one of us knew at least one other person. The impulse to sit near acquaintances was already defeated by a seating system devised by the teacher and based on some as-yet-unknown principle.

After introductions, Miss O'Malley said, "Now, I expect that you will get to know one another at recess; there will be little time for socializing in the classroom. Today we are going to plunge right into our studies and then have a little talk at the end of the day. You will all be accelerated by at least one grade, some of you by a grade-and-a-half or two because we are confident of your ability to perform at a higher level than your peers. In addition to studying most subjects a year earlier than you normally would, you will be trained in special subjects you did not have at your old school: French, pre-algebra, rapid reading, and choral reading. You will have more homework than you have ever had before, an average of three hours each week night, with two nights' homework on the weekends. You will have to work very, very hard, and I will accept no excuses other than illness for unfinished homework. If you receive failing grades on your tests and do not perform your homework well, you will be removed from these classes and sent back to your original school. While you are here, you will sit in rows according to your academic performance; we will rearrange the seating every two weeks to reflect changes in your test scores and your oral recitation. Now we will pass out the books."

In a state of mute anxiety, I received my books and carefully wrote my name in pencil on the inside cover as directed. First, an English book. It was just the regular sixth-grade text — spelling and vocabulary — and I'd already seen it and thought it wasn't too hard. This was my best subject, and it would be fun not to be bored. Then came the geography book: Europe and the Middle East. Wait a minute, I thought. What about South America and Africa, which were done in fourth and fifth grade? Wasn't I going to study them? How was I supposed to know about those countries if I just skipped over them? Would I have to catch up by getting books from the library? Before I could even clearly form this question, the math book appeared. Figuring square roots! Again I cringed. I hadn't even got through the long division! How as I going to learn this? By the time an abacus was circulated (for figuring math?) along with a French book filled with line drawings and assorted gibberish, my heart had sunk completely.

The morning's lessons began. First English, and an assignment to analyze and diagram twenty-five sentences. Next math and twenty-five review problems. Then French, and a different teacher. Madame Bem, a huge young woman with tiny curls bounded into the room, exclaiming "Bonjour, mes enfants! Je suis enchantée de faire votre connaissance. Nous parlons seulement Francais, et pas de tout Anglais!" My relief at having an hour with a teacher who seemed considerably warmer and kinder than Miss O'Malley was tempered by the fact that Madame Bem refused to speak any English whatsoever. We had to guess that she was greeting us, that she was asking our names, and that we were supposed to reply. I hurriedly wrote on a card the phonetic pronunciation of what we were being asked to say — "Ju mop pell Barbara" — and waited for my turn to struggle with the strange sounds and to be corrected — gently but repeatedly.

After the French lesson, we were released to go to lunch. The cafeteria was new and sterile smelling. I missed the mixed smells of tennis shoes, baloney, and old cork floors. I wanted to stay with the few girls I knew, but Mary gulped down her food, grabbed a baseball bat and ball and left to organize a quick game; Gina had brought one of her books and just scowled at me when I tried to start a conversation; Linda went to sit with several other girls who all had very neat lunchboxes and pretty dresses. So I spent that first lunch hour observing the girls and boys with whom I would spend the next eight years — if I made it.

The boys seemed more confident and less intimidated by the new school than did the girls. In fact, the morning's lessons clearly caused some real anxiety for several girls. Molly was nauseated, and Christy kept wetting the ends of her long hair in her mouth and then twisting them in knots. Little Kathy Nakomura's fingers trembled in concentration over her work. Even dauntless Mary twisted her mouth in resentment as assignments were piled on. At lunch the girls who knew one another whispered about the morning in tense tones of indignation and puzzlement. The boys, however, were very lively and excited, and not at all preoccupied with the morning's events. It seemed to me that they ought to be showing some effects other than boisterous delight after such a miserably difficult beginning. Could it be that they somehow liked the challenge? Could the same events that caused self-doubt among girls actually spur the boys on to self-confirming competitiveness?

After lunch we had "choral reading," during which we recited poetry in unison and with exaggerated precise pronunciation and inflection. "Hot cross buns," we chanted vigorously, and "bells, bells, bells, bells, bells, bells, bells . . ." we repeated emphatically. It was strange, but not difficult. After choral reading, a Mr. Peel took over the class for the art lesson. He lectured about tapestries and instructed us to create on paper a design for an attractive tapestry. We labored with our colored pencils; he strolled among us. When we had finished, he examined each drawing and then flamboyantly tore several in half, exclaiming that they were too "symmetrical" and that those kinds of designs quickly became boring. He was intensely and vocally critical of most of our work; nearly all of us had to redesign our tapestry at least once. What might have been a pleasant lesson was soured by his cutting remarks. It seemed that he came down hardest on Linda: "Boring! Ordinary! You've simply copied your neighbor, haven't you?" Then he quickly turned and profusely praised Richard's underwater scene, and went so far as to laugh at Eddie's "Aliens Eating Their Lunch," and to pat him on the back. "Good idea. Try to be neater."

For our last lesson that day, we had another guest teacher, a "reading specialist" introduced as Mrs. Coffey. She told us that President Kennedy was a rapid reader, that he could read five newspapers in the time most people took to read one. Scientists, she said, needed to read great numbers of books and articles just to find a few needed facts; rapid reading was a necessity. She then introduced her tachistoscope, or pacer — a projector that showed one phrase or sentence at a time in succession with a control allowing her to vary the speed. She said she wanted to get our basal reading rate by setting the pacer faster and faster. She told us to read as fast as we could and to raise our hands when we could no longer read the sentences. The sentences would tell a story, and our comprehension would be tested afterwards. We started at 150 words per minute, which seemed rather unnatural and crawly. Nobody raised a hand, but when the speed increased to 250 words per minute a few hands went up, followed by more hands with each change in speed. I dropped out soon, no longer able even to think of bluffing my way through the coming quiz. Faster and faster the words flew on the screen, till at last, at some eerie pace like 750 words per minute, Gina put up her hand with an air of sullen resignation. This exercise ended the coursework for the day. Miss O'Malley reviewed for us our assignments for the next day, and then gave us The Little Talk.

"Boys and girls, for many of you this has been the most difficult school day you've ever had. You will have many more difficult days. In two years you will be doing high school work; in tenth grade you will be doing college work. By the time you are in college, you will be able to take advanced courses that will help you to enter your careers.

"You were chosen for this program because you are gifted. What does being gifted mean? It does not just mean that you scored a 140 + I.Q. It means that each of you has a special gift — yes, a gift from God — of intelligence. Because it is a gift, you must use it well. You must use it to serve your country. For many years the Russians have been training their young people in science and mathematics. Now they are ahead of us because of their gifted young scientists; they were able to achieve space flight before we did. The free world must catch up with the communists. To do this, we need many fine scientists and leaders. You must study very hard, not for yourselves, but for your family, your school, and your country.

You will have the best books, the best teachers, the most up-to-date curricula — in short, the finest education our country can provide. In return you are asked to give your best efforts, and to commit yourself completely to your education. You are the hope of our nation and the pride of our schools. You are the leaders of tomorrow."

The boys beamed. The girls looked at their folded hands and were embarrassed.

Eighteen years later, soon after I had taken my first position as an assistant professor of educational psychology, I received an invitation to our high school reunion. It was to include the students from our special classes from fifth grade on as well as another group of gifted students who had joined us in high school. Although I had lost track of my classmates after high school graduation, rumors did reach me: Mandy and Debbie "had to get married" soon after high school graduation, I heard. The fate of a "shotgun wedding," I also learned, befell Jessie, but no baby turned up after her unexpected marriage. So at least three of the fifteen girls were married in their teens. To my knowledge, none of the boys had married so young. Word had it that my old boyfriend Eddie was a doctor and that Mike was a lawyer. Jerry had followed his brilliant brother into the foreign service. As for Mary and Gina, I didn't quite believe the things I heard — something about Mary's sanity, and something else about Gina leaving her Ivy League school after an "unhappy experience."

Even though I might already have spotted a pattern in these rumored events, I didn't. I was saddened and worried by some, and amused by others. My overwhelming feeling about the reunion was embarrassment. I felt almost certain that the majority of my gifted classmates would be scientists and leaders of their communities. After all, such was the goal of our training.

By this time, I knew that our education had been an exemplary one. Generally, only about one-third of gifted children receive any special programming. And only a small minority of teachers of the gifted actually have training in gifted education. Many gifted programs are no more than a few hours a week of "enrichment activities," which are often not very challenging. Our program had been the rare exception: one that provided a full-time series of challenging academic activities led by trained educators of the gifted. Given my awareness of the special nature of my school, I was ashamed to have entered the "soft" science of psychology. Compared to the lofty careers I imagined for my classmates, psychology seemed frivolous. So with some trepidation, I decided to accept the invitation, and prepared to make the best of it.

The reunion was in the same hotel that we'd rented for our senior prom; then, it had been a high school student's idea of elegance. Now, ten years later, it seemed corny and tacky, a "Starlite Dome" penthouse lounge with too much atomic age decor. The summer night was hot, and the air conditioning didn't work. The place was packed; my class-mates — "Track I-A" students, expanded in high school by the addition of students from other districts — were 44 of this class of 630. About two-thirds of the class had returned for the reunion, and my gifted group was well represented.

At the door I was greeted by the organizers, all three members of my group: Eddie the doctor, Mike the lawyer, and Jeff, now a well-to-do businessman. Replying warmly to each in turn I said that "Yes, I was married; I was a psychologist; my husband was a psychologist; no, no children yet." Then, clutching the reunion booklet titled "Where Are They Now?" I was swept up in a wave of vaguely familiar faces.

In that sea of acquaintances, I found my old friends. First I saw Linda. She was seated at a banquet table, and I could see that she was pregnant. She wore a lacy, pastel maternity blouse; her hair was held loosely back by pink ribbons. She blushed and patted her tummy frequently. Surrounded by other women who seemed, from their ges-tures, to be comparing pregnancies, she was as popular as ever. As I went over, I recognized those around her: Kathy, the math wizard; Molly, who'd been the high school newspaper editor as well as a talented singer; and Sherry, a timid and nervous perfectionist who had excelled in French and had taken private Chinese lessons. I spoke to Linda, and received a pleased squeal of recognition. "How are you? As you can see, I'm expecting! What about you?" "No, not yet," I said. "Well! Kathy has *two* kids — a boy and a girl — and Molly has a little girl, and Sherry *thinks* she's expecting." At this everyone laughed. I said that I certainly hoped to have children, but that I had wanted to wait until I was established in my career. "Well, don't wait too long! Hey — sit with us!" I sat down.

It was not the conversation I had expected, though on reflection, I found it normal enough. In fact, that was the problem. It was quite normal. I consulted my booklet under each name. Linda Ackerman: first-grade teader, retiring now to have a baby, married to Marty Kellerman. Kathy Brown: high school math teacher for the Army, married to Bob Worcester, an Army aerospace engineer (oh, no, I groaned, she married *him*). Molly Schuster: degree in journalism from University of Missouri, not working at the present time, married to Rick Hanowitz. Sherry Speth: homemaker and volunteer, married to Nick Martin, director of Christian Youth Choir. The entries were not at all what I had expected of gifted women.

The sight of a tall figure approaching in a flowing white evening gown interrupted my reading. Big Mary had crossed over to my table. "Kerr, a bunch of us want to talk to you." I excused myself and followed her to some overstuffed chairs in the bar where most of my old volleyball team members were seated. Big, strong, eager girls, they had hung around with Mary throughout high school.

"Kerr, we have a question for you. You're a psychologist, right?"

"Right — uh — "

"OK. Well, *I'm* currently trying to get employed — hard to get a good job when you've been through what I have. Jeri clerks at the bank. Lori is a nurse. Nan — what are you doing? Oh yeah, she's back in the community college. OK. What I want to know is this: Why aren't we the leaders of tomorrow?"

"Well — I don't know — there's sexism, discrimination . . ."

"No, that's not what I mean. I want to know, if we're so smart, why didn't wonderful things happen to us? We want you to find out." Suddenly, Gina was there, too, fixing me in my tracks with her intelligent eyes. "Mary's right. You're a psychologist; you should be able to study us. You could find out if the I.Q. scores and all the business about our bright futures was just garbage."

"Well, that's not my area of research — "

Mary almost shouted, "Kerr — make it your area, OK? Look at us! You think it's not important that we're a bunch of has-beens at age

29? Find out what happened."

Now, from fifth grade on, I had always done what Big Mary told me to do! This time was no exception.

After the reunion, I went back to the University of Nebraska educational psychology department and changed my area of research to the career development of gifted and talented. I began to read as many books and articles as I could find in the field of guiding the gifted. Several post-Sputnik books particularly helped me understand the basic nature of giftedness and the role of gifted education, including Paul Torrance's *Gifted Children in the Classroom* (1965) and *Guiding Creative Talent* (1962), and John Curtis Gowan's *The Education and Guidance of the Ablest* (1964). Several newer books pointed to an awakening interest in the social, emotional, and career concerns of gifted children. Barbara Clark's *Growing Up Gifted* (1979) gave clear insights into the meaning of giftedness to the child and to society. Nicholas Colangelo's and Ronald Zaffran's *New Voices in Counseling the Gifted* (1979) brought together the viewpoints of many new psychologists and educators on the guidance needs of the gifted. Lynn Fox (1976; 1979; 1981) at John Hopkins University was writing many articles and books on mathematically precocious girls. A symposium at John Hopkins University chaired by Julian Stanley resulted in a book reviewing the history and current work of gifted education in *The Gifted and the Creative: A Fifty Year Perspective* (Stanley, George, and Solano, 1977). Later, *Guiding the Gifted Child*, by Webb, Meckstroth, and Tolan (1982), was to set out for the first time, with simplicity and clarity, the major problems of gifted children along with specific strategies parents and teachers could use to help these children.

These recent books showed that after a decade and a half of neglect, gifted children are at last receiving some attention from the helping professions. Most of the authors are emphatic on this point: that the gifted child will not always "get by" without guidance. Intelligence alone doesn't guarantee a life of smooth sailing. Many authors describe the conflicts gifted children experience as a result of unrealistic expectations of others or of themselves. Others delve into the peer relations and social isolation of the gifted child and explore the many strategies gifted children use to cope with their differences. All of the authors deplore the lack of knowledge about the complexities of the development of the gifted child, and all plead for more research to help in understanding these complexities.

Now that I had reviewed books and articles on gifted students generally, I began the long process of reviewing the literature on gifted women, a process that turned out to be unexpectedly difficult. I wanted not only to learn about what had happened to my classmates, but also to contribute new knowledge through research. Within a month of the reunion, I had designed and mailed a questionnaire to each of the female graduates of my high school's 1969 Accelerated Learning Program.

To work with the career development issues affecting gifted young women, I created the Guidance Laboratory for Gifted and Talented at the University of Nebraska. Here, my staff and I could counsel and provide career guidance to over 300 adolescents each school year. While learning of their plans and dreams, we could observe their progress toward achievement. We compared girls' and boys' reactions to counselors' questions, and devised interventions that would encourage girls and boys equally in their aspirations. More recently, we extended the program to counseling adults, enabling us to study striking differences in the career development of gifted women and gifted men.

This book has come from five years of research and practice in the area of gifted girls and women. In these pages, I have distilled my understanding of what happened to these little girls who years ago were waiting at the bus stop in St. Louis, heading for the "gifted school" in the distant neighborhood to become the "Leaders of Tomorrow." Here, too, are my admonitions, suggestions, and pleas for those parents and grandparents, teachers and counselors to prevent shelved hopes and dampened dreams in yet another generation of smart girls.

# Bibliography

Clark, B. *Growing Up Gifted.* Charles E. Merrill, Columbus, Oh., 1979.

Colangelo, N., and Zaffran, T. T., Eds. *New Voices in Counseling the Gifted.* Dubuque, Iowa: Kendall/Hunt, 1979.

Fox, L. H.; Brody, L.; and Tobin, D. *Women and Mathematics: The Impact of Early Intervention Programs Upon Course-Taking and Attitudes in High School.* Baltimore: Intellectually Gifted Child Study Group, John Hopkins University (ERIC Document Reproduction Service No. Ed 188 88), 1979.

Fox, L. H.; "Career Education for Gifted Preadolescents." *Gifted Child Quarterly* 20: 262-273. (ERIC No. EJ 151 429), 1976a.

Fox, L. H.; Tobin, D.; and Brody, L. "Career development of gifted and talented women." *Journal of Career Education* 7: 289-298, 1981.

Gowan, J. C., and Demos, G. D. *The Education and Guidance of the Ablest.* Springfield, Ill.: Charles C. Thomas, 1964.

Stanley, J. C.; George, W. C.; and Solano, C. H. *The Gifted and the Creative: A Fifty-Year Perspective.* Baltimore: The John Hopkins University Press, 1970.

Torrance, E. P. *Guiding Creative Talent.* Englewood Cliffs, N.J.: Prentice Hall, 1962.

Torrance, E. P. *Gifted Children in the Classroom.* New York: Macmillan, 1965.

Webb, J. T.; Meckstroth, E. A.; and Tolan, S. S. *Guiding the Gifted Child: A Practical Source for Parents and Teachers.* Columbus: Ohio Psychology Publishing, 1982.

Dr. Lynn Fox, Professor of Education at Johns Hopkins Evening College, author of many articles on gifted girls and gifted girls' math achievement, has this to say about her mission and her concerns about attitudes toward math:

I took math education as an undergraduate and did my student teaching in junior high. After a masters in education I moved to Washington, D.C. with my husband where I worked at the National Center for Educational Statistics. I became involved with the Task Force on Women.

In 1971, Julian Stanley needed two doctoral assistants at the study for mathematically precocious youth; my background in math education led to that job. It was clear that there were fewer girls in the high-scoring range for math achievement tests. Also, fewer girls wanted to be accelerated. I thought it was related to junior high dynamics — it wasn't O.K. to be good in math.

We needed to reinforce a positive image of females in math.

So, we began an all-girls algebra class for mathematically talented girls. Usually in algebra classes, a few girls would huddle in the back. We wanted to create a more social atmosphere. In our special class, we had female role models and we emphasized the usefulness of math to society.

We found it was important to invite parents of gifted girls to special programs: their attitudes toward girls and math matter.

I just do not want to accept the idea that women are less able in math — this is so distressing to me as a person! I don't attack the biological studies of differences between males and females. But I believe in my heart — I feel so strongly that women are not getting the support they need to achieve in mathematics. This is why in 1980 I wrote *The Mathematical Mystique*.

People keep telling girls they are equal to boys and forcing them to compete with them in math. But women have such a long history of negative attitudes from others and discouragement that this isn't fair. Girls may need special support for math achievement.

I want to continue my research in this area — maybe a survey of professional women, of stress points. One of the reasons for my being able to achieve as much as I have is that I have an incredibly supportive and pushy husband! So, these kinds of factors need to be considered in studying women's achievement.

# 2

# Looking for the
# Leaders of Tomorrow

Developing a fifteen-minute questionnaire that would illuminate eighteen years of career development and personal adjustment is no easy task. The questionnaire ultimately sent from the newly established Guidance Laboratory for Gifted and Talented contained only ten carefully selected questions, but plenty of writing space (see fig. 1). Certain demographics were important: college attended, marital/family status, current location, and employment. More importantly, though, we wanted to know how these gifted women saw themselves, their development, career goals, attainments, and life satisfactions.

To start with, I wanted to understand how parents reacted to their daughter's identification as gifted, so I asked "What did your parents tell you about participation in the Accelerated Learning Program?" The teachers in the students' original schools surely influenced the girls' perceptions of their giftedness, so I asked "What did your teachers tell you?"

Memory records our life experiences inaccurately; we recall the joys of childhood, but tend to alter actual events — as do our parents — to fit with current world view and self-concept. We all mend and polish our past. Each of us seems to carry around a "Story of My Life" that can be narrated as a fairly coherent series of events linked by recurring themes. Every psychotherapist knows that this story, this world view, profoundly affects how we behave on a daily basis and how we make decisions. In fact, our current perceptions of our life events, more than the events themselves, shape actions and reactions. Knowing this, I constructed my questions to reveal how my classmates explained to themselves what being gifted had meant to them.

To find out how the women thought their career goals had been shaped, I asked "What were your career or life goals at graduation from eighth grade, from high school, and from college?" and "What is your current career goal?" and added extra space for explanations.

---

What did your parents tell you about participation in the Accelerated Learning Program?

What did your teachers tell you?

What were your career goals at
.... graduation from eighth grade?
.... graduation from high school?
.... graduation from college?

What is your current career goal?

How has your marriage history affected your career goals?

How has the birth of children affected your career goals?

What positive effects did the Accelerated Learning Program have on your life?

What negative effects did the Accelerated Learning Program have on your life?

In order to qualify for the Accelerated Learning Program, you scored in the upper 5 percent on I.Q. tests and achievement tests, a category generally referred to as "gifted." How do you feel about this label? What impact, if any, has this label had on you?

Are you happy?

What would you change, if anything, if you had to live your life over again?

---

**Fig. 1. The Nebraska Survey of "Sputnik School" Gifted Women**

Career development studies tell us that specific career goals for average students change from junior high to senior high to college, but become stable after about age sixteen. Gifted students show less stability in their interest patterns, and experts have attributed this to their multipotentiality — their ability to select and develop any number of career goals (Sanborn et al., 1976). Confronted with an abundance of options, gifted students may vacillate and dabble, fearing to commit themselves to one career. I suspected that the career development of gifted girls might be even more complex, reflecting indecision and abrupt change uncharacteristic of their male peers.

Hoping not to "lead the witness" too much, I asked "How has your marriage history affected your career goals?" and "How has the birth of children affected your career goals?" Marriage and childbirth traditionally have a major impact on a woman's career development, far more than they do for men.

How had their special education in gifted school affected them? We asked straightforwardly "What positive effects did the Accelerated Learning Program have on your life?" and "What negative effects?"

Surely their rigorous education made a difference in the lives of these women, leading to lifestyles shaped by their intensive elementary and secondary education. Thus, noting that every student in the Accelerated Learning Program was required to score in the upper 5 percent on I.Q. and achievement tests, the questionnaire probed, "How do you feel about this 'gifted' label, and what impact, if any, has this label had on you?"

Finally, we asked about life satisfaction: "Are you happy?" "What would you change, if anything, if you had to live your life over again?"

In developing a survey for my women classmates, I had no intention of generalizing the results to all gifted women. I was only interested in this group of gifted women — women who had experienced a "model" education and who had graduated from high school at the beginning of the upsurge of feminism. *I wanted to know why superb schooling in the late 1950s and the heightened awareness of women's potential in the late 1960s did not produce women of greater accomplishment.* I mailed twenty-five surveys and received eighteen in return; four other classmates were briefly interviewed by phone, and partial information was gleaned from reunion booklets on two more. These replies, I felt, would explain the surprising career and life development of my classmates. I did not know that it would later become evident that the patterns displayed by my gifted friends appeared again and again in other studies of gifted women.

The content of the survey responses was fascinating, though at first I enjoyed simply reading for style and format. Half the women wrote long accompanying letters. Most interview responses were quite lengthy; clearly our questions had stimulated significant reflection.

The responses were not only long, they were complex. Feelings were explored frankly; the answers made it plain that the survey itself was leading to new awarenesses. There were intuitive explanations of the motivations of self and others. My one-time classmates eloquently discussed value issues, constructing both sides of a particular conflict fairly and thoroughly, then working through to some statement of resolution. All responses displayed extraordinary literacy and sharp, discerning wit. The style of the survey responses confirmed that the promise of youth was fulfilled, at least in the sense that this bright group of females had matured into articulate, psychologically sophisticated, knowledgeable members of society. The accompanying letters made delightful reading. As I read them over and over, I pictured the little girls I had known, now grown into thoughtful, fascinating women. Their responses typified the manner of expression of leaders and thinkers. The actual content of the surveys, therefore, was all the more surprising.

## Basic Facts

Six of the twenty-four women who gave information about their education had not earned their bachelor's degrees by age twenty-nine.

Twelve had received only bachelor's degrees; half of these were in education. Three had earned master's degrees (one in zoology, one

| Women | | Men | |
|---|---|---|---|
| Highest Degree | Career Status | Highest Degree | Career Status |
| J.D. Law | Lawyer | J.D. | Attorney |
| M.D. | Physician | Ph.D. | Ethnobotanist |
| M.S. Zoology | Homemaker | Ph.D. | Chemical |
| M.A. Education | School teacher | | engineer |
| M.A. Dentistry | Grad. assistant | M.D. | Physician |
| M.A. History | Teaching | J.D. | Lawyer |
| | assistant | M.H.A. | Hospital |
| B.S. English | Homemaker | | administrator |
| B.S. Education | School teacher | M.S. Eng. | Engineer |
| B.S. Education | Homemaker | | manager |
| B.Mus. Music | Homemaker | B.S. + B.A. | CPA |
| B.A. Business | Account | B.A. | Personnel |
| | representative | | officer |
| B.A. Education | School teacher | B.S. | Actuary |
| B.A. | Insurance agent | B.B.A. | Manager |
| B.A. Journalism | Homemaker | B.S. | Electrical |
| B.S. Education | Homemaker | | engineer |
| B.A. Education | School teacher | B.A. | Cellist |
| B.S. Med | Physician's | B.B.A. | Business |
| Technology | assistant | B.A. | News |
| H.S. | Homemaker/clerk | | director |
| H.S. | Dental assistant | | |
| H.S. | Craftsperson | | |
| H.S. | Auditor | | |
| H.S. + L.P.N. | Homemaker | | |
| H.S. | Craftsperson | | |

(One respondent omitted educational data.)

Fig. 2. **Educational and Career Attainments of Students in the Accelerated Learning Program**

in education, one in pre-dentistry). Among us were one with a medical degree and one with a law degree.

Basic information on fifteen of the twenty men who had graduated from the Accelerated Learning Program that year allowed us to compare educational attainment. All had received at least their bachelor's degrees. In addition, these men held three master's degrees (two MBA's and one in anthropology), two Ph.D.s (botany and chemical engineering), two J.D.s, and one M.D. The educational attainment of these men was clearly superior to that of their female classmates.

The trend of less achievement for women became more pronounced as we examined information about current occupational status. The largest number of women were "homemakers." Eight of the twenty-four women were at home, usually with children. Four were employed as nurses or medical technicians, and four as teachers. Two listed "craftsperson" and "arts and crafts" as their occupations. Two were graduate assistants. Representing the higher degrees, one was a practicing physician, one a lawyer, and two were businesswomen.

In contrast, all of the men were in professional or semiprofessional occupations. Figure 2 shows six business/management personnel, three engineers, two lawyers, one doctor, one news director, one musician (cellist) and one ethnobotanist. None was unemployed.

Over half of the men and women had stayed fairly close to home or had returned to St. Louis. Fourteen of the twenty-four women were then married, eight were single, and two were divorced. Of the fifteen men, eleven were married, and the other four had never been married.

## Denial of Giftedness

A particularly curious finding of our survey was that most of the women preferred to deny that they were gifted or special in any way. Though identified amid much publicity as gifted, and schooled for years in classes and tracks clearly labeled as being for the gifted, these women still repudiated the label.

"I have never really believed I was gifted," said Linda. "I think it was all a mistake!"

The more scholarly approach of a teacher with some advanced training in testing and measurement was "It's a well-known fact that I.Q. tests are inappropriate measures of intelligence; they mean nothing."

Another said "I don't believe in treating intelligent children differently — neither did my parents."

"I can't remember any big 'to do.'"

Several seemed simply to have ignored or forgotten: "I guess I've never thought much about it." "I forgot about the label." "I don't think I've ever known what 'gifted' meant, and so I didn't pay much attention."

One acknowledged a certain fear: "You know, I think I was so afraid of the idea of being gifted that as soon as I got away from that crowd by attending college, I felt very relieved, as if the pressure was off and I could just be normal."

The most ironic response came from a woman who said "I do *not* feel different; my life is, to my knowledge, materially and emotionally unaffected [by giftedness]." She went on, however, to lament that "[Gifted classes] enabled me to skip an introductory class or two in college. But I also skipped classical literature . . . somehow I never read Homer, a lack which I feel deeply." I wondered as I read this, how many "average women" (as she claimed to be) feel deeply the lack of Homer.

What caused this cheerful insistence on normality that I kept seeing? Is it truly forbidden in polite society to speak of one's own intelligence? Is giftedness so taboo in such a society that the same woman who boasts of running five miles a day would not dream of disclosing how many books she could read, how fluent she might be in a foreign language, or how extensive might be her knowledge of genetics. Our survey, however, was private and confidential, and no public disclosures were to be feared; besides, the fact of our education was no secret among *us*. Of what use was it to prove to me that it had all been a mistake? As a psychologist, I was familiar with the clinical defenses of rationalization ("Gifted people accomplish great things. I've accomplished very little. Therefore, I must not be gifted after all!") and of denial ("I don't feel *anything*! I'm *not* angry about this! I'm *happy*!"). But I was not dealing with a group of neurotics. For the most part, these were psychologically healthy women, and these kinds of defenses seemed incongruous with their otherwise penetrating and comprehensive self-analyses.

## A Conspiracy of Silence

One clue to the denial of these women emerged in the responses to the question: "What did your parents tell you?" It seems that parents either told their little girls nothing at all about their giftedness or felt a strong need to put them in their places. Most of the answers to "What did your par;ents tell you?" were similar:

"Nothing."

"Funny, I can't remember them saying anything."

"Absolutely nothing."

"They told me not to get a big head."

"They reminded me that I was just lucky and that this was nothing to brag about."

"I think they were worried I would become conceited — and the fact that my brother had not been identified as gifted made it hard to talk at home about my special school."

The last of these responses suddenly made me aware of the conflict of feelings parents must have felt: first, pride that their child was somehow special, a child of superior intelligence; then, puzzlement: What did this mean? What were Mom and Dad supposed to do about it? Did this mean special treatment — in a family where all the kids till now had received equal treatment? Certainly not! What if she came to *expect* special opportunities? What if we couldn't provide them? She would just have to learn that she's not so special. That she'd better not "get a big head" — and so on. At first, I imagined that this part was the same for gifted girls and gifted boys. Eventually, the differences become clear. Perhaps the little girls had acquiesced, and the boys hadn't. Whatever the reason, the girls had come to agree with their parents and to share their denial of special talents. All this may be related to the long-recognized observation that girls are more obedient and more compliant with parental attitudes throughout childhood and adolescence than are boys. The girls perceived quickly that an attitude of humility, or at least indifference to "special treatment," was the best means of securing parental approval, that most powerful reward of childhood. Whatever the reason, the adult women had largely come to agree with Mom and Dad that being gifted was definitely *not OK*.

## Lowered Sights

The process that began in childhood of "learning one's place" continued, as could be seen by the lowering of aspirations over time. The average elementary school girl has already experienced the sex role stereotypes of her society. When asked what she wants to be when she grows up, she typically replies "nurse," "teacher," or "mother." This was *not* true, even in 1960, for these gifted girls. According to their memories of what they had wanted to be, the eighth-grade girls of the Accelerated Program included in their number an aspiring paleontologist, lawyer, doctor, "traveler," and writer, two would-be scientists, and only a sprinkling of nurses (one) and teachers (two).

By twelfth grade, four girls had firmed and narrowed their ideas. One scientist saw herself as an electrical engineer. The other scientist now wanted to be a physician. A nurse had changed her career goal to "vocal performance." Another's aspiration had changed from "start a career in international relations and help the revolution!" to "get a boyfriend!" All the rest except one who maintained an interest in teaching had become "don't know" by high school graduation. Most respondents were emphatic about their confusion at the time they graduated from high school: "I really had no idea what to do with my life." "Now I was an adult! What was I supposed to do?" "I was very uncertain."

Five years after high-school graduation, what were the goals of these gifted women? In fact, they hardly held career goals. Curiously, those who did, displayed only vague, compromised goals that lacked direction.

"I had fallen into accounting . . ."

"Teaching, but maybe marriage . . ."

"To help others or to serve God."

"My husband I were completely uprooted. My school goals were confused and undefined."

"Just to be happy."

". . . seemingly stuck in a no-win situation — always having to work at whatever job I was qualified for (with one year of college credits, to earn the most money I could get to survive)."

"Get over a traumatic love affair so I could finish my thesis."

By this time five years after high-school graduation, half of the college graduates planned to teach (usually wherever their husbands might be located). A few were on their way to other, well-paid, high-status professions: one had entered medical school, one an engineering graduate program, and one a law school.

Ten years after high school graduation, four were teaching, four were nurses and technicians, and eight were unemployed outside the home.

The trend was clear: Career goals were juggled, lost, confused, compromised, or downgraded, and only rarely pursued in a determined, progressive way.

## Adjustment to "Reality"

One would think that individuals who had found it necessary to change aspirations radically and compromise goals dramatically would feel at least some dissatisfaction. The following sad, self-aware comment I thought would be typical:

> ... My main gripe was that I was 'special' then; but becoming a mediocrity in the real world was a disappointment. It's taken me this long to come out of the rock bottom pits from that reunion. I knew many of my friends and acquaintances would be doing great things with their lives (I never have). I can't be too hard on the [Accelerated Learning] program. The lack of career counseling really left me wanting. I was armed with lots of knowledge, good grades, recommendations, and prestige, yet my parents' example of 'life is' (that is, that life is something to be grudgingly endured if you're not sleeping or escaping) overpowered the option of doing something constructive with this real opportunity to change the impending fate. It also sealed my failure complex since I didn't become anything near a physicist or a senator.

This response, however, was one of only two ambivalent replies to the questions about happiness. It was accompanied by a wry and poignant letter, describing the struggle to learn and to understand the nature and meaning of the writer's failure to live up to expectations from self and others. It had the ring of truth, and I heard it. It was from Big Mary. The other ambivalent response was from Gina.

> Am I happy? This is tough. I think I have much more fury and anger than happiness in my life. . . . This last broken engagement wracked me so that I find it difficult to write about. I want to get a hold of my life, you know, take charge and go to find what *I* want. . . . Somehow, those classes never taught me failure or how to accept being second or how to gracefully admit defeat. . . .

Gina, too, was struggling with the conflicts between her goals and the expectations of others — especially of men.

The disappointment and bewilderment in Mary's and Gina's letters were understandable responses to events in their lives. Schooled to believe that great accomplishment was inevitable, they found after graduation that the real expectations were for a successful marriage and acceptance of the kind of career goals that would not interfere with a timely wedding. Caught between their earlier dreams and the pressure of finding a man, they had ended up, at least for awhile, dissatisfied with both their achievements and their relationships. In the responses of the other women to questions about happiness, disappointment, at most, was muted. Apparently, most of them were very happy with their life patterns. At first, I was puzzled. If the majority of these gifted women were unemployed or underemployed according to normal standards for men, why were they so happy? Why were the complaints of lost dreams and unrealized potential so few and so feeble?

The answer lies in the crucial, elementary fact about gifted individuals that has emerged from research on gifted individuals: *Gifted people are generally well-adjusted* (Terman and Oden, 1935). As children they are happier, healthier, and more socially adept than are other children. As adolescents they are more fun-loving, more popular, and more athletic than others are. As adults they are content, integrated, and easy to please. It would seem logical to conclude that the gifted woman's tendency to be well-adjusted makes her cheerful despite underemployment, that she is free of resentments toward people who openly or unwittingly discouraged her or failed to encourage her to achieve her full potential, and that she endures personal heartbreak with a smile or a shrug. She has a long history of being a "good girl." Most gifted girls are well-behaved in class and helpful at home, and they are praised for this. Gifted young women in high school are usually congratulated for being sensible but "sweet."

They continue to be rewarded for their sociability and good humor long after peers, parents, and even professors have lost interest in their academic achievement. Being well-adjusted in a society in which women are expected to achieve less than men, in which marriage and child raising are viewed as major accomplishments demands calm adjustment, and the gifted woman complies. Also, because she is psychologically hardier than her "average" peers, the gifted woman may deal creatively with conflicts between her original goals and societal expectations and is, therefore, less likely to complain about her lifestyle than is the average woman. Only those gifted women whose coping skills have not been adequate, or who have encountered extraordinary barriers and humiliations — like Mary and Gina — will cry out in anger that *something is wrong.* The others generally will continue, at least through young adulthood, to adjust to life as it is.

## Patterns of Adjustment

Although the group of gifted women I had surveyed and interviewed was small, four distinct patterns of adjusting to giftedness emerged from my repeated readings of their statements. With some hesitation, I have labeled these patterns, recognizing their superficiality, but feeling nonetheless that insights into behaviors that shape lifestyles emerge from the categorizations: Happy Homemaker, Disposable-Career Woman, Lone Achiever, and Dual-Career Coupler.

### The Happy Homemaker

At twenty-nine, she is married and has two children; she stays at home and she likes it. She resents those who say that homemaking isn't work, because she has made a full-time job of it. She knows her skills as a homemaker are crucial to her husband's success. She understands his career and what he needs to do to rise higher on the professional ladder. She helps him with reports and presentations, revising, typing, and even rehearsing with him. She entertains his associates and gets to know their spouses because she understands the importance of the informal social network to his future.

Her children are the best-dressed and best-behaved children in the neighborhood. Their Halloween costumes are the most original and the most carefully sewn; their Valentines are handmade and charming. She reads child development books to help her plan appropriate experiences for her children. She takes their education seriously, helping with their homework and planning activities to reinforce their learning.

She tries to be a gourmet cook and a brilliant decorator. She has created in her home a beautiful and lively environment. She is proud of what she has accomplished, and knows that her money sense and planning made it possible for her and her family to have all this.

Sometimes she worries about a life without her husband, or how she will adjust when her children are grown. She has given so much to others that she isn't very good at giving to herself. She sometimes thinks she could have done more, and she is aware that she may not be realizing her full intellectual potential. She knows that life is full of compromises, however, and that she chose this life — and so she decides to be happy.

## The Disposable-Career Woman[1]

At twenty-nine years of age she has just dropped out, is about to drop out, or has just returned (temporarily perhaps) to her job as teacher, nurse, or office worker. Problems of identity are nagging her (just who is she anyway — ex-teacher, homemaker, ex-homemaker?), but she thinks she has found a lifestyle that allows her to have a limited career, yet accompany her husband and leave her job when he and the children require it. She would stay home with the children, at least until they begin school, and would excel as a mother and homemaker (becoming a happy homemaker) if the family could afford it. Her husband's career is more important than her own — implicit inasmuch as his education was completed first, or they moved to his first job site. When she is working, she takes her job very seriously. As a teacher she is superb, planning her curricula and trying out techniques she reads about in education literature. She may be bored with her mediocre colleagues, but she hides it. As a nurse or medical technician, she dislikes being under a doctor's or dentist's authoritarian thumb, but she is proud of her profession and aware of its importance to

[1] I want to thank my graduate assistant, Jan Deeds, for her creation of this term and the concept behind it.

medicine, and she works hard to improve her position and the status of her profession. As an office worker, she is ambitious, even a perfectionist, rising quickly to leadership positions such as office manager or executive secretary. She is often bored with other office workers, but maintains pleasant relations nonetheless and tries to enliven a dull environment with her creativity. She's not sure what the future holds for her because she is unsure whether she will have more children and how her husband's job changes will affect her.

## The Lone Achiever

Approaching thirty, she is about 90 percent sure that she wants to remain single and commit herself to her profession. She has her first professional job or is nearing it, and she loves being at last in the work for which she has trained so long. She has never found a man she could love, one as intelligent as she, and she can't imagine loving a man less intelligent. Or she has tried a relationship with someone less intelligent or less ambitious, and it just didn't work out. She's beginning to be pessimistic about relationships with men, because even casual liaisons seem to lead to one or both partners feeling threatened by the other. On the other hand, she has established a warm and loving community of friends who care about her as a person and respect her as a professional. If she can maintain these close friendships, she feels she has the support system to carry her through life. She is a dedicated professional who believes that medicine, law, research, or business management is a twenty-four-hour-a-day, seven-day-a-week commitment.

## The Dual-Career Coupler

She is twenty-nine years old and exhausted but happy most of the time. She and her husband are both professionals who take their careers seriously. They may be colleagues in the same profession, in which case no clear line divides their relationship at work and from their relationship at home, or they may be in different professions but know quite a bit about what the other does, since work furnishes a major topic of conversation. They are tired most of time, not only because they are workaholics but also because they are trying to share all the household tasks. If they don't have children, they wonder how they will survive when they do. If they do have children, they have learned quickly to employ competent household help and have made loving, enriched child care their top budget priority. Their schedules are so tight and planned so far in advance that an unexpected work-related trip or a child's illness can throw their entire lives into temporary chaos.

Because tenure tracks and promotion ladders wait for no one, or because her patients/clients desperately need her, she can take only minimal time out to have a baby, a few weeks perhaps. Then she is left even more physically tired than she was before her child was born, and if she is breast feeding she is rueful that biology has temporarily made equality impossible in the division of labor. She wants to be the best mother possible as well as a successful professional. Some people think she is trying to do too much, but she feels she must do all that she is capable of doing.

In figures 3-6 are quotations that seem to fit my classmates in each of the four categories. Some are cliches; some are novel insights. All display a diversity of values and opinions that characterize today's gifted women.

These four patterns occur frequently and are unmistakable. Yet at least two other patterns are missing.

The first invariably draws notice. It is a married lifestyle in which the woman is the primary breadwinner and/or has the stronger career orientation, while the husband stays in the home caring for the children. None of the gifted women in my survey was engaged in this lifestyle.

A second pattern, even more unusual, involves a "self-actualized" lifestyle. First described by Abraham Maslow (1967), it represents the person whose career has fully blossomed, often in a unique or self created way. Self-actualized people care little for external evalua-

I am happy being a homemaker because:

I can put my "gifts" to use
being the best wife and
mother possible.

I am going to raise gifted
children!

I'm *not really gifted.*

Scripture tells me I belong in
the home, serving my husband.

It's more fun!

My husband is gifted and needs
a talented wife to support him.

My children's need for a mother
at home is more important than
my selfish need for a career.

I can accomplish just as much
through volunteer work.

I could never get a job up to
my abilities in this economy
anyway.

**Fig. 3. The Happy Homemaker**

tion — that is, other people's opinions of their worth as workers or
human beings. They are totally absorbed in the process of living, in
creating meaning in their lives through their work and involvement
with humanity.

Intellectually gifted people would seem to be the most apt candidates
for self-actualization. Although some of my classmates may have been

---

**I want to be a (teacher, nurse, office worker) because:**

I can go wherever my husband goes.

Our society needs gifted
teachers now more than ever.

I don't have to invest a lot of
time and money in an education.

I can quit anytime I want to.

I don't mind not being in the
spotlight as long as I can make a
contribution.

I want a career, but I don't want
to compete with my husband.

I don't think I have what it
takes to get a higher degree.

I can go back to [teaching,
nursing, office work] after my
children are grown.

---

**Fig. 4. The Disposable-Career Woman**

laying the groundwork for this lifestyle, none had yet attained the
autonomy, intensity, or creativity of the self-actualized lifestyle. Yet I
believe that all of my classmates, men and women, had the potential
for this full flowering of talents. Many of the women in this group had
learned to deny their gifts in the same way others denied them; they
had learned to lower their sights and to adjust to "reality." Guidance
for these women had been inferior or nonexistent. In most cases, no

---

**I'm happy being single and career-oriented because:**

Even though I get lonely,
I'm doing something meaningful.

                                                    I haven't found a man who could
deal with my success.

I'm not ready to involve myself
in marriage or family until I'm
established in my profession.

                                                    I haven't found a man who
is my intellectual equal.

I've decided that my friends
provide all the support I
need for my lifestyle.

                                                    My career requires that I
commit myself to it full time.

My career involves a great deal
of travel.

**Fig. 5. The Lone Achiever**

adult had affirmed the gifts of these women, raised their aspirations, or challenged them to attempt self-actualization.

Having learned a little about the failure of gifted girls, I thought I needed to understand more about what facts leads to personal success. I found much of it in the biographies of eminent, gifted women. Summaries of seven of their lives, how they achieved self-actualization and career success form the next chapter.

34

---

**I'm happy in a dual career couple/family because:**

Even though I'm exhausted sometimes, my life has great meaning.

I feel like I have it all.

I enjoy having a husband who is
also an intellectual companion.

I don't believe I could be
a good wife/mother if I
gave up my career.

I invested a lot in my education,
and don't want to waste that
investment by dropping out.

Even though it's very hard to have
good jobs for both of us, we always
*try* to treat our careers equally
seriously.

I believe we can find competent,
loving child-care for the time we
must be away from our children.

**Fig. 6. The Dual-Career Coupler**

## Bibliography

Maslow, A. H. *Motivation and Personality*. New York: Harper, 1954.

Sanborn, M. P.; Engels, D. W.; Pfleger, L. R.; and Rodenstein, J. M. "Career Education of Gifted and Talented Boys and Girls." Madison, Wisc.: Research and Guidance Laboratory, University of Wisconsin (ERIC Document Reproduction Service No. ED 148 077), 1976.

Terman, L. M. and Oden, M. H. "The Promise of Youth." *Genetic Studies of Genius*, Vol. 3, Stanford, Calif.: Stanford University Press, 1935.

# 3

# Eminent Women

Despite countless barriers that have kept many gifted women from rising to their peak, some do not stumble and fall. Why? Why is it that a few gifted women do accomplish extraordinary feats? And how does a gifted woman become an eminent woman?

To learn about the background, characteristics, and experiences of gifted women who reached the top, I used the approach available to me: that of case or biographical study. A true empirical approach would be founded on research that begins by drawing a random sample of eminent women, then tests them on a variety of objective measures, and finally questions them by means of standardized interview schedules. Such research was outside the scope of my endeavors and has not been done by anyone else (Albert, 1983). Until it is, case studies provide the only resource for understanding what makes achieving women extraordinary and how they overcame barriers they faced.

I examined the biographies of thirty-one eminent women, selecting a group whose lives spanned from the middle nineteenth century to the present, and who represented the wide varieties of lifestyles chosen by gifted, eminent women.

To read them is to be overwhelmed by the unique power of brilliant women to create new directions in art, science, literature, politics, music. Of these thirty-one biographies, only seven are excerpted here as capturing common themes and powerful, substantive tenets. A complete list of the thirty-one women appears at the end of the chapter.

## The Women

### Marie Curie: Scientist

Marie Curie, youngest of five children, was born as Marya Sklodovska in Warsaw, Poland in 1867 to two hard-working, loving school teachers, suffering with friends and other family members in constant resistance to the tyranny of Russia. Marie's parents were well trained in the pedagogy of the day and perhaps because of that were frightened by their daughter's precocity. Having learned her alphabet by playing with her older sister, she was reading well at four. She also had an extraordinary memory, remembering clearly at age four events that had happened several years before, and was fascinated by her father's physics apparatus. Marie's childhood was marred by tragedy. Her mother was slowly dying of tuberculosis and her father's economic status declined steadily because he refused to be subservient to Russian authorities and because he became involved in a naive and unfortunate financial speculation. Marie's closest, oldest sister died of typhoid when she was nine. Marie had a gift for total concentration and, throughout these dark days, continued to perform remarkably at school. When she read, she was oblivious to everything else, much to her family's amusement.

After her mother died in 1878, Marie's father took over the care of the children as best he could. All four children were brilliant; the family's life centered on intellectual activity, with every member teaching or attending school. It seemed natural to this family to want to know everything about chemistry and physics, to speak five languages, and to read Greek and Latin. Reading aloud was the main family entertainment.

Marie believed as a girl of seventeen that service to Poland was more important than marriage or personal ambition and that the best way to serve her people was to educate the poor so that they could not be easily tyrannized. She joined the Floating University, an underground community of Polish scholars dedicated to educating individuals beyond high school so that they could go on to teach others. She carried on her work quietly and remained independent despite the strong ideologies of her companions. When she became dissatisfied with the intellectual progress she and her siblings were fashioning in their makeshift academic environment, she made a deal with her older sister: Marie would get a permanent, well-paying job as a governess to put Bronya through medical school; then they would reverse roles.

Marie's first job as a governess was miserable, with a selfish, bourgeois family who rejected her when she and the elder son fell in love. The family refused to allow them to marry, and forced Marie into humiliation. Marie felt buried alive in this household, but nonetheless continued to read and study voraciously — physics, philosophy, literature and whatever else she could find. She wrote often to her family and longed for home in Warsaw.

After three years, her exile was over. She returned to her father and the Floating University; she was excited and happy to have a tiny laboratory, obtained through a friend. Working in her free time, evenings, and Sundays, she reproduced her great experiments in chemistry and physics. During this time, she was once again disappointed by her former love's timidity; although they were still in love, he was still afraid to marry her against his parents' will. She broke with him and made the decision to pursue the university education that her sister, now a doctor in Paris, wished to help her with at the Sorbonne.

At the Sorbonne, Marie eagerly began to pursue knowledge. Living on a few francs a day, she nearly starved to death, not only because she was poor (increased by her desire to live alone in a quiet room rather than in her sister's noisy house) but also because she frequently forgot to eat, studying constantly. She often fainted from weakness, and had to be revived by friends and family who tried vainly to get her to take better care of herself. Her extraordinary academic performance — and encouragement from a friend — led to a scholarship that rescued her from further starving for the sake of money for her studies. Marie had determined never to marry after her first disappointment. However, when she met physicist Pierre Curie at a friend's house she knew that this man could fulfill her great intellectual and emotional needs. They fell very much in love and were nearly inseparable during their years together. Pierre Curie was a renowned scientist in the area of crystallography; but when Marie proposed for her doctoral research to investigate the newly discovered phenomenon of emissions from certain minerals (later to be named by them "radiation"), he threw himself wholeheartedly into helping her with her projects.

Over their years of collaboration, they discovered polonium and radium, revolutionizing the whole periodic chart; revealed the effects of radium on cancer; and changed the direction of science through their theoretical and experimental work in atomic physics and chemistry. The couple received the highest awards of the scientific community, including the Nobel Prize.

They had two children whom they adored. From all reports, Marie Curie found a way to be an excellent, devoted mother while continuing her established level of intensity in her work. She hired nurses and helpers who lightened many tasks while freeing her to nurture the children's emotional and intellectual growth. Pierre shared in child care as he shared in Marie's scientific work.

Pierre's tragic and sudden death in a traffic accident changed Marie Curie's personality forever. She was disconsolate and emotionally weakened; she became withdrawn and almost unreachable to any but her dearest friends and family. In Pierre, she had lost not only a husband but a major source of fulfillment for her intense intellectual hunger. Ironically, Marie achieved worldwide fame during this tragic time. She was plagued with callers, letters, and demands for her time. Her shyness and sadness made public appearances grievously painful, but she consented to a tour of America in return for an offer of a gram of radium for her laboratory (radium was the most expensive material in existence). This trip weakened her physically and spiritually, and she gradually sank into ill health, although she continued her work. At the time of her death, she was still attempting to complete an experiment.

## Gertrude Stein: Writer

Gertrude Stein was born youngest of five children in 1874 to Amelia Stein, a homemaker, and Daniel Stein, who owned a wholesale wool business with his brother. After quarreling with his brother, Daniel Stein took the family to Vienna; he soon returned to the U.S., leaving his family to move to Paris. Gertrude went to kindergarten there, learning to speak French at age four. In time, Daniel brought his family back to America, where they lived briefly in Baltimore with Amelia's Orthodox Jewish parents before relocating in San Francisco. In San Francisco, Daniel had a high-paying job with the cable car company, enabling his family to live in a large house with servants. Gertrude had governesses and special lessons.

By first grade, Gertrude was more interested in reading and nature than in school. After their mother became stricken with cancer, Gertrude and her beloved brother, Leo, spent most of their free time in the library, then walking and talking about what they had read. Their father, who had always been nervous and unsettled, became even more difficult to live with because he was now forced to run the household; so Gertrude and Leo spent a great deal of time away from home. After Amelia's death, when Gertrude was fourteen, Daniel became tyrannical and disorganized. His death, three years later, was not overly upsetting to Gertrude.

Gertrude's elder brother, Michael, who was doing well in business, took over the support of his younger brothers and sisters. He also supported Gertrude's and Leo's love of literature and theater, and sent them to Radcliffe and Harvard, respectively, to pursue their academic goals.

At Radcliffe, Gertrude dressed her short figure in odd dark clothes and a funny hat and immersed herself in a world of ideas at neighboring Harvard. She studied with the great philosophers George Santanyana and Josiah Royce and was considered the best student of early psychologist Hugo Munsterberg; psychology was especially appealing to Gertrude because through it she was able to study thought, consciousness, and language. She was fascinated by automatic writing, and experimented with herself, her close friend Leon Solomon, and then hundreds of subjects. William James, pragmatic philosopher and psychologist, stimulated her intellectually as no other scholar before, and with him she studied language and what is now called "altered states of consciousness" and engaged in many heated discussions. By ordinary standards, she was a careless writer, her thoughts and emotions rushing ahead of structure in most of her work.

In college, Gertrude had an active social life; with her wit and infectious laughter, she made friends easily. She went to galleries, opera, and theater and participated in boat rides and picnics. Upon graduation she knew she wanted to be famous, but she didn't know *how* she wanted to get there.

She tried medical school at Johns Hopkins, satisfying her affinity for science and responding to the challenge of being one of the first women medical students. She lost interest quickly, however, in this technical field and performed poorly. To her, boredom was worse than anything, and she left medical school to go to Europe with Leo, returning only briefly to do brain research, and then going back to Italy and England. Always during her travels, she visited museums and read in all the great libraries of the world.

Back in New York, she decided that she would be a writer, and began her first novel. For a year she worked on the novel in New York and then moved to Paris to 27 rue de Fleuris, an address she would make famous. It was in the heart of the artists' and writers' district, where a renaissance of creativity was taking place. Here in Paris, where she had always been comfortable, she began her career as a writer and as an arbiter of taste in the arts.

She finished her first novel, but did not wish to publish it; she had proved to herself that she could write a novel, and that was enough. She and Leo began to collect art for their apartment from among the works of new, extraordinarily talented painters. They understood the impact of Cezanne's talent long before anyone else did, and they helped the penniless Matisse by paying him the price he deserved for his works.

In 1905, Gertrude met Pablo Picasso and began a lifelong friendship; she championed the cause of his movement, Cubism, and advertised his genius to all who would listen. His remarkable portrait of her was created over three months during which she posed for him.

After finishing her novel, Gertrude translated several of Flaubert's works and wrote three short stories, seeking to accomplish in writing what the modern painters were doing in art: the creation a new form, with rhythms mirroring real life and with each element as important as the others. While some friends were enthusiastic, publishers were not; in fact, they didn't understand at all what she was trying to do. Even the "vanity press" that agreed to publish her works for a fee had great misgivings about her unusual phrasing and odd use of punctuation.

She began an extraordinary novel, *The Making of Americans* (1925), which told the history of one family as the prototype of all families, written in her new, repetitious rhythmic style. During the writing of this novel, she met Alice B. Toklas at a party. Alice was immediately struck by Gertrude's genius and was greatly attracted to her. Howard Greenfield, one of Gertrude Stein's biographers, says that "Gertrude needed someone to believe in her, and Alice needed someone in whom to believe." They became constant companions, and Alice moved in with Gertrude and Leo. Alice typed Gertrude's manuscript, helped arrange her schedule, and ran the household. Gertrude and Alice came to love each other deeply and lived as lifelong partners. In 1925 Gertrude completed *The Making of Americans* and some brilliant "portraits" in writing; then she traveled in Spain and Italy. She wrote the "portrait" of Mabel Dodge, a wealthy patron of the arts, while she visited her in Italy. Mabel had it printed and sent it to 300 people who generally responded they believed Gertrude had gone crazy. Her brother, Leo, simply thought she had no talent; he had also apparently grown indifferent to her in general, and she no longer needed his closeness now that she had Alice. He moved out and they divided their great art collection amicably.

Gertrude's fame grew even though she had not yet been officially published. Her salon was always filled with the great artists, writers, and thinkers of the day. Mabel Dodge promoted her and John Lane agreed to publish her *Three Lives*, the short stories she had written about three women.

During World War I, Gertrude and Alice worked for the war effort, driving supplies and opening supply depots. American servicemen loved her although they did not know who she was. After the war, the homeless and disaffected writers that Gertrude labeled "The Lost Generation" found hospitality and encouragement from her. Sherwood Anderson was encouraged by her, and in turn praised her as a great, original American woman. She helped Ernest Hemingway, reading his manuscripts and offering critique. They became intimate friends, he shared his deepest concerns with her, and she and Alice were god-mothers for his son. Eventually, however, they had a quarrel that ended their intimate relationship but began a rather unusual, widely-publicized feud that was to last throughout their lifetimes. Hemingway seemed not to be able to accept Gertrude and Alice's lesbianism. F. Scott Fitzgerald, however, whom Hemingway had introduced to Gertrude, became her great friend and also benefited from her criticism and encouragement. During this period, Gertrude published in small magazines and lectured; for a long time, however, she did not receive the fame for her work that her proteges did.

In 1932, she wrote her first book that could be easily read by the public. It received fairly wide distribution. She wrote the humorous account of her and Alice B. Toklas's lives, in *The Autobiography of Alice*

*B. Toklas,* and it was serialized in the *Atlantic Monthly.* It was a huge success, and her publishing obscurity was over.

She collaborated with Virgil Thomson on an opera called *Four Saints in Three Acts,* which opened in combination with a Picasso show and was so popular that extra cars had to be added to the train to Hartford where it played. She lectured across America, charmed reporters, and was entertained at the White House. Everywhere people were surprised that the avant-garde writer was a warm, witty woman who could explain perfectly well how she composed her book.

She and Alice now had a large country house in Belignin, in France, as well as a new apartment in the city. When World War II came, they went to live in the country house, oblivious to the danger they were in as American Jews. Their French neighbors protected them, however, and even the German soldiers quartered in her house did not know who she was. When the American Army invaded France, she was overjoyed, and returned to Paris to open her home to American soldiers. She lectured at American bases in Belgium and Germany, where she was always received warmly.

In 1936 Gertrude became ill with cancer. She died a short time later, with the first copy of her loving narrative of American soldiers, *Brewsie and Willie,* in her possession, and Alice B. Toklas at her side.

## Eleanor Roosevelt: Human Rights Activist

Eleanor Roosevelt was born in 1884 to an affluent New York family. From the first, she was considered an "ugly duckling"; her mother subtly communicated to Eleanor her displeasure in having a child so little resembling the beauties of the family and concentrated her attention on her two younger brothers. However, Eleanor's father, Elliott, favored her, and she loved him as deeply as only a lonely, sensitive child can love. When he was at home, they were inseparable.

Eleanor's happy relationship with him was not to last, however. He had a severe drinking problem, and the family sent him away. When Eleanor was eight her mother and brother Elliott died suddenly of diphtheria. From then on, she lived with her grandmother, where her father could visit occasionally. She read and spent her time in a world of her own, without friends or loving family. She was alone and frightened most of the time.

When, at ten, she learned of her father's death, she was desolate and unbelieving. As an adolescent she could not overcome her sadness and her feelings of not belonging. She was educated poorly but expensively for much of her childhood, finally being sent to a French school in England headed by a Mademoiselle Souvestre, a talented educator and enlightened, opinionated woman. Here at last Eleanor was able to catch up on what had been a spotty education.

Back in New York after three years, she felt suffocated by the necessity of "coming out" in a New York society that terrified her. Yet, she had been raised to be completely submissive to the rituals of society and knew no other life than one in which one's material needs were completely tended by others and in which a woman had no responsibilities other than to visit and be visited. She was kept completely ignorant of relationships or marriage.

After her coming out, she saw her cousin Franklin frequently; when he asked her to marry him, she agreed because it was the thing to do. He seemed to recognize the strength, honesty, and ability in her that she did not yet recognize in herself.

They were married in 1905; her uncle, President Theodore Roosevelt, gave the bride away. After the honeymoon, they lived in homes prepared and arranged by Franklin's mother. Eleanor now became completely dependent on her mother-in-law for all decisions — and wondered why she was often unhappy in this situation.

For ten years, Eleanor was either expecting children or recovering from childbirth. She was a conventional society matron during this period. Her husband advanced from his law practice to political activities to government service. When he became assistant secretary of the Navy, Eleanor accepted the burden of social responsibilities, and she forced herself to participate in the daily round of visits that seemed so necessary.

World War I changed her life. Suddenly all women were expected to be part of the war effort. Volunteering in a canteen in Washington, Eleanor learned that hard work agreed with her. She also learned that she could be effective in changing some of the conditions that forced people to live in suffering. She was galvanized by a visit to the federal insane asylum; the sight of demented men wandering about unattended and uncared for provoked her to work for better conditions. She persuaded the Secretary of the Interior to work in Congress for appropriations and encouraged charitable organizations to fund improvements for the hospital.

It was this experience that created a new woman of Eleanor Roosevelt. Even when the war was over, her life as a socialite was finished. Her life as an agent of social responsibility had begun.

The sudden affliction of infantile paralysis in Franklin, crippling his legs for life, also signaled great change. Eleanor was forced to become a well organized and autonomous planner for the family. His mother wanted Franklin to retire to life in her home as an invalid, but Eleanor fought against this, establishing her first independence from her mother-in-law. She herself became active in politics partly to reinvigorate her husband. She persuaded him to run successfully for the office of New York governor. After the crash of the stock market and through the deepening depression, she and FDR increased their national political activity, believing that there were jobs to be done.

When he became president, Franklin D. Roosevelt provided political solutions to problems besetting the nation; Eleanor provided personal solutions. She rode cross-country to see poverty and despair with her own eyes and to bring hope. Whether she spoke to women garment workers, coal miners, or jobless veterans, she listened and talked to Americans about their concerns. She was tireless and ubiquitous. Eleanor Roosevelt had lost all fear, it seemed. She dared to work for change in areas where even her husband held back, such as civil rights for blacks and freedom for interned Japanese Americans. She was not afraid to be seen speaking with Communist youth groups, because she wanted to hear their views, and she wanted to give them hers.

When Hitler's power grew, she decided she needed a keen understanding of the crisis in Europe. Using her contacts, she became an astute observer, advising and supporting her husband with unique talent. Her understanding of political events was matched by her unique charisma. She used her powers to persuade the American people of the horrors of fascism and nazism. Dictators hated this honest and outspoken woman who, like Thomas Jefferson, despised "all tyranny over the minds of men" — whether that tyranny was right or left wing, ally or nonally.

During the war she traveled 25,000 miles in the Pacific theater visiting soldiers at bases and hospitals. When her husband died before the end of the war, she imagined that her opportunity to be of service was finished; to the reporters after FDR's funeral she said, "The story is over."

But it was indeed not over. For the next fifteen years until the end of her life, she acted, says Archibald MacLeish, as "the conscience of the nation."

President Truman appointed Eleanor ambassador to the United Nations. To the surprise of many, herself included, she elevated this assignment into a crowning achievement. She fought avidly for the rights of refugees the world over. She insisted that the United States uphold the right of the state of Israel to exist. She chaired the United Nations Commission on Human Rights, developing and attaining passage of the Universal Declaration of Human Rights. This document has become the foundation for individual freedom around the world, and has shamed tyrants everywhere.

She later said that her autobiography might show how much a woman "of no great talents" can achieve if she can overcome timidity and fear.

Margaret Mead: Anthropologist

Margaret Mead was born in 1901 to a "very advanced mother" who was a sociologist working on her Ph. D. and a father who was a professor in the Wharton School of Finance and Commerce at the University of Pennsylvania. She grew up in an academic environment, playing in her father's office and listening to constant talk about university politics. Her mother interrupted her graduate work to raise Margaret, her brother, and her two sisters. Her mother's child-raising was loving but by the book; lacking imagination, she simply provided the proper food, home, activities, and education and remained very involved in the many liberal causes that typified New England Unitarians like herself.

Margaret's father was somewhat of a rascal, although Margaret claimed she was always a match for him. He was interested in the concrete side of economics, and liked to be involved in financial schemes and watch economics in action. He was often short of funds, and seldom honest about it. His many minor eccentric rebellions irritated Margaret, but drew out the best in her; she claims it was he who taught her how to think like a scholar. He was flippant about her major life decisions, but in the long run supportive. He tried to prevent her from going to college by saying she would only get married anyway (the real reason was his lack of money); but when she graduated from college, he was proud of her and the Phi Beta Kappa status she had achieved. He tried to prevent her from marrying her first husband by offering her a trip around the world; she married anyway, and he still sent her around the world later — to Samoa, where she was able to do her first great work.

Throughout her childhood, the family moved around; Margaret learned that a home was wherever you made it. As a child she was never dressed in a typically feminine way and was allowed to engage in far more adventurous play than was her frail brother. Her elementary education was mostly carried out by her paternal grandmother, a superbly intelligent woman who rose to be a teacher and principal in a time when few women worked. Margaret claimed that this self-assured, creative, independent woman was a decisive influence in her life. She noted that the two women she grew up with were both mothers and professional women; so she never felt that brains were unsuitable in women. Margaret was an independent scholar from childhood, reading and writing much of the time and managing easily to pass the achievement tests to enter high school. Although she felt different in high school, because of her unusual family and education she made a strong and successful effort to adapt.

At De Pauw University, however, the rigid sorority system excluded Margaret — for being a New Englander, an intellectual, and a non-Evangelical Christian, and for not having the right clothes. Here she had experienced her first feelings of rejection. The pain of being an outcast also had a positive effect: In this comparatively mild way, she learned first-hand about underlying racism, religious hatred, and all forms of elitism. She fought back, taking the leadership positions she could and making the best of the situation until she could leave after a year for the more congenial environment of Barnard.

Margaret also had learned at De Pauw that she preferred a same-sex rather than coed education; she had experienced the conflicts women feel in competition with men and expressed her experience in this straightforward manner: "This made me feel that coeducation was thoroughly unattractive. I neither wanted to do bad work in order to make myself attractive to boys nor did I want them to dislike me for doing good work." At Barnard, Margaret found the intellectual opportunities she had hungered for and a gifted and warmly affectionate group of students with whom to live. She exchanged poetry with her friends, organized seminars on burning issues of the day, became interested in the social sciences and was fascinated by anthropology. Ruth Benedict, assistant to Professor Franz Boas (together they gave birth to the field of anthropology), offered her "the opportunity to do work that *matters*," and she chose anthropology as her life's work.

Throughout college, Margaret had been engaged to Luther Cressman, a young man five years her senior and a friend of her adolescence, who intended to be a minister. She and Luther married (an egalitarian marriage, in which she kept her own last name) and they went through graduate school together, she in anthropology and psychology and he in sociology.

When her dissertation was completed, she wanted to do her field work immediately, and Luther had graduate work to do in Europe. Boas persuaded Margaret to do her work on adolescence, and she persuaded Luther to allow her to go to Samoa. At the time, Samoa seemed far too distant and dangerous for a lone woman, but Margaret insisted that she could manage.

She did manage; she threw herself into her work, investigating how the Samoans dealt with adolescence in the female. She was "adopted" by a chief and his family. She invented new techniques in the field and was stimulated by her findings.

Her meeting with New Zealand psychologist Reo Fortune, on the boat returning home, came at a time when Margaret was filled with the excitement of her discoveries and Reo with that of his work in psychology. Fascinated with each other's ideas, and thrown together for dinner by the ship's steward, they fell in love. She returned to Luther, however, and thought over her relationships.

Margaret had learned from her doctor that there was a strong chance she could not have children. She had chosen her first husband because he would be a good father. Reo, on the other hand, would be a better colleague. Since she would be devoting her life to her work, she reasoned, it would be better to be married to Reo. This pragmatic decision seems to have sat well enough with Luther, and so they parted.

She and Reo married; Reo redirected his interest to anthropology; and they arranged their separate sources of scientific grants to allow them to do field work in New Guinea together. Meanwhile, Margaret's first work, *Coming of Age in Samoa,* was a popular as well as scholarly success, and she had been hired as curator for anthropology at the American Museum of National History in New York City, where between field trips, she enjoyed seeking new objects and rearranging collections. Her next book, *Growing up in New Guinea,* was also a success.

She and Reo went on to study sex roles in culture with the Arapesh and Mundamagor; however they found the work unsatisfying in that their major questions were not being answered. The marriage was also beginning to be strained by such problems as Reo's lack of sympathy for Margaret during the fevers that anthropologists in the tropics must endure. After she had spent a difficult time in the field, her meeting with anthropologist Gregory Bateson, in the New Guinea village in which he was working, was another turning point for Margaret Mead. The ideas she and Gregory developed on sex and temperament furnished the theoretical bridge she had been seeking in understanding problems of similarities in behavioral patterns across cultures. Again, intellectual excitement seems to have led to love for her.

She and Reo divorced, and she and Gregory went to Java to work in Bali together. Here they performed comprehensive work using new technology that formed a basis for much current field work.

Margaret Mead changed her mind about children after her marriage to Bateson, largely as a reaction to the negative effects she saw in cultures that rejected children. She was determined to have a child in spite of physical risk and miscarriages and, at last, was successful. She had to fight for the right to natural childbirth, to breastfeed and to be with her child more often than the rigid hospital schedule allowed, but her perseverance won out and she was able to have her baby her way.

This daughter, born late in Margaret's life, was to be her only child, but she treasured her role as a mother and found little difficulty in continuing her work as well. For thirty more years, Margaret continued to produce new anthropological findings from the field and to improve the collections of the American Museum of Natural History. Her name became a household word; she was much in demand for public appearances because she was able to communicate so easily the pleasure to be found in understanding other cultures. She popularized anthropology, and she helped create a deep understanding of the commonalities in development, temperament, and relationships that bind human beings together.

## Georgia O'Keeffe: Painter

Georgia O'Keeffe was born a second child in what was to be a family of seven children, in 1887 in Sun Prairie, Wisconsin, to an Irish father and Hungarian mother. Her mother loved books and had wanted to be a doctor; her father farmed a large piece of land, ran a dairy, and raised livestock. Perhaps predictably, Georgia retained a visual memory of the first time she was taken outside. As a child, she had a great deal of freedom, had a make-believe house of her own invention, and wandered happily through the countryside. Her mother took a strong interest in her children's mental development, reading them the classics and arranging for private art lessons, but was otherwise somewhat aloof. Georgia herself seemed sometimes to draw back from others, preferring to play by herself. She liked being different, and refused to dress or act like her sisters or other little girls. She loved to play with her father, who was more affectionate and lively than was her mother.

Georgia entered school early and was recognized as an intelligent and curious child. She asked questions constantly. She was always being admonished for having "crazy notions." Later she was to say that "I decided that the only thing I could do that was nobody else's business was to paint." She was completely confident that she could do anything she wanted and was not ashamed to be a female — as a girl, she even insisted that she *knew* that God was female.

At fourteen she was sent for a year to a very exclusive girls' school, Sacred Heart Academy, in Madison. Although it was very restrictive, Georgia adjusted because it gave her intellectual and cultural stimulation. She performed well (better in her other subjects than in art) and later also excelled at Madison High School. It was from an art teacher there that she learned that she could paint.

When her family moved to Virginia, she was content to go along.

There the Wisconsin family was not easily accepted, but Georgia did not seem to be bothered. She was enrolled in an excellent boarding school for girls featuring a modern education rather than "finishing." She was admired by the other students for the extraordinary plain suits and severe hairstyle that made her a striking figure. She was also greatly admired for her artistic ability; other girls would stand and watch her paint. Georgia accepted their admiration but remained an independent spirit, responding also to the influence of her teacher, Elizabeth May Willis, who discovered her great talent and encouraged her.

This teacher strongly guided Georgia toward further development as an artist, and was instrumental in getting her to enroll in the prestigious Chicago Art Institute. Here she applied herself seriously and received high honors after the first year. An attack of typhoid fever, however, prevented her from returning the next year. After a year at home, she went to the Art Students' League of New York where Elizabeth Willis had gone. She studied under the famous William Merritt Chase, who taught her how to use the artists' materials in new ways.

In New York she met her future husband, Alfred Steiglitz, whose gallery was the most daring, avant-garde establishment of its kind. During Georgia's year at the Art Students' League, his controversial gallery featured a completely new concept in art in the sculptures of Auguste Rodin.

Upon returning home after summer school, Georgia learned that her father's business was failing. He became involved in a number of ill-fated business ventures, and gradually lost the family savings. As a result, Georgia looked for a job.

She worked unhappily as an illustrator in Chicago, hating the city and the tedium of her tasks. After two years and a bout of measles, she returned to Virginia. Her mother was stricken with tuberculosis, and her parents' marriage, strained by illness and business failure, fell apart. Georgia's mother moved with her remaining children to

Charlottesville where she operated a boarding house. Her father followed there, and tried to start a creamery. These misfortunes seem to have affected Georgia's personality; she became even more reserved and introverted than before.

Georgia went to summer school at the University of Virginia where she studied under Alan Bement, who taught her much about the aesthetics underlying art. It was Bement who helped her to find a job teaching art for the Amarillo public schools in Texas. At the time, Amarillo was a wild frontier town with shootouts and brawls and a surrounding landscape that astounded and attracted Georgia, who took long walks alone in the desert. Using modern techniques, she taught art to children and resisted the Texas law requiring uniform, old-fashioned art textbooks. In the summers, she returned to the University of Virginia to teach summer school and study with Bement. After seven years of saving and planning she was able to return to New York to continue her training at Columbia University Teachers' College.

Alfred Steiglitz's New York Armory Show in 1913 had turned the art world on its head. Hundreds of avant-garde European and American paintings had been displayed, and the age of modern art had begun. Georgia O'Keeffe was open to the new world, and she was excited about painting in colors. She received excellent grades in her painting courses — her teachers considered her one of the best students ever — but she paid little attention to her education courses. The influence of modern art in Steiglitz's gallery, Steiglitz's "laboratory of ideas," the gatherings where he challenged artists to paint what was in their minds, and the new aesthetic theories of Charles Dow at Columbia University were having a profound effect on Georgia O'Keeffe. She realized that she might be able to make a career as a painter.

Yet for immediate economic reasons, she again took a teaching job, this time in the sleepy town of Columbia, South Carolina. This position provided the solitude and free time to encourage a great breakthrough. She decided to give up all the influences of others, to give up color, and to return to basic black lines on white paper. She intended to recreate what was in her mind and, behind her locked door, she created her first great abstractions with charcoal. She continued working with simple lines and shapes, always being true to her visions and, upon finishing a work, often thinking how very much she would like it to be appealing to Steiglitz, whose independent opinion she valued above all others. She was elated and excited, completely herself. She would always remember this time as a peak of her life.

She sent a roll of her drawings to an artist friend, who was so astonished by their originality that she took them to Steiglitz. This was a momentous event: Steiglitz is said to have cried, "At last, a woman on paper!" Steiglitz believed that these abstractions were the first brilliant expressions of the feminine intellect in art; he wanted to share his reactions with her in person.

A new job offer of teaching in Canyon, Texas, contingent on her taking more courses at Columbia University Teachers' College, gave Georgia the excuse to leave South Carolina and return immediately to New York. There Steiglitz arranged a show for her abstractions which, as he had foreseen, caused a sensation. He firmly encouraged her to continue her new work, and she was buoyed by his encouragement and the great public response.

Her blossoming career and Steiglitz's encouragement helped her to get through the difficult time of her mother's death and the final splintering of her family. She also gradually gave up on a romantic relationship at this time, believing that love would interfere with her creativity at this point in her life.

She moved to Canyon, Texas, to teach and absorb the beauty of the landscape she had come to love. It was the extraordinary changing beauty of the desert canyons and sky that impelled her to pick up her water colors and to paint abstractions that burst with desert colors. These paintings made up her first solo show.

Steiglitz was greatly attracted to Georgia O'Keeffe, as she was to him. She impulsively visited New York where she modeled for him; the photographs he made of her were to become famous. Their attraction increased, and Georgia returned to New York to live with him. (He was married, unhappily, to a rich woman.) This was the beginning of a long creative partnership of independent artists. Alfred Steiglitz and Georgia O'Keeffe seemed to have an intensifying effect on each other's work in those days; she painted more and more daring, erotic, colorful abstractions, and he photographed into brilliant images every inch of her austere beauty.

Steiglitz's wife divorced him, and he and Georgia married. She had wanted children, but he persuaded her that children would diminish her work. She decided that her art must receive her primary attention. For eleven years, spending winters in New York and summers at Lake George, Georgia created the paintings that were to make up the first period of her work as one of the greatest American artsists.

However, Georgia felt stifled and miserable in the contained environment of Lake George and the man-made environment of New York City. She longed for the open spaces and unusual beauty of the Southwest. After many struggles with Steiglitz, who was frightened by the idea of separation from her, she went to Taos, New Mexico for the summer, where the great second phase of her work began. For the rest of O'Keeffe's and Steiglitz's life together, Georgia lived "like Persephone": winter in the cold north with her husband, and summer in the Southwest alone with her work. Her paintings of bones, skulls, and flowers became famous for their strange juxtapositions of life and death, color and absence of color. Along with Eleanor Roosevelt and other distinguished women leaders, she was named one of the most outstanding women in America by *Good Housekeeping* magazine. Although much sought after for her opinions and conversations, she remained independent, holding off all people but a few friends and known by her acquaintances for her sarcasm and "sharp edges."

After Steiglitz's death, she moved permanently to Abiqui, New Mexico, where she furnished her adobe home precisely and in exquisite simplicity. There she painted until her eyesight began to fail, at which time, encouraged by a young artist friend, Juan Hamilton, she took up sculpture. Like the Renaissance artists who assigned parts of their work to others, she also hired painters who painted at her direction. She died recently at the age of 99.

## Maya Angelou: Writer, Dancer, Political Activist

Maya Angelou was born Marguerite Johnson at the beginning of the depression in California. Her mother, Vivian Baxter, was separated from her father, Bailey Johnson, when Maya and her brother were three and four years old; and at that time they were sent to live with their paternal grandmother in Stamps, Arkansas. Maya and her adored brother, Bailey, were to spend most of their childhood in this small, completely segregated town. Maya could remember very little contact with whites at all, although she remembers being infuriated that white children called her grandmother by her first name. Her grandmother kept a general store that managed, through her determination and good direction, to stay afloat during the depression and beyond.

Maya and Bailey were brought up strictly and piously; their lives centered on schooling and church. Maya loved to read, although her reading material also reflected her isolation from whites: She read almost exclusively black authors. She remembers trying to pass off Shakespeare, whom she loved, as black. Maya and Bailey played adventurous games, and Maya dreamed of a more exciting life, chafing as a child against the racial prejudice that dampened her dreams.

For a brief time when she was eight, her mother took her back to live with her in St. Louis. She learned much in the large St. Louis black ghetto where her mother lived, but her stay ended in tragedy. She was raped by her mother's boyfriend (who was later found murdered, possibly in revenge for this act). Maya survived by turning inward and closing out the world with silence; eventually she was returned to Stamps.

In Stamps, Maya continued her education under the watchful tutelage of her grandmother; but she was also sent to a Mrs. Flowers for instruction in the finer points of being a young lady. Mrs. Flowers embodied Maya's idea of absolute elegance and poise; she was the black community's answer to rich white women. She wore lovely voile dresses, was always fragrant and cool, and spoke with such precision and beauty that Maya loved to listen to her. She gave Maya books to read and poems to recite. She made Maya feel special: "I didn't question why Mrs. Flowers singled me out for attention . . . all I cared about was that she had made tea cookies for *me* and read to *me* from her favorite book." As a grown woman, Maya would always remember Mrs. Flowers when she needed to call upon reserves of grace and intelligence.

Maya's teen years were sometimes difficult and unsettled. She lived at various points with her father in California, her mother in San Francisco, and with nobody at all as a runaway in a junkyard. In San Francisco, where she spent her adolescent years, she won a scholarship to the California Labor School, where she showed a great flair for the dance and drama courses she took in the evenings while she attended high school. She received high marks, and loved school so much that she hid the fact of an unexpected pregnancy until her graduation, when her baby was almost full term. At sixteen, she was a mother with a need to support herself and her son.

She tried work as a streetcar conductor, a cook, and a waitress. She says she got "cocky" and tried to manage a house of ill repute. Trapped by her desire for a man to take care of her, she established a relationship with an older man who seduced her and persuaded her to work for him as a prostitute. Maya sank lower and lower into a state of cynical degradation, held there by her belief in her man's love. When he clearly showed himself to be a pimp and a hypocrite, she felt betrayed and alone. At this point, she might have lost forever the chance to realize the potential of her intelligence and strength; she considered using heroin. Only the concern of a hopeless addict, who wanted to show her the final, horrid consequences of being a user, saved her. He took her to a "hit joint" where miserable and dying addicts like himself were a graphic example of where she was headed.

Maya decided to return instead to work and to lessons, learning all she could about dancing, singing, and acting. She sang with a number of bands and hoped to land a serious acting job. Her break was a chance to play in "Porgy and Bess" for the touring company scheduled to entertain in Europe for the U.S. State Department. "Just imagine how I felt," she said in an interview: "Me, a poor black girl, in Paris." From this point on, Maya's life became a series of challenges that she met with vigor and intelligence. She became a citizen of the world, teaching dance in Rome and Tel Aviv. Maya decided to move with her son to the likeliest place for success in her field: Hollywood. There she sang and danced at the top night clubs, and there she met Billie Holliday, who at the end of her career, felt a sad attraction to Maya's stability and spent a great deal of time in Maya's home.

Her next move was to New York where, as a member of the Harlem Writers' Guild, she sharpened her already considerable writing abilities under the discipline of the Guild's harsh but fiercely supportive criticism. She wanted to do something to support the efforts of the civil rights leaders and of her people, who were rising everywhere against racial injustice. Together with Godfrey Cambridge, she produced, directed, and starred in *Cabaret for Freedom*, a show at New York's Village Gate that brought together the most powerful black talents into a great national success. Maya was justifiably proud, never having had any experience in production or funding; she was just spreading her wings. Not long after, she starred as the White Queen in Jean Genet's *The Blacks*. This extraordinary play, which lashed out at racism on the part of blacks as well as whites, was a sensation; most of the players were or went on to be black leaders in theater and film

These were not to be her only experiences of having to draw upon untapped wells of creativity within herself. Her success as an organizer had been noted by New York leaders of the Southern Christian Leadership Conference (SCLC); as a result, at thirty-two she was asked by

Rev. Martin Luther King to be the northern coordinator of the SCLC. She wanted more than anything to succeed in this position, and threw herself wholeheartedly into the work of the organization.

It was in this position that she met Vusumzi Make, a South African freedom fighter who was seeking support in the United States for his political work on behalf of his people. Maya fell immediately in love with him; their shared commitment formed a foundation of an ardent relationship. Vus Make made it clear that one reason he had come to America was to find a strong wife, and he felt Maya was the right woman from the first.

She married Vus and went with him to Africa, where she lived a new life as the wife of an important politician, diplomat, and warrior. Her friends were the wives of ambassadors and politicians; she lived with her son and Vus in comparative splendor in this high-level political world. Not satisfied to be kept in splendor, she found a job as an associate editor for an English-language mideastern newspaper in Cairo. Vus objected strongly, but her desire to act on her abilities prevailed. She set out to learn everything about the field of journalism, and succeeded in learning the trade.

This conflict with Vus over her work was to become one of many: He wanted her to be a traditional African wife, and he wanted for himself the privileges of African husbands, which often included permission to seek multiple sexual relationships. Maya could not tolerate his infidelity or the role prescribed for her. They quarreled frequently, and after a six-month trial agreed upon in a traditional African palover ceremony, they separated.

Maya decided to go to Ghana, where her son could attend an excellent university. There, among free black people, she felt all the traces of humiliation of her upbringing in a racist society fall way. She worked for a newspaper in Ghana and committed herself to her career as a writer.

Her autobiographical books written in the late sixties and seventies — beginning with *I Know Why the Caged Bird Sings* — along with her poetry established Maya as a major American writer. She now lives in New York where she continues her work for her people and her art. She has been called a Renaissance woman; she believes that she is one of the few who was fortunate enough to have her gifts released while many suffered in silence.

Beverly Sills: Singer

Beverly Sills was born Belle Miriam Silverman in 1929 in an all-Jewish section of Brooklyn. Her mother, a homemaker, played opera records all day and, as a tiny child, Beverly memorized them and sang along. Her mother believed that all little girls should be able to sing, dance, and play the piano, so Beverly was sent to at least three lessons every Saturday morning. Although her father, an insurance company executive, was not enthusiastic about Beverly becoming a child performer, he allowed her to appear frequently on the weekly local radio program featuring talented children. She loved show business, and her mother supported her in her interest, taking her to auditions for children without pushing her.

At seven, she was renamed Beverly Sills and was given a singing part in a Twentieth Century Fox movie during the child-star craze begun by Shirley Temple. The movie was not a wild success, but Beverly's interest in singing was established. She could perform whole arias beautifully in imitation of the great stars. Her mother decided to take her to the best vocal coach known to her, Estelle Liebling, the "Coach for the World's Greatest Voices." Estelle had never taken children, but upon hearing Beverly (as well as knowing she and her mother had traveled three hours to get there), she agreed to give brief lessons at no cost.

Estelle bcame a second mother to Beverly, taking her career in hand and training her extraordinary operatic talent in a careful, comprehensive way. She arranged for Beverly to audition to sing for a weekly radio program on CBS where Beverly's success led to frequent appearances and national recognition. Her father continued to support her appearances because of the total education she was receiving; he paid for her language lessons as well as her special music lessons.

Despite appearances in soap operas and theatrical productions, Beverly's great love was opera. All through her adolescence she attended opera frequently, learned a vast repertoire, and read voraciously the plots of operas and the literary backgrounds for the plots.

Her father wanted her to have a traditional high school education, but when impressario J. J. Shubert wanted to send Beverly on tour with a light-opera company, he agreed to allow her to finish high school in the Professional Children's School in Manhattan. And when she won a math scholarship to Farleigh Dickinson, he was overjoyed; but she refused it in order to begin her serious opera performance and training. Ending her long, happy career in "showbiz," she set about her lessons, with Estelle with energy and enthusiasm. Before long, she debuted with the Philadelphia Opera Company, and toured with the Estelle Liebling singers.

When her father died of lung cancer, she was on her way back from a tour of South America. She and her mother moved to a small apartment where they lived when they were not touring. Her mother was a capable and loving companion, making Beverly's costumes throughout her career.

A tour with the Wagner Opera Company, where many opera greats got their first start, was the beginning of her operatic career. She sang Violetta in forty La Traviatas, learning acting techniques and personal management techniques that would make her a true professional.

After many straight, serious, and unsuccessful auditions for the New York Opera Company, Beverly did an amusing, half-angry audition demonstrating that she did indeed have "personality." She was hired by the company, and devoted herself happily to her roles.

While she was on tour in Cleveland, newspaper editor Peter Greenough became attracted to her and successfully attracted her to him. He was a married man in the midst of divorce, a father, and a non-Jew, and so had a great deal to overcome with her mother. He courted them both, and after his divorce, Beverly's mother willingly agreed to their engagement and marriage. Their marriage has been a happy one, with Peter strongly supporting her career and Beverly enjoying the role of wife and mother to Peter's two daughters when she was at home between tours.

She wanted children of her own and had a girl, Muffy, and a boy, Bucky, twenty-three months apart. She had taken a leave of absence from the City Opera for a period of childraising and homemaking in a large house in Boston. However, soon after the birth of their second child they learned that Muffy was profoundly deaf and then that the second child was severely retarded. The parents began a search for the proper schooling and help that would allow the children the fullest development of their abilities.

Her friends, Sarah Caldwell of the Boston Opera and Julius Rudel of City Opera, encouraged her to continue her singing — especially her lessons — in spite of her family tragedies. She did return to singing. She since has said that her children's difficulties have brought her inner peace; if they were strong and brave despite their handicaps, she could not be any less.

She went on to become a great American opera singer in a time when Americans had to struggle to be perceived as competent as Europeans. For years she was prevented from singing with the Metropolitan Opera mainly because the Met's director objected to American singers. One of her mentors, Edgar Vincent, helped her to get a role at La Scala. She sang all over the world; she went mad as Lucia di Lammermoor in hundreds of places. "Queens, mad women, country girls, army mascots — I sing 'em all," she said. She met heads of state and sang at the White House. Her charming, bubbly personality (which had led to her nickname "Bubbles" as a child) made her an approachable classical singer to many Americans who had never attended an opera and succeeded in creating many new opera-goers.

When Beverly experienced personal difficulties, she worked harder; in this way, she maintained her great emotional strength and avoided self-pity. When she was asked to be the chairman for the Mothers' March on Birth Defects, she took her role seriously, and found it to be one of her most rewarding challenges.

After the retirement of the imperious director Rudolf Bing from the Met, Beverly at last made her debut there in 1975. She had proved the point that one could become an international opera star without the Met, and now she had that too. At the peak of her career in the late seventies she decided to give up singing before her voice gave up (as happens normally in older middle age) and devote her energies to directing the New York City Opera. She thus began a successful second career in which she has continued to perform flawlessly.

## The Eminent Women: An Analysis

Did the eminent woman in our study truly transcend the barriers to achievement that defeat so many other gifted women? If so, how did they manage to do so?

Clearly, the routes these eminent women took to attain their successes are as varied as are their personalities. Some themes that emerge are paradoxical. One might speculate, for example, that an eminent woman must have been blessed with loving, intelligent parenting; but many had at least one ineffectual, absent, deceased, or irresponsible parent. One might expect that gifted girls would show their genius early; but many went undiscovered and unnoticed as children. One might further reason that all these distinguished women benefited from an excellent education and that they performed as well academically as gifted girls generally do. Instead, many received intermittent schooling, and many performed brilliantly only in their areas of interest. Finally, one might expect that these women would have to struggle against sexism and their own inner doubts throughout their lives. Somehow, however, virtually all of these women decided at some point to ignore potential limitations of traditional sex roles and to refuse to acknowledge that a problem existed for them because of their gender.

Instead they charged ahead. It seems then that several factors set these eminent women apart not only from women in general but also from thousands of gifted women who do not achieve eminence.

## Time Alone

As girls, all of these gifted women had time alone. Whether the solo time was by choice or by necessity hardly matters. Georgia O'Keeffe seemed typically to prefer aloneness, and her parents allowed her to explore the world by herself. Eleanor Roosevelt was isolated by circumstances that left her in the homes of relatives who knew little about providing for the social needs of a child. Marie Curie's intellectual hunger was so insatiable that it drove her to withdraw into private concentration even in the midst of a busy family. Maya Angelou was isolated by violence and fear of others.

This alone-time may have accomplished several things. First, it encouraged these children and young women to read and think, to nourish their intellects. Second, it gave them practice in spending time alone and in experiencing personal fulfillments. They learned to set their own goals, to evaluate themselves and to reward their efforts. Many adults may never create any art, music, literature, or work of enduring value simply because they are unable to be alone. This surely holds for those whose need for companionship and company is very strong. For most of us, productivity requires time to be alone, a time to be able to expand, to be free from distractions while, at the same time, actually being content. Alone-time may have freed some of our "eminent women" from the negative stereotypes, which are such forceful influences in adolescent peer groups.

## Voracious Reading

Most of these talented women spent much time alone absorbing worldly information and diverse ideas through reading. All were prolific readers in childhood. Eleanor Roosevelt described how her childhood reading took her into unusual worlds, often unpopular with disapproving adults; she even found that if she asked questions about some controversial point in a book, the volume quickly disappeared. She said she looked for Dickens' *Bleak House* for weeks! Many celebrated women such as Eleanor Roosevelt and Margaret Mead found great breadth in their reading material. Others, such as Georgia O'Keeffe and Beverly Sills, enjoyed reading intensively within their interest areas, even if it meant neglecting other responsibilities. Their reading patterns differed, and also served different functions. Reading provided them a means of immersion in a loved subject. It offered an escape from a tense family situation for some. Whatever the primary motivation for reading, the result was that these women grew up under the influence of great thinkers, expressive advocates, and articulate personalities. It is easy to forget that a child, especially one who is gifted, may be as affected by the voices of authors as by those of family and friends. Genius sometimes seemingly emerges out of nowhere. Parents of distinguished individuals are often quite ordinary. For many gifted children, books take over the informational and guidance role that is elsewhere played by the family and school. For talented women, the books they devoured were by authors who thus became their counselors, teachers, and sometimes even parents.

Being Different or Special

All illustrious women in our study felt different or special, in both positive and negative ways. For those whose gifts were apparent early, adults could not help but communicate their admiration — or occasionally irritation — at the little girls' precociousness. Marie Curie was aware of her intellectual giftedness from an early age; her schoolmates amused themselves by testing her extraordinary memory. Beverly Sills was a prodigy at seven, starring on a nationally broadcast radio show. The unusual responses of peers and adults to these children must have impressed upon them their special qualities. Surely a child who is intellectually in the upper 3 percent of the population but is in a school system designed primarily for the other 97 percent, is likely to feel and appear different from others.

Some of the gifted women were aware early that they differed because they belonged to an unusual family. Margaret Mead sometimes wished that she could have a *normal* family; she often felt embarrassed by her mother's progressiveness and her father's eccentricities. Gertrude Stein set herself apart from her unhappy, explosive family. Eleanor Roosevelt mourned not having a real family.

For some of our celebrated gifted women, feeling different was heightened by their appearance; Eleanor Roosevelt looked quite plain, Gertrude Stein stout, while Georgia O'Keeffe possessed striking, sharp features. These different features somewhat set them apart. There is, and there has always been, an "ideal" physical model of a woman; at one time it was a flat-chested, bobbed-hair flapper, at another, a snub-nosed, long-legged athelete. Noted women often come nowhere near the physical ideal and instead emphasize their mental gifts.

## Individualized Instruction

These eminent women received individualized instruction as children, often in their areas of future fame. Language lessons, art lessons, music lessons, at-home scientific experiments, and home schooling were methods of individualizing education for the gifted girls who became illustrious women. This kind of training for girls was once more common than it is today; but the distinguished women described here seemed to have had an especially large part of their education individualized. By allowing these women to proceed at their own faster pace, individualized instruction probably kept boredom at a minimum, while at the same time advancing their knowledge and skills. In addition, individualized instruction was often provided by a person who also functioned as a mentor and/or model and who communicated clear attitudes and expectancies about learning and achievement.

## Difficult Adolescence

Many of the eminent women studied experienced embarrassing

social awkwardness in adolescence. Only one — Beverly Sills — was truly sociable and popular during her adolescence. (It may be no coincidence considering that she was the only performing artist.) Margaret Mead was treated cruelly by the sorority system, feeling ignored and unpopular. Eleanor Roosevelt dreaded her coming out and felt dismayed by her lack of social skills. Georgia O'Keeffe held companions at a distance much of the time, rejecting others to avoid risking rejection.

But an awkward adolescence compounded other experiences for these women. First, it emphasized their sense of separateness, which often was rooted in a lonely childhood. Second, it left in them a lasting understanding of the costs and benefits of nonconformity. Third, it increased their time alone and encouraged them to focus inwardly on their dreams and achievements. Finally, for Margaret Mead and Eleanor Roosevelt, it stimulated compassion for and identification with the suffering of oppressed or unaccepted people.

## Separateness/Ability to Avoid Confluence

Many women view themselves entirely or primarily as a part of someone else. In a relationship some women may even experience confusion about their own interests and values, and those "borrowed" from their partner. Some women seem incapable of saying "I," but say instead "*We* feel happy"; "*We* like Tom's new job." Psychotherapists call this *confluence,* from the Latin words meaning "to flow with"; confluent people confuse their own and others' feelings. Their egos flow into those of others.

The eminent women studied seemed to have largely resolved or unraveled the confluence enigma by the time they began their life's work. Many always felt separate from others; these women have always had a clearly unique sense of self. Margaret Mead, Georgia O'Keeffe, and Gertrude Stein seem to have grown up with firmly established, even powerful, identities. Marie Curie struggled through a confluent, unhappy romantic attachment before she understood and appreciated her own identity. For Eleanor Roosevelt, her sense of separateness and her own identity emerged only after she began to accept herself as capable of having goals not necessarily tied to her husband's. When Eleanor visited the asylum and observed the misery of the inmates, she knew *her* goal was to do something about the problem. From that moment, she devoted her energies to helping the poor, disenfranchised, and those who live in fear, not because these represented Franklin's political needs but because they represented her concerns. Husband and wife formed a creative partnership, with Franklin supporting Eleanor's interests. After Franklin died, she proved that her own commitment to human rights was lifelong.

## Taking Responsibility for Oneself

One great decision altered the course of Eleanor Roosevelt's life: to be guided by her own actions and beliefs. She determined that her own identity, her convictions, her values were meaningful and worthwhile. Major single events and decisions similarly shaped the lives of many other distinguished women.

Existential philosophers refer to this sort of decision or event as "taking responsibility for one's own existence." Each of the thirty-one women studied did just that. None was satisfied to identify herself in relationship to another person; each identified herself as a woman working on ideas or tasks.

## Love Through Work

An early feminist of Georgia O'Keeffe's youth said, "First you must find your work; then you will find your love." This axiom held for most of these women. For many, their romantic lives were so entwined with their intellectual lives that the two were inseparable. Margaret Mead chose all three of her primary romantic relationships because the partner fit her work at that period. Less pragmatic was the relationship of Georgia O'Keeffe and Alfred Steiglitz; their early relationship combined the ecstasy of romance with the delight in the new images they were creating. The intensity of the relationship of Pierre and

Marie Curie was founded on the reality of mind touching mind as well as heart touching heart. And without her work, Gertrude Stein could not have attracted Alice B. Toklas who exclaimed that "a bell rang" telling her that she was in the presence of genius when she met Gertrude, evoking intense feelings and making her want to stay by her side.

## Ability to Fall in Love With an Idea

Related to the sense of separateness and to existential responsibilities is the ability to fall in love with an idea. This concept was first used by creativity researcher Paul Torrance, to explain the process by which creative individuals choose their life's work. It is certainly related to the motive described by Nietzche as being stronger than love, hatred, or fear: the capacity to be *interested*. Falling in love with an idea is more than being able to identify an idea or subject that is personally exciting; it results in a lasting, often intense, absorbing life interest that ultimately leads to an expansion of that idea or subject. All the eminent women described had that ability: Marie Curie nearly starved to death because she immersed herself so totally in the study of physics; Georgia O'Keeffe locked herself into a room with charcoal and paper; Gertrude Stein wrote a novel of hundreds of hours of work to prove to herself she could do it. Each of these is certainly an example of a woman in love with an idea. This ability, and the intensity involved, is almost certainly at the heart of the success of eminent women.

## Refusal to Acknowledge Limitations of Gender

The distinguished women studied not only typically denied limitations of their gender, they often seemed to deny their limitations as human beings! Surely all knew the sex-role traditions of their society and the expected limitations on feminine accomplishment that they imposed; they seemed to deliberately ignore these limitations. Just as Margaret Mead said she was always aware that brains were not unsuitable for women, most of these women characteristically assumed a stance of equality with men even when faced with strong resistance. Similarly they denied any inferiority of their sex; Georgia O'Keeffe was furious when she was called "the greatest woman artist" because she did not see any reason for "woman" to be used as a qualifier.

## Mentors

Most celebrated women have had mentors, men or women who have nurtured their talents and provided them access to a profession. A mentor is not just a tutor or a coach, but rather is an individual who takes an abiding and intense interest in the person as well as in the talent. Mentors identify with their protege's successes and support them through their failures. The close personal relationship of the mentor and protege can become parental in nature, or may evolve into a romantic attachment.

Mentors to eminent women always seem to have access to the highest level of their profession. This does not mean that eminent women succeed only because "they know somebody." Rather, their talent is great enough to impress a member of the inner circle of a profession. A certain amount of luck may go into finding the mentor; but in the end, it is the giftedness of the woman that attracts the mentor. Beverly Sills's Estelle Liebling is an example of a maternal mentor, for whom Beverly was "family." Franz Boas was a paternal mentor for Margaret Mead. Mentor Alfred Steiglitz developed a romantic relationship with his protege.

It is possible, even likely, that without their mentors, many gifted women would not have achieved eminence. Historically excluded from most professional elites, women more than men need mentors to gain distinction. Mentors open the network of power that guides professions and guilds. Even in areas relatively open to women, a mentor is often necessary to strengthen the chances of a superbly skilled but unaggressive woman to reach the top.

## Thorns and Shells

Many of the gifted women needed to "grow thorns." Often, their predilection to excellence caused them to be impatient with and biased against the ordinary and mediocre. Their intensity expressed itself as intolerance, self-righteousness or arbitrary insistence, even with their peers. Gertrude Stein and Georgia O'Keeffe were sarcastic and sharp-tongued. Margaret Mead could be brusque.

Those who do not grow thorns seem to grow shells instead. Marie Curie never overcame her shyness; she was always uncomfortable except among a small group of friends and family; the stress of her public appearances certainly contributed to her ill health. Eleanor Roosevelt, with substantial effort, did overcome her timidity in order to speak out for others; but she retained a personal modesty that made it difficult for others to know the private woman behind the public person. Maya Angelou gave up the shell she had taken on as a child, but retained an assertive wit.

Again Beverly Sills is the exception; her bubbly personality seemed to need no protection, possibly because she always knew what it was to be accepted and admired. Her life suggests that it is not female giftedness, per se, that produces thorns and shells, but rather others' reactions to this female giftedness.

## Integration of Roles

Most of the illustrious women studied chose to integrate myriad tasks in their lives, stemming from their roles as leaders in their field, as wives, as mothers, as companions. Most of the mothers made use of nurses, governesses, and household help, as one would expect. Yet the evidence suggests that the eminent women who were also mothers were as committed to parenting as they were to their work. Marie Curie took her first baby everywhere with her — hiking, traveling, studying — happy to be sharing her life with her daughter. Margaret Mead fought to have natural childbirth and breastfeeding on demand at a time when social mores and hospital rules were strictly against these practices. Her work as an anthropologist gave her a knowledge of what was best for her baby, to which she held firmly despite pressure by the medical profession to bottlefeed on a strict schedule, to ignore the infant's cries, and to require the mother to be isolated from the child for the first few days. Fortunately, her friend, the famous pediatrician Dr. Benjamin Spock, helped to support her in her choices. Beverly Sills found new strength through coping with her children's disabilities. She made sure not only that they felt her deep love but also that their future was secure, establishing financial trusts for the best care and education for her children. She extended her love to all children as chairperson of the Mother's March of Dimes.

As wives, these women frequently showed as much dedication in their relationships as they did in their careers, and often went "the extra mile." Eleanor Roosevelt nursed Franklin through the pain of his illness and planned his psychological rehabilitation with insight and determination. Marie Curie, even while contending with her loneliness and grief, finished the research her husband was working on at the time of his death and saw to it that the findings received the proper exposure.

None of these women were complaining "superwomen," either self-pitying or martyrs; instead they were strong women who decided calmly, if boldly, to use life to its fullest.

## Conclusions

The characteristics of these eminent, gifted women reveal much about ingredients for success. Alone-time, a perception of being different, a sense of separateness, and even thorns and shells all seem to make it possible for a gifted woman to work, undistracted and unafraid. These conditions isolate and protect her from the daily barrage of stereotypic sex-role images and media commands. They protect her from powerful peer pressures to conform, comply, and adjust to being a female. These conditions feed on each other; alone-time leads to feeling different and separate, which leads to thorns and shells which lead to time alone and so on. . . .

These conditions *hurt* sometimes. The difficulty of adolescence for gifted women seems to be compounded by aloneness, separateness, and difference at a time when most young people want nothing so much as to blend perfectly with their popular peers. Yet experiencing loneliness as a girl may lead to acceptance and even delight in aloneness as a woman.

Voracious reading, individualized instruction, and mentoring nurture female genius on the way to fame. Clearly, a standard, unadorned, public school education is not likely to spark the route to eminence for gifted women. Not that public school instruction is bad for gifted women, it is simply not enough for those with a chance for dazzling achievement in adulthood. Most schools allow little time for the intensive reading that gifted girls want; in fact, students are likely to get in trouble for reading outside material. The slow pacing and teaching to the lowest common denominator in the regular classroom essentially constitutes a waste of the precious learning time of gifted girls. Individualized instruction, especially concentrating in children's major fields of excellence, is imperative for nurturing intellect and talent in gifted girls. In one-on-one instruction, gifted girls are released from pressures to conform to the group, to act dumb, or to await information passively.

Mentoring provides the important link between education and a career for eminent women. A good mentor is a model, sharing trade secrets and protecting the protegé from sex discrimination.

Love through work, successfully integrating roles, and balking at limitations of gender all helped ensure that most of the eminent women in our study received the support they needed for their rigorous lifestyles. These findings suggest that gifted women can be bold and daring in pioneering new horizons in partnerships and mothering, just as they pioneer within their own intellectual domain. These conditions allow gifted women to "have it all."

Finally, the decision to assume responsibilities for one's self and the ability to fall in love with an idea are distinctive properties of gifted women. "Eminent women" are cheerfully obsessive and adamantly committed to their ideas. These ideas make them free and fearless: They can face (and enjoy) aloneness; they have confidence in the paths they have chosen; they can ignore opposition or they can meet it with firmness or ferociousness. Society has many ways of attacking and "muzzling" the gifted woman simply by ignoring or deriding her. A gifted woman in love with an idea is well armed.

## Bibliography

Angelou, Maya. *I Know Why the Caged Bird Sings.* New York: Random House, 1969.
  *Gather Together in My Name.* New York: Random House, 1974.
  *Singin' and Swingin' and Gettin' Merry Like Christmas.* New York: Random House, 1978.
  *The Heart of a Woman.* New York: Random House, 1981.
  These autobiographies comprise an important addition to American literature as well as provide many insights into what it is like to be young, gifted, black — and female. The story of Maya Angelou's struggle to realize her potential is compellingly and vividly told in the trio.
Curie, Eve. *Madame Curie.* New York: Doubleday (Pocketbooks), 1965.
  A poignant and fascinating biography of a great scientist by her daughter. This book provides looks at the insatiable intellectual curiosity of the scientifically gifted girl, and the struggles that have always been encountered by gifted women in their search for knowledge. This biography tells the love story of two people brought together by common work and mutual intellectual respect.
Greenfield, Howard. *Gertrude Stein: A Biography.* New York: Crown Publishers, 1973.
  This is probably the clearest and most objective biography of a woman who inspired much subjectivity. Gertrude Stein's unusual childhood and education are well described, as is her gradual self-discovery as a writer and patron of the arts. The many photographs — especially those of Gertrude in her art-laden salon — are delightful.

MacLeish, Archibald. *The Eleanor Roosevelt Story.* Boston: Houghton Mifflin, 1965.

This great American poet has written a lyrical tribute that became a film of the same name. This book, with only a few pages of text and many brilliantly illustrative photographs, captures the emotional response of a nation to one of its beloved citizens.

Mead, Margaret. *Blackberry Winter: My Earlier Years.* New York: Simon & Schuster (Touchstone Books), 1972.

A readable autobiography applying Margaret Mead's anthropological viewpoint and methods to the study of her own life. She shows how kinship, community, schooling, marriage, work, and childbirth shape intellectual and emotional life. Her life provides one example after another of the ultimate sense of autonomy and separateness needed by women in order to achieve.

Roosevelt, Eleanor. *The Autobiography of Eleanor Roosevelt.* New York: Harper Publishers, 1958.

In three volumes, this story of Eleanor Roosevelt's life covers the time from her birth through her triumphs in the United Nations. It can be read as the story of an underachieving, emotionally troubled gifted girl who blossomed into a far-sighted, active humanitarian when seized by the possibility of commitment to a cause. It is a modest but eloquent record of the thoughts of this great woman.

Sills, Beverly. *Bubbles: A Self Portrait.* New York: Bobbs-Merrill, 1976.

An autobiography by the bubbly, indomitable soprano. In words and pictures, the story of this musically and dramatically gifted woman comes alive. The path from Brooklyn, N.Y. to the stage of the Met is realistically presented; it would provide good career education for any vocally talented girl.

Stein, Gertrude. *Everybody's Autobiography.* New York: Random House (Vintage Books), 1973.

A stream-of-consciousness, chatty, hilarious ramble through the life experiences of the author, but not for the reader who wants quick facts. Much of this book is incorporated in the one-woman Broadway play "Gertrude Stein, Gertrude Stein, Gertrude Stein." It is one of the most accessible of Gertrude Stein's books.

## Supplemental Bibliography

Albert, R. S. *Genius and Eminence.* New York: Pergamon Press, 1983.

Barry, J. *Infamous Woman: The Life of George Sand.* New York: Doubleday and Co., 1977.

Bell, Q. *Virginia Woolf: A Biography.* New York: Harcourt, Brace, Jovanovich, 1982.

Blanchard, P. *Margaret Fuller: From Transcendentalism to Revolution.* New York: Delacorte, 19  .

Bourke, White, M. *Portrait of Myself.* New York: Simon & Schuster, 1963.

Bradford, S. *Harriet Tubman: The Moses of Her People.* Gloucester, Mass.: Peter Smith, 1981.

Bullett, G. *George Eliot: Her Life and Books.* New Haven: Yale University Press, 1948.

Davis, A. *Angela Davis: An Autobiography.* New York: Random House, 1974.

DeBeauvoir, S. *Memoirs of a Dutiful Daughter.* New York: Harper & Row, 1958.

DeBeauvoir, S. (1962). *The Prime of Life.* New York: Harper & Row, 1962.

Douglas, E. I. *Margaret Sanger: Pioneer of the Future.* New York: Holt, Rinehart & Winston, 1970.

Goldman, E. *Living My Life.* New York: Knopf, 1931.

Hale, N. *Mary Cassatt: A Biography of the Great American Painter.* New York: Doubleday, 1975.

Harris, T. F. *Pearl S. Buck: A Biography.* New York: John Day Company, 1969.

Hellman, L. *An Unfinished Woman.* New York: Little, Brown & Company, 1969.

Huxley, E. *Florence Nightingale.* New York: Putnam, 1975.

Johnson, T. H. *Emily Dickinson: An Interpretive Biography.* New York: Atheneum, 1980.

Kramer, R. *Maria Montessori.* New York: Putnam, 1976.

Lindbergh, A. M. *Bring Me a Unicorn.* New York: Harcourt, Brace, Jovanovich, 1972.

McDonagh, D. *Martha Graham.* New York: Praeger, 1973.

McFarland, D. T. *Simone Weil.* New York: Unger, 1983.

Meir, G. *My Life.* New York: Putnam, 1975.

Plath, S. *The Journals of Sylvia Plath.* Hughes, T., Ed. New York: Dial Press, 1982.

Reid, R. *Marie Curie.* New York: Dutton, 1974.

Robinson, P. C. *Willa: The Life of Willa Cather.* New York: Doubleday, 1983.

Sahgal, N. *Indira Gandhi: Her Road to Power.* New York: Ungar, 1978.

Schultz, G. D. *Jenny Lind, the Swedish Nightingale.* New York: Lippincott, 1962.

Sitwell, E. *Taken Care Of: The Autobiography of Edith Sitwell.* New York: Atheneum, 1965.

Tims, M. *Jane Addams of Hull House.* New York: Macmillan, 1961.

Wagenkencht, E. *Harriet Beecher Stowe: The Known and the Unknown.* New York: Oxford University Press, 1965.

# 4

# Major Works and What They Tell Us

Major writings devoted entirely to gifted women are sparse although obscure studies and writings, undiscovered by librarians or through computer searches do exist. (I hear about them intermittently from parents and teachers of gifted as I travel around the country.) Just how much has been written about gifted girls and women? Little enough to be read by one person during one academic year.

Five major works most clearly illustrate the development of gifted girls and women. The summaries here describe only their scope while later chapters emphasize more specific findings.

### Study Number I: Terman's Gifted Women

Long before education of gifted children in the U.S. was born as an idea meriting special attention, psychologist Lewis Terman pleaded his case to upgrade education of the gifted so that society would take better advantage of what he believed to be one of its valuable national resources.

Terman's landmark studies, beginning in 1921 at Stanford University, initiated a new understanding of the gifted. Using recently developed I.Q. tests with children at an average age of 11, he reevaluated these subjects five times during their lifetimes until they reached an average age of 62. His findings fill five volumes, entitled *Genetic Studies of Genius*. They destroy the myth that the brilliant youngster is peculiar, unhealthy, and doomed to insanity. In *Terman and the Gifted* (1975), May V. Seagoe, his biographer, notes that Terman turned the first furrow in the field of giftedness by studying factors that influence achievement and by attempting to find traits that characterize children of high I. Q.

The popular psychology of the early 1900s in America abounded in stereotypes of intelligent individuals. Many people believed in "early-ripe, early-rot": that the bright precocious child would surely wither by adolescence. Bright children were characterized as sickly and puny, nearsighted from reading too much, and clumsy and incompetent at physical and athletic activities. Common belief held that intelligence went hand in hand with personal and social maladjustment. Little wonder then that a negative and disapproving concept of giftedness emerged. The more intelligent a child, the more physically, socially, and psychologically deficient he or she was thought to be.

In this climate, Lewis Terman and his colleagues determined to learn the truth about the nature, the development, and the life of the "genius." Working from a test devised by French psychologist Alfred Binet to separate mentally deficient children from average and above average children, Terman developed an intelligence test that he believed would measure "the ability to acquire and manipulate concepts." The Stanford-Binet (named for the original test and the university where Terman made his home) became the first and, eventually, the most widely used individual intelligence test.

Terman and his four colleague-interviewers (all female psychologists or graduate students later to become professionally eminent psychologists in their own right) set out to identify, on the basis of the Stanford-Binet, the top 1 percent of school children in the major California school districts.

Thus, in 1921 and 1922 the interviewers asked hundreds of teachers to nominate their brightest students for testing. A total of 1,528 children were identified; the amount of data gathered was awesome. Each child was administered an individual intelligence test, the Stanford achievement test, a general information test, seven "character tests" (measures of personal and social adjustment), and a test of interest in and knowledge of play. Beside all of this, thirty-four anthropometric measures (height, weight, etc.) were completed, along with medical exams, a home information blank, a school information blank, an interest blank, a two-month reading record, an assessment of socioeconomic status, and a case history. Rarely in history has any group of children received more in-depth investigation.

Some surprising facts quickly emerged. Although school achievement of these children was generally high, it was not as high as had been predicted. Then came the startling evidence that their social adjustment was not only better than had been predicted, but better than that of average children. Even physically, gifted boys and gifted girls were "superior"; they were taller, stronger and more athletic than their peers. The myth and stereotype of the intelligent, awkward, weakling had been put to rest.

## Study Number II:
## Women Presidential Scholars —
## Where Are They Now?

Felice Kaufmann, Ed.D., an educator of the gifted pursuing her dissertation research at the University of Georgia, performed a unique follow-up study of the Presidential Scholars of 1964-1968. This study differed distinctly from Terman's. First, the subjects were members of a quite different generation, and the largest ever born — the Baby Boom group, born in the early 1950s. They were about two generations removed from Terman's gifted women. Second, far more than either Terman's subjects or mine, these Presidential Scholars probably inhabit a rarified intellectual realm. With only two Presidential Scholars chosen from the top-ranking National Merit Scholars in each state, many of these people have minds that are literally one-in-a-million. All were in the top one-tenth of 1 percent of the nation in academic achievement. While Terman's gifted were "moderately gifted," the Presidential Scholars, as a group, were "highly" or "profoundly" gifted, terms given to people with scores at 150 and above on I.Q. tests.

Dr. Kaufmann sought to learn what had happened to this extraordinarily intelligent group. She assumed that regular contact had been maintained with the Presidential Scholars; after all, weren't they a key national resource? The records of the Presidential Scholars were kept in the U.S. Office of Gifted and Talented, now defunct. Finally, she located the records in Washington and made a shocking initial discovery. No contact had been made with these scholars since they had first been recognized at the White House!

What had at first seemed like straightforward research turned into grueling detective work. Kaufmann made thousands of phone calls and visits, hounded families, friends, and acquaintances of Scholars, and enlisted the aid of Found Scholars in locating lost Presidential Scholars. Within a year she had located 501 (83 percent) of the Presidential Scholars, and sent each a forty-one item questionnaire.

The 322 subjects who responded were representative of the entire group of Presidential Scholars, and the data seemed accurate and valid. The results were intriguing. The career development of the Presidential Scholars reflected the turbulence of American society during the late sixties and early seventies, with many gifted individuals in nontraditional careers. Most of the Presidential Scholars had participated in the counterculture. Even so, the level of educational and professional attainment for the group as a whole was extremely high. The gifted women had achieved more than those in the Terman study, but still were poorly paid compared to gifted men. And, these highly gifted women had marriage and childbirth rates that were low compared to the general population. Kaufmann's findings document how a group of highly gifted women born five decades after Terman's women have fared in their career and personal development.

## Study Number III:
## Never Catching Up:
## The "Realization of Potential" Study

Josefina Card and her colleagues studied bright people born after 1945 and found that two major factors account for sex differences in achievement. The first factor — early socialization had been recognized for some time. Earlier researchers had shown that girls are subtly taught to relate their failures, but not their successes, to ability. Boys, however, are taught to perceive their successes as a reward for their abilities, but their failures are viewed as the result of bad luck. Over the years, girls lose their confidence in their achievement ability; boys by contrast gain confidence. Such differences in early socialization by parents, teachers, and others has been shown to have striking impact on achievement, resulting in women failing to realize their potential.

However, Card and her colleagues at the American Institutes of Research in Palo Alto, California, believed that the differences in realization of potential for men and women were so great that some additional factors must be present. They focused their attention on another aspect — the difficulty for women in traditional roles in American society to devote time to the achievement-related roles of student or worker. From a "human capital perspective," one has only so much time and energy capital to invest. Whatever life patterns lessen a person's investments in intellectual, physical, or social development will reduce the likelihood of further achievements. For women, marriage and parenthood typically reduce drastically the time and energy they might otherwise invest in education and in the work place. By contrast, men traditionally have less conflict between family responsibilities and their investment in education or work.

Card and her colleagues studied this second factor through follow-up data on 4,035 Project Talent high-school students. They expected to find sex differences in realization of potential in all socioeconomic levels; rich or poor, a woman's greater responsibilities for homemaking and childrearing would likely decrease her achievement. They further suspected that the difference in achievement for men and women would increase with age; women would become progressively less able to participate in careers. Third, they believed that the future of women with high potential would be most affected, because they could have "gone further."

To measure realization of potential, one must first estimate that potential. Card and her colleagues developed an "achievement potential composite," which gave a score for each child based on five existing measures of actual achievement, including academic aptitude, as measured by ninth-grade achievement scores; high school grades; how the child reacted to parents' expectations; how the child viewed the expectations of friends for his or her education, ranging from "will quit high school" to "professional or graduate school"; and the child's own expectations, ranging from "definitely will not go to college" to "definitely will go to college."

Actual achievement was measured six to ten years later by combining educational attainment, annual income, and job prestige. By comparing predicted achievement with actual achievement, the authors obtained a Realization of Achievement Potential (RAP) score for each person.

As predicted, the average man showed a positive realization of potential; the average RAP score for the women was negative. Sex differences in average educational attainment and average salary were striking. Average prestige differed, but only moderately because more men were in very low- or very high-prestige jobs, while most women were in average-prestige jobs.

The prediction that poor and rich women alike would be underachievers turned out to be true. Socioeconomic status had little influence on realization of potential, even though the poor subjects began with less potential.

Subjects in the highest 25 percent of achievement potential produced the most impressive findings. As the author notes, "These were individuals who showed early signs of being able to succeed in obtaining a good education and a prestigious, well paying job. Failure on the part of these talented individuals might result in keen losses to society."

In the group of the highest achievement potential, women fell the farthest behind men. Women with average potential achieve less than men with average potential, while high potential women achieve far less than high potential men. Strikingly clear also were the hindering effects of marriage and childbirth on achievement, particularly for those women with the highest potential. The more children gifted women bore, the more difficult it was for them to realize their potential in career attainment. The importance of the Card study lies not only in its description of women who underachieve, but also in its clarification of the economic and environmental reasons for their underachievement.

## Studies Number IV and V:
## The False Choice — Career or Family

The conflict between the need for achievement and the desire for family seems to recur in studies of the lives of gifted women. Two research studies have focused on that classic, but perhaps unnecessary, conflict.

The first is an unusual but interesting study by Norma Jean Groth on declining achievement in gifted women. This obscure study, now on a barely readable microfiche, was presented at the national convention of counselors in 1969. It was a true "cross-sectional" study; the samples of gifted subjects represented different age groups. Gifted 10-14-year-olds were drawn from a summer institute for gifted; gifted men and women, 15-70, were drawn in 1968 from Los Angeles MENSA, an organization for the gifted.

Groth was interested in how gifted males and females compared on the need levels as described in Maslow's hierarchy of needs. Maslow's model notes that needs arrange themselves in a hierarchy. When basic needs are unmet, they dominate behavior until they are satisfied, and a person moves from one need to another, one step at a time. The needs begin with the physiological and then progress to safety, love and belonging, self-esteem and finally to self-actualization. Maslow observed that one cannot successfully meet any of these needs until the prior need has been met. Therefore, an individual is not likely to be free for creative activities (self-actualization) until he or she has met all of the other basic needs. Only at the level of self-actualization are individuals able to utilize their full potential, Maslow believed. He encouraged individuals to seek lifestyles that met needs at each level until the need for self-actualization emerged into the forefront.

Groth assessed the level of needs simply and straightforwardly by having each individual list three wishes. She then determined the highest level on Maslow's hierarchy of needs that applied to the wishes. In this way, she was able to discover just how far gifted girls and women had progressed in meeting their needs and striving toward more complex goals.

Gifted women and gifted men both progressed and regressed considerably over their lifespan. However, the pattern of progression and regression of females was especially interesting in the light of the Terman study and the Realization of Achievement Potential study. Women studied appeared to have strong self-esteem, or achievement interests until the age of fourteen. At that point, desires for love and affection became much stronger; in effect, a kind of regression took place. The intense need for love and affection continued in women until the age of forty, when self-esteem regained importance. Men, on the other hand, tended to maintain strong interests in achievement throughout adolescence and adulthood, until retirement age. This study has important implications for gifted females at particular ages; there may be critical periods during which gifted females are more or less likely to experience needs toward achievement.

In the second study of "career vs. family," Judith Rodenstein and Cheryl Glickhauf-Hughes at the Guidance Institute for Talented Students in Madison, Wisconsin, noticed that gifted girls in particular were caught in a conflict because they were reinforced for their abilities while simultaneously being taught that traditional passive female roles are the acceptable ones for them. Paradoxically, there were increasing numbers of women in the 1970s and 1980s who were successfully combining career and family. Many were gifted women who had participated in the Guidance Institute as high school students. The authors decided to follow up women who had participated in the Institute since 1957 in order to understand how "integrators" (women who combined family and career) differed from single career women and women who were homemakers. The 201 gifted women located had been born in the 1950s, and were between 24 and 35 years of age at the time of the study.

Several questions were asked: What kinds of parental influences are associated with a gifted woman's choice of the career-focused, homemaker, or integrator role? What early career interests are linked to the choice of career-focused, homemaker, or integrator? What personal traits and behaviors are precursors of the three different roles?

Rodenstein and Glickhauf-Hughes carefully defined the terms *career-focused, homemaker,* and *integrator,* and subsequently categorized their subjects accordingly. They then found that there were important differences among the groups. Career-focused women had had more scientific interests; homemakers had had more social interests. Integrators fell between the two. All of the girls had parental support for their choices but, surprising, career-focused girls apparently ignored both positive and negative feedback from parents. The study results clearly disproved the myth that career and homemaking could not be successfully combined and the data collected shed light on the type of upbringing, education, interests, and traits that foster this lifestyle.

## Bibliography

Card, J. J.; Steele, L.; and Abeles, R. P. Sex Differences in Realization of Individual Potential for Achievement. *Journal of Vocational Behavior, 17*

(1980): pp. 1-20.

This is a scholarly article rich with information.

Groth, N. J. "Vocational Development for Gifted Girls." ERIC Document Reproduction Service No. ED931747, 1969.

The microfiches at any college or university library should contain this paper, presented at the American Personnel and Guidance Association.

Kaufmann, F. "The 1964-1968 Presidential Scholars: A Follow-up Study." *Exceptional Children, 48,* 2: 1981.

The information about sex differences has to be gleaned from between the lines.

Rodenstein, J. M., and Glickhauf-Hughes, C. "Career and Lifestyle Determinants of Gifted Women." In *New Voices in Counseling the Gifted,* N. Colangelo & R. T. Zaffran (eds.). Dubuque, Iowa: Kendall/Hunt 1979.

This contribution to the only anthology of work on counseling gifted ends the myth of the home versus career choice.

Seagoe, M. *Terman and the Gifted.* Los Altos, Calif.: Kauffman, 1975.

A scholarly, interesting biography.

Sears, P. S. and Barbee, A. H. Career and Life Satisfaction Among Terman's Gifted Women. In *The Gifted and Creative: A Fifty Year Perspective,* J. Stanley; W. C. George; and C. H. Solano (eds.). Baltimore: Johns Hopkins University Press, 1977.

An interesting and readable study with plenty of charts to show the way.

Terman, L. M. Mental and Physical Traits of a Thousand Gifted Children. *Genetic Studies of Genius,* Vols. 1 & 2. Stanford: Stanford University Press, 1925.

Terman, L. M. The Gifted Group at Mid-Life. *Genetic Studies of Genius,* Vol. 5. Stanford: Stanford University Press, 1959.

All of these volumes are dry reading. However, they contain an impressive amount of data.

Terman, L. M. and Oden, M. H. The Promise of Youth. *Genetic Studies of Genius,* Vol. 3. Stanford: Stanford University Press, 1935.

Terman L. M. and Oden, M. H. The Gifted Child Grows Up. *Genetic Studies of Genius,* Vol. 4. Stanford: Stanford University Press, 1947.

# 5

# Bright Beginnings:
# The Gifted Girl

Katie's lavendar skirt and T-shirt are as soiled as if they've been worn all day although it's only 9:00 a.m. at her daycare center. Since her mother brought her at seven this morning, she has rolled across the floor like a tank; she has piled up the milk crates with Timmy and Josh and tumbled down from the top; and she has bitten Ben on the chin when he fell on her, starting a free-for-all.

Miriam likes her Brownie troop, shopping at the mall, and making cookies with her mom. But none of these compares to reading horse stories and galloping around the house on her stick horse named Grits. She likes to imagine that she is a famous horsebreaker, renowned for her ability to tame the wildest stallion.

Jennifer has been told that she has an I.Q. of 165, but she doesn't want any special recognition for this. She hopes her test score will let her get out of a few boring classes at school so she can read in the school library. She thinks being a librarian must be heaven.

These are three gifted girls: definitely child-like, recognizably female — but somehow different from most other girls. Like birds in the spring, they are in their most colorful phase. Later on, they will blend in with other girls and women, perhaps so much that their gifts might never be spotted. But for this brief time of childhood, gifted girls may be enthusiasts, scholars, clowns, and dreamers. Few educators or psychologists have studied the gifted female in this bright and florid phase, from preschool to junior high.

Most of the available knowledge about the gifted girl comes from Terman's long-range study. The girls, like the boys in that study, were healthier, taller, and stronger than were average youngsters. They were as happy and well-adjusted (or more so) than average children were, and they had more "social knowledge" than did average children; this means they knew how to read subtle cues in interpersonal situations and understood group dynamics at an early age. In short, they understood people, and they knew what people wanted of them.

They displayed more leadership ability, rising naturally to leadership positions in children's groups. They were more achieving — but not extraordinarily more — than were other girls in school. Their families were somewhat higher in socioeconomic status and often had more education than did those of average children; but many gifted girls were born to working-class families with low education levels.

What about differences in simply identifying boys and girls as gifted? More boys than girls were identified by Terman — 116 for every 100 — even though the Stanford-Binet had been constructed in such a way as to attempt to minimize sex differences.

Boys' and girls' scores were combined in the original standardization group; therefore, it is likely that the disproportionate number of boys was a statistical fluke. In all studies of the Stanford-Binet I.Q. test, no evidence of sex differences in scores has been found. In the revisions and restandardizations of this test, care continues to be taken that the test will select an even number of girls and boys (Lutey & Copeland, 1982).

At first testing, psychological sex differences appeared to be *less apparent* within this gifted group than across the population as a whole. Gifted girls tended to like the same school subjects and play activities as gifted boys did. They were more like gifted boys than they were like average girls in many interests and activities, the tests showed. This explains why so many eminent women, as children, enjoyed the company of brothers and other boys. The biographies of eminent women are full of images of girls who loved active, exciting, outdoor play. As a girl, author Willa Cather rode her pony over the prairie all day long; Margaret Mead built villages in her back yard. Gifted boys and girls did seem to show differences in upbringing. The boys preferred adventure stories; the girls preferred straight fiction. *Amazing Stories,* an early science fiction magazine, was a favorite of the boys, while the girls read *Good Housekeeping.* The boys enjoyed science and math in school; the girls enjoyed English. Girls liked dramatics; boys liked leadership activities. Girls were more easily influenced by disappointments than boys — at least they displayed a greater tendency to admit such influence. Girls mentioned their mothers as a major influence in their lives six times more often than boys did. Both Terman's boys and girls exhibited the patterns of sex differences demonstrated by the population as a whole.

Although gifted girls were more like gifted boys in many ways, they nonetheless maintained attitudes, values, and social behaviors expected of girls, apparently to prevent them from being perceived as markedly deviant from the norm. Being a well-adjusted gifted girl meant being similar enough to the average to avoid notice and gain approval. The highly gifted girls sometimes did not seem to be as adjusted, or as concerned about approval.

Like their male peers, highly gifted girls were sometimes loners without much need for recognition, as Felice Kaufmann's study documented. This may explain why eminent women, as girls, spent so much time alone. Some of the comparisons and contrasts of males and females in Kaufmann's study yielded unexpected results. A high percentage of the girls were second-born females in their respective families. Most of the female Presidential Scholars were from suburbs and small cities rather than from rural or urban areas. Perhaps urban and rural gifted girls are blocked from high academic achievement by the scarcity of educational resources characteristic of many rural and inner-city schools. Rural schools may also add pressures to conform, which prevent gifted girls from displaying their scholarly abilities. As girls, the female Presidential Scholars generally did not have remarkably high career goals. Even so, they maintained outstanding academic achievement — the highest possible throughout school. They seemed to love learning for its own sake, a trait that may have been for them, as it was for the eminent women studied, the beginning of developing a sense of mission or vocation.

A commonly held belief is that the relationship among parental influences, career, and lifestyle choice is a simple one. That is, many believe that more encouragement and modeling will automatically produce a stronger career orientation in girls. However, while many parents are eager to support their gifted daughter's achievement, it is often surprising to them how unresponsive their daughter is to their encouragement. Similarly, many parents who actively discourage and deny their daughters' talents are simply ignored. This was Gertrude Stein's and Margaret Mead's strategy when their fathers discouraged them. As the Rodenstein and Glickhauf-Hughes study showed, most of the parents of the gifted girls were supportive; but the actual occupations of the parents did not influence whether the gifted girls become career-focused, homemakers, or integrators. Not much relationship existed between the parents' support for accomplishments and the lifestyle that was chosen, and the amount of encouragement given to pursue education or career plans seemed to make little difference. Interestingly, the career-focused gifted women rarely paid attention to parental support for a career choice. These results can be better understood in the light of my findings about parental ambivalence toward girls' giftedness. Parents may have been "encouraging"; but the encouragement may have been so minimal, or so ambivalent, that the women who became career-focused were only those able to ignore the mixed signals they were getting. The career-focused may have had very strong inner direction and sense of purpose.

Finally, Norma Jean Groth's study of the wishes and needs of young, gifted girls seems to agree with Terman's psychological profile of such girls. She interviewed a large sample of ten-year-old gifted girls in order to determine at what level of need they were functioning. Clearly, the basic needs of food and shelter were met for these girls and, most likely, the need for basic security was, too. What interested Groth was how gifted girls would respond to the higher order needs, which range in complexity from affection to self-esteem to self-actualization.

When asked to tell stories about wishes they had, the girls most frequently told stories or described wishes related to achievement. At age ten, they were actively attempting to fulfill needs for self-esteem; they were intensely interested in successes in school or in clubs that could contribute to their self-esteem. Relationship issues, such as the desire for girlfriends or boyfriends, were clearly not as important to gifted girls as achievement issues. Many teachers and parents of younger gifted girls can be reassured by these results — particularly that gifted girls at this age may survive quite well with many books but few friends.

## Summary

The four major studies cited include most of the knowledge about preteen gifted girls. They afford only glimpses of their lives but, because they are based on well-designed research, they are probably accurate glimpses. The subjects of these studies ranged in ability from bright girls in the upper 25 percent of achievement potential to highly gifted girls in the top one-tenth of one percent on standardized achievement tests. From this research emerge some key dimensions, as well as answers to some basic questions about the experiences of younger gifted girls.

Key Points:

— Many gifted girls were superior physically, had more social knowledge, and were better adjusted than were average girls.
— In their interests, gifted girls were more like gifted boys than they

were like average girls. Even so, they usually maintained enough behaviors of others girls so as not to seem too "different."

— Gifted girls were more strongly influenced by their mothers than were gifted boys.

— More highly gifted girls were not as likely to seem well-adjusted.

— Highly gifted girls were often loners without much need for recognition.

— Highly gifted girls were often second-born females.

— Suburbs and small cities produced more female Presidential Scholars than did rural or urban areas.

— Highly gifted girls aspired to careers having moderate rather than high status.

— Highly gifted girls had high academic achievement.

— Actual occupations of parents did not affect gifted girls' eventual choice of an occupation.

— Career-focused gifted women may have had to be indifferent as girls to all pressures or encouragments in order to pursue their interests straightforwardly.

— Gifted girls at age ten expressed wishes and needs for self-esteem.

— Gifted girls were interested in fulfilling needs for self-esteem through school and club achievements.

## Questions and Answers

*Do gifted girls have common early childhood experiences?* Sex differences in young gifted girls and boys are less apparent than they are in the population as a whole. This means that young gifted girls are more likely to enjoy the play activities enjoyed by boys. The gifted girl may not necessarily be a tomboy, but she is likely to be more active than other girls are, to be a little more interested in adventurous play, and to prefer the company of boys. She may like dinosaurs and science fiction, "Dungeons and Dragons," and computer games more than most girls do.

She may be more sensitive than other girls are and more sensitive than gifted boys — especially to disappointments. Her sensitivity may show in irrational or frequent worries and fears, upsetting nightmares, or easily hurt feelings.

Despite these sensitivities, gifted girls are likely to have excellent social knowledge and therefore are able to be "well adjusted" — if they so choose!

In other words, gifted girls usually know what they need to do in order to fit in. Commonly, this means that they will read girls' magazines, will participate in feminine play activities such as playing house and playing school, and that they will behave much as average girls do most of the time. Gifted girls will readily participate in traditionally feminine activities, even if they aren't crazy about them, simply because they are usually cheerful, friendly and compliant little people. They want to please, and they accurately read that society will be most pleased with them if they are not too different from other little girls.

There is some evidence from the Terman study that the brighter the girl, the more likely that she may *not* choose to please. Some highly gifted girls may choose social isolation over conformity if none of their true interests coincide with those of their peers. Some gifted girls observe the results of a lifetime of attempting to please, and decide to do differently. This conflict is observed beautifully by Harper Lee (1966) in a scene in *To Kill a Mockingbird* in which the little girl, Scout, decides that ladies in bunches always filled her with vague apprehension and a firm desire to be elsewhere.

*Are there typical family patterns of gifted girls?* It seems gifted girls can happen to almost any family! There is no evidence that girls of working or professional mothers are more likely to be gifted than girls whose mothers stay home — or vice versa. Birth order may be related to giftedness in girls, but the findings are unclear and complex. Terman's gifted were more often first born; Kaufmann's highly gifted were more often second born.

94

*Do gifted girls have any academic experiences in common?* One of the most common findings of the major studies was the superior academic performance of gifted girls. They not only outperform average girls and boys, they consistently outperform gifted boys in grade school and high school. They receive higher marks than gifted boys do at least until just past high school graduation; the more highly gifted young women continue to get better grades than young men in undergraduate years. Like average and lower-performing girls, gifted girls prefer English and humanities to the sciences. Unlike average girls, quite a few gifted girls excel in and enjoy math. Gifted girls tend to participate in many school activities, although there is some tendency to prefer dramatics to the leadership activities preferred by gifted boys. Gifted girls are interested in school achievement and seem to meet their need for self-esteem through their achievements.

As a result of their behaviors and attitudes, the typical teacher seems to like gifted girls and vice versa. This generally leads to contentment in the school environment. Gifted girls, in elementary school, are off to a bright start.

## Bibliography

Card, J. J.; Steele, L.; and Abeles, R. P. "Sex Differences in Realization of Individual Potential for Achievement. *Journal of Vocational Behavior, 17*: 1-20, 1980.
A scholarly article rich with information.
Groth, N. J. "Vocational Development for Gifted Girls." ERIC Document Reproduction Service No. ED931747, 1969.
The microfiches at any college or university library should have this paper, presented at the American Personnel and Guidance Association.
Kaufmann, F. "The 1964-1968 Presidential Scholars: A Follow-up Study. *Exceptional Children*, Vol. 48, 1981.
Information about sex differences needs to be gleaned from between the lines.
Lee, Harper. *To Kill A Mockingbird.*

Lutey, C. and Copeland, E. P. "Cognitive Assessments of the School-aged Child." In *The Handbook of School Psychology*, C. Reynolds and T. Gutkin (eds.). New York: Wiley, 1982.

Rodenstein, J. M. and Glickhauf-Hughes, C. "Career and Lifestyle Determinants of Gifted Women. In *New Voices in Counseling the Gifted*, N. Colangelo & R. T. Zaffran (eds.). Dubuque, Iowa: Kendall/Hunt, 1979.

Seagoe, M. *Terman and the Gifted*. Los Altos, Calif.: Kauffman, 1975.

Sears, P. S. and Barbee, A. H. "Career and Life Satisfaction Among Terman's Gifted Women. In *The Gifted and Creative: A Fifty Year Perspective*, J. Stanley, W. C. George, and C. H. Solano (eds.). Baltimore: Johns Hopkins University Press, 1977.

An interesting and readable study with plenty of charts to show the way.

Terman, L. M. "Mental and Physical Traits of a Thousand Gifted Children." In *Genetic Studies of Genius*, Vols. 1 & 2. Stanford: Stanford University Press, 1925.

Terman, L. M. "The Gifted Group at Mid-Life." In *Genetic Studies of Genius*, Vol. 5. Stanford: Stanford University Press, 1959.

All these volumes are dry reading. However, they contain an impressive amount of data.

Terman, L. M. and Oden, M.H. "The Promise of Youth." In *Genetic Studies of Genius*, Vol. 3. Stanford: Stanford University Press, 1935.

Terman, L. M. and Oden, M. H. "The Gifted Child Grows Up." In *Genetic Studies of Genius*, Vol. 4. Stanford: Stanford University Press, 1947.

A gifted woman relates the story of her I.Q. test.

"I was nine years old, in the fourth grade, when my teacher suggested that I be tested for our school's gifted program. I had no idea what giftedness meant. I had always performed near the top of the class academically, but I did not feel special. I don't remember my Mom and Dad saying much about the test except that it was too bad my older sister didn't get a chance to take it. I was indifferent, nonchalant — until the lady who was to test me came to get me out of class.

"Then suddenly, I don't know why, I was struck with terror. Somehow, I knew *my whole future* depended on this test. I felt stage-fright, or something like that.

"We went into the teachers' lounge. I'd never been there before, and I was awed by this private sanctum where they ate, smoked, and talked.

"The lady who had come to get me was definitely a Very Important Person, you could tell by the way she walked — confidently and quickly, and the way she was dressed — in a heavy, beautiful woolen suit. (Later, I learned that she was the superintendent of schools.)

"She was kind and encouraging, but otherwise not very conversational. She opened her briefcase and took out the tasks I was to do. I promised myself I would remember all the questions and tasks so I could check the answers later, but I didn't remember much.

"I do remember a vocabulary test, in which the administrator asked me to simply say as many words as I could think of. I realized I needed to sound "smart" so I started naming all the dinosaurs I could. Only after the thirtieth five-syllable name did I realize she was counting each word. So I quickly changed strategy, barking softly as many little words as occurred to me, in a blur of eloquence.

"I also remember stringing beads, and repeating long strings of numers backwards. There were cards with pictures: 'What's wrong with this?'

"I thought I'd gotten nearly everything right until she asked me what "shrewd" meant. I said "mean," *knowing* I was wrong, and very frightened about having messed up.

"The test was over soon after that.

"I think I found out the very next day I was gifted. My very best friend, my only *real* friend, my funny, modest, hardworking pal Jenny was not. Our lives would forever be different. She insisted on carrying me around on her shoulders at recess, yelling 'She's gifted! Hooray!' I was so very embarrassed, and sad, and puzzled — and proud."

# 6

# The Adolescence of the Gifted Girl

For the first time in her life, Stacey is not worrying about getting straight As. She is becoming increasingly popular among her seventh grade peers, and her best friend says that Sean Davis, the most popular boy, likes her and wants to go with her. Stacey can't think about much else.

Tonya was one of the highest scoring students in the Talent Search in mathematics in her state, and she attended special summer institutes for the gifted during the last two summers. She loves the summer institutes, where she has made some good friends, but she hates coming back to her high school, where she is unpopular and considered weird. She wants to get out of high school as soon as possible, enter college early, and study medicine.

Jodie has received a National Merit Scholarship, and has applied to and been accepted by Bryn Mawr and by Stephens College. She has decided to attend her state university instead because she thinks she wouldn't like a women's college and because she'd like to stay closer to home. Also, at the state university she's being rushed by the sorority her best friend is in, which is her boyfriend's little-sister house. Going away to college with strangers just seems too scary.

The major research studies paint an interesting portrait of the gifted girl's adolescence. She is still achieving academically, but is also beginning to have different needs and to respond to those needs. Or, she's become so concerned with conformity and the "right" clothes that she daydreams while her grades slide drastically.

In the years 1927-28, the gifted boys and girls of Terman's study were followed for the first time by his associate, Melita Oden, who had taken over the study. The gifted group members had maintained their superiority; most had entered college and were succeeding academically. Their social lives seemed normal, and they were active in extracurricular pursuits.

Some unusual findings emerged, however, and some clear differences between gifted girls and boys appeared on I.Q. tests as well as in other areas. As a group, the gifted adolescents dropped an average of nine points on their individual scores; but the decline in scores was five times larger for the girls than it was for the boys. Girls scored thirteen points lower than they had at the time of the original testing; the boys scored fewer than three points lower. This striking difference makes it highly improbable that the gender difference was due to chance. In fact, the group I.Q. test and the achievement tests yielded similar results.

Paradoxically, Oden noted, parents failed to see a decline. Parents of gifted girls believed their daughters had maintained the same level of ability as the gifted boys had. Their beliefs were likely based on school marks, because the girls had continued to receive high grades.

Terman and Oden were clearly ambivalent about these sex differences in I.Q. in gifted adolescents. In *Genetic Studies of Genius,* they speculated that "It may be due to male superiority or to the nature of the test. It may be that elements of the test are such as to capitalize on training more often received by boys than girls."

What was happening? It seems unlikely that inherited "male superiority" could explain differences at seventeen and eighteen years of age when these differences did not exist six years previously. Only some traumatic change could alter genetic potential. Apparently not entirely satisfied, Terman and Oden suggested that the I.Q. tests emphasized training more often received by boys than girls. Yet another possibility, not suggested by Terman or Oden, is that the girls had decided *not to try* on the I.Q. test. Though the girls may have felt it socially acceptable to continue to receive high marks in school and to achieve in extracurricular activities, they may have found the label "gifted" unacceptable, knowing this would be the price to pay for a high score on an I.Q. test. Since gifted girls are good adjusters, they adjusted — and may have begun to deny their giftedness.

Terman's gifted young women did continue to perform admirably in school. More women than men earned the fifteen high school recommending units (A or B grades) required for admission to top-ranking colleges and universities. More women than men held honor society membership. Even though a year younger than their peers of average intelligence, more than a quarter of the women held important elective offices in high school.

Many modern parents may feel discouraged that their bright daughters do not fit this pattern and are so clearly underachieving academically. It may well be that gifted girls go through periods of underachievement more often now than in the 1930s when educational coformity was expected more than peer conformity. The effects of those expectations continued into college.

After high school, 87 percent of the men and 84 percent of the women in Terman's study entered college, a remarkable proportion considering that only 30 percent of the general population graduated from high school during this period.

Whenever young women were enrolled, however, they continued their high achievement in college. More women than men achieved a B average or better. As had been true in younger years, the gifted women's interests were closer to men's interests than they were to those of average women. Few gifted women chose education as a major, even though one-fourth of college women overall chose teaching. Gifted women more typically chose social science and "letters" majors than did college women in general.

The issue of conformity versus achievement was highlighted by the Kaufmann study of highly gifted girls from which a composite picture of adolescent Presidential Scholars emerged. The study showed them to be loners and nonjoiners, high achievers without much regard for recognition. The picture seemed to match that of other studies of highly gifted. The highly gifted are never quite as "normal" socially as are the moderately gifted; they seem to be more concerned with self-actualization — being all they can be — than with adjustment.

In the study, school interests reflected an increasing difference between teenage gifted boys and girls and, apparently, in how they came to view themselves. Boys preferred careers in physical sciences; the girls preferred humanities, although many of the same girls also were interested in math. Occupational goals differed markedly. The boys aspired to high status careers (doctor, lawyer, professor); the girls aspired to moderate status careers, such as business and secondary school teaching. Significantly, more men attended highly selective, top universities and colleges, although an abundance of scholarships would have made it equally possible for the women to attend these institutions. As a result, more men went on to prestigious graduate schools. It is clear that many of the highly gifted women of this study, despite their abilities and despite recognition and encouragement, had somewhat lower aspirations than did the men by the time they were seniors in high school.

The bright girls in the Realization of Potential Study, like those in the Terman study, maintained higher grades in high school than had their male counterparts. As a result of grades and achievement tests, they had started out with slightly better achievement potentials. They were more advantaged than the boys in other ways: they had college-educated parents more often, and in high school rated themselves higher on positive personality traits than did average girls. Their advantage did not last, because of a critical shift in adolescence from achievement needs to relationship needs, a change highlighted in Groth's study. When fourteen-year-old girls were asked about their wishes, they told different stories than did the ten-year-olds. At fourteen their wishes centered on friendships and romantic attachments — finding the perfect boyfriend. Between twelve and fourteen years of age, girls showed higher "maturity valence" than boys; that is, they were more concerned about self-esteem and self-actualization than boys were. This may explain why younger gifted girls talk so excitedly about challenging careers — paleontology, space exploration, etc. — at least until age thirteen. With the great emphasis on love needs at fourteen, however, girls' "maturity valence" suddenly dropped and continued in decline until they were forty, when it began to rise again. The major shifts in psychological needs of gifted girls probably account for the conflicts felt by so many eminent women as adolescents. It is likely that society's emphasis on the impossibility of combining love and achievement forces many gifted girls to become preoccupied with their relationships rather than personal achievement.

During the period when the girls studied were most concerned with relationships, the males, on the other hand, were more interested in careers. From fifteen to twenty years of age, the boys revealed that the self-esteem need was strongest, and measures of older groups showed continued interest. The boys, therefore, were motivated to pursue careers, and they received much encouragement for this focus. The inner lives of gifted teenage girls and boys are indeed very different.

What influences the roles gifted girls eventually choose? Rodenstein and Glickhauf-Hughes were able to extract background elements from the women's adolescence that helped account for their chosen life-styles. The career-focused women, the homemakers, and the integrators of their study were different in important ways as adolescents.

During their career development, the career-focused group women often were unaware of or indifferent to their parents' attitudes toward their career goals. These women defined their career goals during high school and continuously strived toward them. This single-minded pursuit of goals was indicative of the commitment shown by eminent women to their vocations. Unlike those in the other two groups, they were interested in scientific professions (e.g., physician, dentist, physicist) as well as social occupations (e.g., teacher, nurse). This interest was clear in their earliest career choice and continued through high school and college until the career goals were met, despite their parents' preference for them to pursue social occupations.

From their earliest career choice through high school graduation, the homemakers' main interests were social occupations such as elementary education and librarian, occupations that have traditionally been woman-dominated. They had little interest in the more traditionally man-dominated occupations (e.g., physician, engineer, physicist). Homemakers were supported by their parents, who also tended to choose a limited range of occupations for their daughters.

In their career development, the integrators, like the homemakers, chose social occupations most often. But they were similar to the career-focused women in their frequent choice of investigative occupations. The integrators had overwhelming approval from their parents for their career choices. Although many of their parents chose social occupations for their daughters, some proportion also chose scientific careers.

It seems then, that the degree to which gifted girls embrace social needs and goals may have a strong effect on their eventual lifestyles. As parents of adolescents have ruefully noted, their influence on teenagers' interests is minimal. With gifted career-focused girls, their effect may be even more limited.

## Summary

By early adolescence, many gifted girls have already marked out the path they will take in adulthood. Some, in choosing traditional feminine social activities have become virtually indistinguishable from girls of average intellect. Others, by continuing not only to perform well in intellectual pursuits but also to enjoy them, have learned they can survive being different. Sadly, some have become confused about who they are and what they want, and this confusion may be long lasting. The key points that emerge from the studies about gifted adolescents are:

— Gifted girls' I.Q. scores dropped in adolescence perhaps as they began to perceive their own giftedness as undesirable.

— Gifted girls were likely to continue to have higher academic achievement than gifted boys exhibited until college, when a reversal took place.

— Gifted girls maintained a high involvement in extracurricular and social activities during adolescence.

— Highly gifted girls often did not receive recognition for their achievements.

— Highly gifted girls did very well academically in high school.

— Highly gifted girls attended less prestigious colleges than did highly gifted boys, and this fact seemed to lead to lower status careers.

— Girls in the Realization of Potential study had higher grades than did their male counterparts.

— Girls in the Realization of Potential study rated themselves higher on positive personality traits than average girls did.

— Age fourteen seemed to be a critical time in the life of gifted girls; then a strong shift of lifestyle values occurred.

— The change in values at fourteen was related to strong needs for love and belonging.

— Gifted adolescent girls who became career-focused were interested in scientific, idea-oriented careers.

— Gifted adolescent girls who became homemakers were interested in social, people-oriented careers.

— Gifted adolescent girls who became integrators of career and home-making also chose social careers most often, but were also interested in scientific careers.

— Gifted girls feared that they had to make a choice between career and marriage; however, this was not the case.

## Questions and Answers

*Are there shared experiences in puberty and adolescence?* Yes. Adolescence seems to be a time of crisis for gifted girls. The year immediately preceding puberty is a time of peak interest in activities enhancing self-esteem. This is a time when gifted girls might be very interested in achieving and exploring careers. At this time in life, Terman's gifted girls were still attaining high I.Q. scores.

Soon after the onset of puberty (girls reached puberty at thirteen and fourteen at the time of Groth's study, but now reach puberty between eleven and twelve) gifted girls seem to undergo great change, a restructuring of personality that is far more extreme than the change occurring in average girls. Interest in careers recedes rapidly, to be replaced by intense needs for love and belonging. The gifted girl who recently spent most of her time enthusiastically reading about astronomy and rock hunting now spends her time playing records with her new best girl friend, talking about boys, and preparing for parties. She may continue to receive high marks in school (especially if they come easily), but her social intrigues are more complex. After a few years, a retest on an I.Q. test may show a drop-off, as happened in the Terman study. Few sixteen-year-old girls want to be labeled "gifted."

After a few more years, the intellectual lethargy may show in college grades of a gifted young woman as they gradually begin to fall behind those of gifted young men.

What happens? What starts the decline in academic performance and I.Q. measurement? Blaming it on the physiological changes of adolescence was once popular. Groth quotes research on the "systolic changes" that supposedly lead to less energy for intellectual pursuits. This is a pretty silly idea by present day standards, but it is similar to the blindness shown by so many scholars to the impact of social pressures.

It is more likely that the abruptness of the change in the gifted girl's interests and needs mirrors the abruptness change in society's attitudes toward her. Until puberty, a gifted girl has usually been rewarded and encouraged for her intellectual achievement. Her parents are proud of her astounding marks, her friends admire her abilities, and her teachers profess interest in her. When she becomes an adolescent, her parents begin to worry about her attractiveness to boys and the impact of her giftedness. They want her to be happy, and to spare her the pain of being socially different. They begin to praise her more for appearance than before, while showing greater interest in her social life — perhaps trivializing her intellectual achievement. The gifted girl's peers are caught up in the great panoply of symbols and rituals that surround adolescence in American culture: the current clothes, hairstyles, music, heroes and beauty queens, cars, parties and proms, dating, going steady, sexual awareness, and experimentation with alcohol and/or drugs. In this world, her acceptance depends on knowledge of the current symbols and her adeptness at the rituals. Often the adolescent culture is a closed one; if she doesn't take the plunge and join when she gets her chance, she may be doomed to social rejection and lose the rewards of adolescence.

Most gifted girls are eager to conform and become teenagers almost indistinguishable from the rest. The gifted girl learns to pose as just another pretty, average girl. She may act and look the part so well that she becomes the part. If she knows within herself that she is different, she hopes no one will be able to tell. She debases her vocabulary, squelches her flow of ideas, and learns to hold back when she has something valuable to contribute. If the gifted girl dresses attractively, is interested in boys, is asked out and invited to parties, her parents are relieved and probably show it in their enthusiasm for her social life. If she continues to participate energetically in the rituals of adolescence, her friends will disregard her embarrassingly excellent academic performance. If she is not extremely popular, she may have to "tone down" her academic pursuits in order not to jeopardize her social position.

A few gifted girls won't take the plunge. Some of them are so bright and so motivated that their intellect will simply not allow itself to be eclipsed by social involvement or urges for intimacy. Their thirst for knowledge is so intense, their perception of the world so sophisticated, their need for creativity and productivity so strong that they cannot, or do not, take time to be teenagers. They willingly accept social isolation as the price to be paid for their continued involvement with the world of ideas. The price may be an embarrassment to their parents and to childhood friends who wish they would "get with it"; however, these girls pay little attention to their parents' and friends' wishes for them.

A few others don't take the social plunge because they cannot. A homely gifted girl or one who has been led to believe she is unattractive may conclude that investing time and energy in becoming popular carries too burdensome a price tag and then may not pay off. She may turn to her studies with extra energy, determined that her payoff will be in grades and academic reward.

Many gifted women remember their adolescence as a time of betrayal. One of my fellow graduates remarked:

"Until I was in junior high, my dad was my best
friend. We read together and played chess together.
He was proud of my intelligence and he showed it.
Then, when I entered junior high, he began to show
ambivalence toward my achievements. He still said
'great' when I got good grades, but he began asking
me about boyfriends and praising me for looking
pretty. Somehow this made me feel bad, but I never
could express it. I was just frustrated with him, and
felt betrayed. He just wanted me to be like the other
girls."

It comes as a shock to most gifted girls when the cheering stops for intellectual achievement and is replaced by steady pressure to be feminine and popular. Most of them master their surprise and sense of betrayal, and congenially adopt the expected values and behaviors. A few refuse and must find ways of coping with being alone.

*Do gifted girls share similarities in their career development?* Although gifted girls tend to have lower aspirations by adolescence than do gifted boys, they still differ from average girls in their career interests. For example, fewer are interested in education, and more are interested in social sciences. A steady lowering of career aspirations beginning in adolescence is marked by choosing moderate rather than high prestige careers, attending less selective colleges, and dropping out of graduate and professional training more often than is characteristic of men.

Age at marriage is an important predictor of the achievement of young gifted women; thus the younger they marry, the less they typically achieve. Early birth of children compounds the negative effects of early marriage. Most gifted women do not marry early; among highly gifted young women, marriage is later than average. If a gifted young woman is to establish and maintain a professional career, the timing of marriage and children is crucial.

Several talented women politicians, including 1984 Democratic vice presidential candidate Geraldine Ferraro, responded to the question: "How has being a woman affected your progress toward your career goals?"

### Rep. Geraldine Ferraro

Being a woman has both hurt and helped me in my career. Early on, being female made it more difficult for me to get into law school and get paid equally to men in jobs I held. It was harder obtaining financial backing for my Congressional race. Once in Congress, I found that being one of a very small number of Congresswomen gave me visibility and opportunities I may not have had as one of many hundreds of men, but it was still up to me to prove myself and show I deserved those opportunities. Women are still judged by a higher standard.

### Rep. Lynn Martin (R-Illinois), elected in November 1980

Well, I was a woman before it became popular, but I do believe that while I was growing up few women — including me — had "great" goals. But because of that, I had more time to grow, so I think I was readier when strange twists of fate involved me in politics.

### Rep. Patricia Schroeder (D-Colorado) elected in November 1972)

While the fact that I am a woman certainly has not affected my ability to work towards the goals I have set, at times it has been difficult getting people to take me seriously. After I successfully gained a seat on the House Armed Services Committee as a first-term Congresswoman, some members did their best to ignore me and make me feel uncomfortable.

Congress is very much a male institution, and even after 12 years in office, I am still considered an outsider. However, I think that my lack of membership in the "old boys club" has been an asset, rather than a liability. I believe I have gained the respect of many of my colleagues, while maintaining a clear, outside perspective.

# 7

# The Gifted Woman

Joan is a sociologist working as an instructor at a small private college. She is married to a lawyer. She makes less than most office workers and has an outrageous course load, but she's glad to have a job; many of her friends in the field are unemployed. Also, for her to move to another job — necessarily in another state — would be difficult for her husband, who has established his practice. So, for the present, Joan has few options.

Marie always thought she'd go to college, get married, have babies, perhaps work for a few years. As it turns out, she's thirty-five, single, and on the fast track professionally. She loves her work as a human resources consultant, and her friends — and their children — provide her with all the "family" she needs. Things aren't turning out as she had expected, and she feels her family is vaguely disappointed in her, but she really enjoys her lifestyle.

Carolyn, forty-one, is an Air Force wife of twenty years. She has lived all over the world, raised a large family, and worked as a teacher in six different schools. Still, she is intimidated as she plans to finish the master of arts degree she started twenty years earlier. Her advisor is patronizing; her fellow students are friendly but uninterested in her. She knows that she is more knowledgeable and at least as intelligent as her student colleagues, but she nonetheless doubts herself.

Helen, sixty-three years old, is the wife of a retired bank executive. She has never had to work, but she has been a leader in the League of Women Voters, the Junior League, and many other political and service organizations all her life. Looking back on her life, however, she is unable to point to any accomplishments that her career-oriented daughters respect. She wishes she could do it all over again, using her leadership skills in a profession and being paid for her work; but times are different then, she thinks; no one expected such achievement of her.

Research on gifted adults shows women to have taken different paths from those that men have followed. Most gifted women are achieving less in the way of professional careers than are gifted men their age, and those who are employed in high-level occupations are underpaid. Marriage and children have much greater impact on gifted women's career development than on gifted men's.

Terman's information on the employment of the gifted at their twenty-year follow-up showed strong differences between gifted men and women. Only about 1 percent of gifted men were unemployed, a figure much smaller than that for men in general; the majority of women were unemployed, whether married and calling themselves "housewives" or single. Most women with advanced degrees were working, but even of this group, one Ph.D., one M.D., and one lawyer had relinquished their careers entirely.

Considerable underemployment existed among these gifted women. Only 10 percent entered the higher professions (professions requiring advanced graduate training) or university teaching. Most of the employed gifted women had chosen "disposable" careers: teaching below college level or working in office/business occupations and as service providers such as social worker, nurse, and librarian. Childhood I.Q. scores did not predict level of employment for gifted women; the childhood I.Q. score was about the same whether the woman was employed or not.

Even when males and females held similar occupations, job status

| Percent of Gifted Women | Percent of Gifted Men | Achievements |
|---|---|---|
| 93.0 | 84.0 | Earned "high-school recommending" units |
| 55.0 | 38.0 | Held honor society membership |
| 27.0 | 20.0 | Held important elective offices |
| 87.0 | 84.0 | Entered college |
| 87.0 | 77.0 | Achieved at least a B average in college |
| 66.5 | 69.8 | Graduated from college |
| 39.8 | 47.6 | Continued for graduate study |
| 14.2 | 31.1 | Earned advanced degrees (Ph.D., M.D., LL.B.) |
| 5.7 | 1.0 | Unemployed in 1940 |
| .5 | 7.5 | Earned $5,000/year in 1940 |
| 11.0 | 86.0 | Employed in professional or managerial careers in 1955 |

Fig. 7. Facts and Figures about the Terman Gifted

was lower for women. Salaries of gifted men and women in identical occupations showed marked disparity (see figure 7).

Five years later a resurvey showed that the percentage of employed women had dropped again. Oden believed this was due to increased marriages and number of children. At this time, after World War II, many women were returning to the home from temporary jobs held during the war. The pattern of low salary and career status remained.

In 1955, ten years later, yet another Terman follow-up portrayed "The Gifted Group at Mid-Life." It described gifted people in their mid-forties, with lifestyles and well-established patterns of social, intellectual, and emotional behavior. For at least half of the gifted women, vocational achievement and actualization of intellectual potential through traditional channels had apparently come to an end; they listed their occupations as homemakers. The authors struggled to characterize these women. Were they to consider women who dropped out as failures? It made no sense. What could they do? In their interpretation of "success," they decided to leave women out entirely. About success, Oden said[1]:

> "The study has been limited to men because of the lack of a yardstick by which to estimate the success of women. By means of rating techniques, it is possible to identify fairly accurately outstanding chemists, astronomers, mathematicians, or psychologists, but no one has yet devised a method for identifying the best housewives and mothers, and this is what the vast majority of women aspire to be. The few women who go out for a professional career do so with one eye on the preferred alternative. Those who make no pretense of wanting a career are willing to accept any reasonably pleasant and respectable employment that will bridge the gap between school and marriage. For some the gap will never be bridged, and the result is that there are highly gifted women working as secretaries, filing clerks, elementary teachers, and telephone operators."

In 1955, one-half of Terman's gifted women were housewives with no employment outside the home. Marriage did indeed seem to be the major factor in determining employment or unemployment; among single women, only three independently wealthy women were not employed; of married gifted women, fewer than one-third were employed. Women who had married did not differ markedly in their educational preparation from those who did not. Women with advanced degrees were predictably more likely to be employed than those with lower degrees.

[1] NOTE: From L. M. Terman and M. H. Oden. "The Promise of Youth." In *Genetic Studies of Genius,* vol. 3, Stanford University Press, 1935. Reprinted with permission.

What occupations did bright women choose? Most frequently, gifted women earned their salaries in elementary and secondary teaching, and next often in office occupations. College faculty positions and higher professions followed. The remainder appear scattered among a great number of occupations. The tendency for gifted women to be in "disposable careers" and traditional woman-dominated occupations was still quite high. When compared to the group of gifted men, the gifted women had disappointing occupational histories. The gifted men were mostly in professional and managerial occupations, such as lawyer, college professor, and engineer. By 1955 the gifted men had steadily progressed to improved status and higher salary jobs. They were more often represented in lucrative professions than were male college graduates in general, and they continued to maintain their vocational superiority.

Although many women had discontinued achievement in the world of work, and therefore compared unfavorably to gifted men, some of these women were pursuing outstanding individual careers. Oden describes some of these superior achievers as follows:

"Several scientists have made important contributions to research to the extent that seven women are listed in American Men of Science. Among the distinguished biological scientists is one who played an important part in the development of the vaccine for poliomyelitis and who is continuing to work in virus research. The social and behavioral sciences include several women who are outstanding in the fields of psychology, education, and social welfare.

"Only one woman is working as a high-level physical scientist. Since taking her Doctor of Science degree, she has worked in private industry where she has successfully competed with men for advancement and is now one of the most highly paid women in our group.

"But not all the conspicuous achievements have been in the sciences. One of our most distinguished women is a gifted poet whose work has received wide recognition and who is rated among the outstanding poets of our day. Others among the women writers are a feature article writer who contributes to leading magazines, two novelists, a member of the editorial staff and an executive editor of a nationally circulated magazine, and still another is the editor of a small literary magazine. Other writers include the author of a successful Broadway play (also produced as a motion picture), several journalists including a reporter and feature writer for a metropolitan daily paper, and several technical writers. One of our women is a gifted painter whose work has appeared by invitation in many exhibits and who has won considerable recognition. Several women have been phenomenally successful in business; two of these are in the real estate business, another is an executive buyer in a large department store, and still another, herself a pharmacist, is the owner and operator of a prosperous pharmacy."

No comparison of vocational attainment is complete without comparing financial status — the pay for labor — for gifted men and gifted women. Income comparison was almost ludicrous. Terman and Oden did not even list an average for gifted men's salaries because the average would have been so unbalanced: earnings of the men ranged from $50,000 to $400,000. Instead, they reported a median income ($9,640) for the total group of men and women. This overall median was almost twice that for employed gifted women ($4,875) with the highest belonging to a female physician making $24,000 and the lowest given as below $3,000.

Education seemed of little help to these gifted women, even though it had benefited average college women graduates; at that time, average women graduates typically could expect to earn 2½ times as much as nondegreed working women. Gifted women graduates, on the other hand, earned only about one-fourth more than did nondegreed gifted women. Curiously, the authors cautioned repeatedly that salary should not be considered the most important measure of success.

One phenomenon gleaned from Oden is particularly revealing. When these poorly paid working gifted women reflected on their lives, many were amply satisfied with their lives and careers. In 1972, Pauline Sears, who inherited the Terman study, sent a questionnaire about career and life satisfactions to the Terman women. The average age of the 430 gifted women who responded was then sixty-two. Ninety-one percent were, or had been, married. Forty-three percent had worked for most of their adult lives; the rest were classified as homemakers. Seventy-five percent had at least one child; 25 percent were childless. Sears and Ann Barbee had predicted that women who were married, with children, income-producing work, and a lifestyle based on a higher-than-average income would report higher satisfaction than those in the reverse group. But when the survey results were in, they wrote that "as with many naive theories, most of these predictions proved false." In this study, persons were labeled "satisfied with their life work" if they indicated that they would make the same choice if they had it to do over again (i.e., to be a homemaker, to have a career most of one's life, to have a career except when raising children, or to have simply worked for money.) The results were complex and striking.

Many of the total sample were pleased with their lives. When divided into heads-of-household (women who were on their own, either single, divorced or widowed since 1960) and non-heads-of-household, the head-of-household group showed the largest number of especially satisfied women. When these two groups divided further into income worker or homemaker, the income workers overall had the largest proportion of extremely satisfied women — and a striking 92 percent of heads-of-household who were income workers were quite satisfied. When these four groups were broken down still further into "no children" or "children," then the group with the largest number of highly satisfied women were the head-of-household income workers with no children. With childless gifted women almost across the board showing more satisfaction, Sears and Barbee wondered if mothers were becoming an endangered species! Clearly, single gifted career women had spent fulfilling lives — despite growing up in an era when such women were often pitied and mocked. By contrast, many gifted women who were homemakers reported a feeling of having missed out on opportunities for challenge and self-development. Heads-of-household homemakers — especially those without children — were the least satisfied women; these were women alone, who had missed the chance to define themselves either through careers or families.

Income had little to do with high satisfaction. Numerous gifted women led satisfied lives despite being in the lowest income category. Whether most gifted women were generally satisfied depended on "an early ambition for excellence in work" and vocational advancement after age forty. The early qualities associated with later satisfaction were self-confidence, persistence, and minimal feelings of inferiority.

The Terman study has important implications for gifted women. By viewing the development of a large group of gifted women over a forty-year span of the twentieth century, one gains a rare perspective and unprecedented insight into the brightest and most promising women of an earlier era and how their world evolved. The Terman study provides clear warnings, hopes, and encouragement for gifted women.

Extraordinarily able gifted women are unusual in several ways besides intellect. As adults they tend to be high achievers, according to Kaufmann. Some in her study were not very socially active. Their marriage rate was surprisingly low, and their childbearing rate correspondingly lower. Despite extraordinary achievements, they did not receive much recognition.

Even though they married relatively late by usual standards, 30 percent of the women (as opposed to 19 percent of the men) were married by age twenty-one. While the Kaufmann scholars' average age was thirty-one, 39 percent of the women and 49 percent of the men had never married. Thirteen percent of the women and 7 percent of the men were divorced by thirty-one. The marital patterns of these highly gifted men and women probably resembled each other more than they resembled those of the population as a whole. Yet, differences remained: The women married more and divorced more, while almost half of the men were single.

Despite these trends, men and women earned an almost equal number of higher degrees (M.A.s, Ph.D.s, L.L.B.s, M.D.s), and high employment levels were typical. Even so, 11 percent of these highly gifted women were unemployed or homemakers, compared to 4 percent of the men.

Men's higher aspirations and more prestigious educational backgrounds seem to have carried them along to higher status careers. The average status of men's first jobs was superior to the average status of women's first jobs. By the time of the second job the gap had widened from fifteen to twenty-two points on a prestige ladder devised by sociologists. But in Kaufmann's more recent survey in 1980, the gap in job status between men and women had narrowed noticeably. It was as if women needed time to "catch up," although the trend of more men choosing professional careers and more women choosing clerical careers continued.

Even in prestigious jobs, equal pay for women remained a pipedream. Kaufmann's women, like Terman's, were woefully underpaid, even when they pursued the same careers as the men did. Men's average income was almost twice that of women. Almost a third of the women in 1979 were earning under $8,000. Some of these women would benefit from equal-pay-for-equal-work legislation as well as comparable-pay legislation. Most would not, because their professional jobs, unlike men's, were most likely to be temporary, part-time, or subject to availability of funds. A physician with only a half-time practice with a medical group, a public administrator hired through federal grant money, or an election year paid campaign director may rate as "high status" positions, but the talented women who fill them will be paid less than people in full-time, permanent, and "hard-money" positions of similar status.

Marriage and childraising have drastic effects on gifted women's career development. Card and her colleagues showed the difficulty of "catching up" after dropping out of careers. After five years out of high school, women with unusual potential were still ahead of high potential men, at least in terms of the prestige of the job they held and their job satisfaction. However, eleven years beyond high school, the picture changed dramatically. Greater job prestige and job satisfaction for the gifted women had disappeared. Instead, men showed significantly higher levels of education; more men were working full time, and had significantly higher incomes. Men's achievement continued to grow, but women's achievement declined as they got older.

The differences between the high potential males and females were consistently higher than the differences in the average groups. In other words, bright women underachieved to a much greater extent than did average women. Clearly, for people with high potential, gender was more important in predicting achievement than was affluence, background, or other factors.

What traits differentiated the high-achieving women from the low-achieving women? Leadership and maturity were the most important factors, along with age at first marriage and the number of children born (Card et al., 1980). Leadership and maturity appeared to be quite important to female success; for male success, job experience carried them to prominence.

Women with high potential for achievement are especially affected by problems of managing work and family, while high-potential men are relatively unaffected. As women marry and families grow, their achievement becomes less, and it is also less likely that they will eventually realize their potential. Perhaps women will return to work as their children grow up, the authors suggested. Even so, they warn: "Sex differences in achievement will not disappear with time. Men's prior investments manifested in terms of greater seniority and experience on the job, should keep them ahead of women for the duration of the cohort's working lives." The most unfortunate aspect of the conflict between career and family is that the current American economic system does not allow talented women to easily "catch up" if they take time out to engage in homemaking or childrearing.

What inner needs of gifted women might impel them to change goals and lifestyles in adulthood? The decline between ages fourteen and forty in career orientation in the females Groth studied was largely due to their high needs for love and belonging. These needs alternated with needs for esteem throughout this period, but in the long run, needs for love and belonging prevailed. The ages of fourteen and forty are milestones in the changing needs of gifted females. At fourteen, a majority of the gifted girls experienced a great surge of wishes centering on love and belonging; this trend continued until forty, at which time needs for self-esteem and self-actualization prevailed. Age forty marked the end of the childrearing phase for most gifted women. Having met their needs for love and belonging, these women began to experience the desire to demonstrate self-esteem through a career and self-actualization through creative activities — a desire that continued throughout their lives. By contrast, males indicated no interest in career needs after sixty.

The conflict of career versus family has repeatedly emerged in studies of women's career development, so much so that many people believe that career and family are mutually exclusive. In fact, until only recently, young women were usually persuaded by counselors that they must make a choice between career or marriage and heard frequently, "You can't have everything." The Rodenstein and Glickhauf-Hughes study has clearly shown that for gifted women the integration of career and family is both a possibility and an actuality, although it is not the only approach that provides satisfaction.

The career-focused group in this study reported much satisfaction from work, and from recognition for accomplishments. The stereotype of a single career woman portrays her as socially inept, isolated, and dedicated solely to her work. Instead, these women reported that they derived much satisfaction from their hobbies and close personal relationships as well as from work. This is consistent with the lifestyles of the single, eminent women we have discussed. Income was not a major source of satisfaction for them, nor were religion, community activities, or children. They viewed personality and good mental stability as critical to their success. They were self-starters and seldom wished to rely on others.

Another element in the stereotypic picture of a career-focused woman is that once she makes her career choice, she will no longer want to choose a homemaker or integrator role. Thirty-eight percent of career women in the Rodenstein study did plan to have children at some point in their lives. So the choice of being career-focused does not exclude the possibility of moving to either of the other two lifestyles as far as these gifted women were concerned.

The homemakers got less satisfaction from their work than did the other two groups. Sixty percent of the homemakers reported satisfaction from their work as compared to 84 percent of the working (career and integrator) groups. Personal relationships, hobbies, and children were very important to the homemakers; most of these women had planned to have children. Despite a common belief that housewives get work-related satisfaction from community activities, community service was not of significant interest to them. Lastly, the homemakers attributed their life accomplishments to significant others, good mental stability, and an adequate education. They did not feel their personalities had affected their choices.

Integrators demonstrate that women can have both a family and career. The myth holds that both cannot exist simultaneously without each interfering with the other. The women in this group, however, reported satisfaction from their work (86 percent) and from recognition of their accomplishments (82 percent). Further, they reported much satisfaction from their personal relationships (97 percent), their children (96 percent), and their avocations (82 percent). They had both career and family, and they are highly satisfied with both.

This group showed characteristics of both the career-focused group and homemaker groups. It is difficult to adapt to this combination, and great mental stability is needed. More than the other groups, integrators thought that good mental stability was an important contributor to their life accomplishments. The women in this group seemed to gain strength both from within and from outside themselves. Family and friends were important, but so was their own strength in persisting toward a goal. Again, the description of this group fits many eminent women who integrated work and family.

## Summary

Research findings suggest that although the combination of career and family may be difficult for many women, gifted women *can* maintain both. Gifted women integrators are more satisfied with their careers than gifted single career women; and they are as satisfied with their families as gifted homemakers. A forced choice between career and family is not necessary for the gifted woman.

Key Points

— Gifted women's academic and vocational achievement compared to that of gifted men continues to decline throughout adulthood.
— Gifted women's I.Q.s do not predict career achievement or employment.
— Most employed gifted women are in disposable careers, and only a small group enter the higher professions.
— Salaries of gifted women are much lower than those of gifted men in occupations at the same level; in fact, in 1955, the gifted women's

median salary at midlife was one-half that of gifted men. However, income is not related to life satisfaction.

— Single, working, childless, gifted women looking back on their lives are highly satisfied as a group.

— Gifted women engaged in income-producing work are more satisfied with their lives than are those who are not engaged in income-producing work.

— Highly gifted women need time to catch up to men.

— Highly gifted men's income has averaged almost twice that of highly gifted women.

— Only a small proportion of highly gifted women were unemployed 15 years after high school graduation.

— Early marriage and childbirth are closely related to low achievement.

— Between the ages of twenty-three and twenty-nine, men's careers accelerate; women's stand still.

— Marriage and childbirth affect the achievement of high-potential women much more than they do that of high-potential men.

— Women who drop out of careers to marry and raise children may not catch up with their male peers for the rest of their working lives.

— Age forty may mark another critical change in lifestyle values for gifted women, as a point in time when esteem needs become highly important.

— Single career women derive great satisfaction from their work, and also enjoy their friends, hobbies, and community activities.

— Homemakers receive less satisfaction from their work than do single career women or integrators. In addition, many do not seem to derive satisfaction from community activities and hobbies.

— Gifted women in the Rodenstein & Glickhauf-Hughes study successfully integrated career and family.

— Integrators are highly satisfied as a group.

— Integrators are more satisfied with their careers than are single-career women and are as satisfied with their families as are homemakers.

— Mental stability and the support of others is crucial to successful integration of career and family.

## Questions and Answers

*How does the conflict between social expectation and personal potential affect gifted women?* All of the women in the studies described felt the conflict between social expectations and personal potential. Much more than women of average ability, they were given two very different messages. On the one hand, they were encouraged to achieve their full potential: They were tested and identified as gifted, sometimes they were given special education, and they received awards for their academic performance. On the other hand, they were encouraged to be feminine: They were discouraged from achieving too much, or achieving in such a way as to interfere with their potential for attracting marriage partners.

As is true for today's gifted women, many were given the unhappy choice of career or marriage by counselors who would never have considered giving that choice to males. Many gifted women are encouraged to take the path of least resistance when they learn there will be no punishment from society for withdrawing from accomplishment. Even though society responds harshly to a gifted male who drops out of education or a professional career, a woman who drops out to marry or raise children, or even to seek a partner, is simply considered to be practical. Finally, many gifted women give up achievement when they learn that their efforts are never going to be rewarded as much as are those of men.

While gifted women are still in school of any sort, their hard work dependably leads to high marks. After graduation, salary is the only "grading system" available. In all of the follow-up studies, gifted women were earning far less than men, usually one-half. They earned less not only in women's professions such as nursing and teaching, but also in the same professions as men, such as college teaching and law. The seeming hopelessness of this situation surely leads many gifted women to devalue their work just as it is devalued by society.

*Are there characteristic ways in which adult women adjust to being gifted?* The lifestyles and the accompanying patterns of adjustment that emerged from the research were very similar to those apparent in the gifted women in my follow-up survey.

It appears that Big Mary, Linda, and Gina, as well as the whole group of young adult gifted women who had been my classmates, were not atypical of gifted women. They had experienced the same kind of childhood, full of promise and the excitement of being special; and like the majority of gifted women, they did not go on to become eminent. They had weathered the crises of adolescence — the change in their parents' and society's attitudes and the choices to be made between the denial of gifts and certain social isolation. They had developed lifestyles that were attempts to cope with two powerful forces: society's inevitable, constant pressure to be feminine, to settle for less, to live through others on the one hand, and their own sense of responsibility for the actualization of their intellect on the other.

It seems true, then, that gifted women today are very much like gifted women throughout this century. In attempts to cope with socialization, career development, and lifestyle, gifted women do, indeed, seem to adopt characteristic patterns of adjustment. The ones so far identifiable are those described by Rodenstein and Glickhauf-Hughes — career-focused, homemaker, and integrator. Each pattern has its own assets and liabilities; every woman must assess her personal gains and losses for adjustment choices. But only if she knows the factors influencing her can she make knowledgeable decisions.

# 8

# Barriers to Achievement

For many years, two myths held that it made little sense to seriously study the career development of women. One assumption was that studies of male career choices would also explain women's, while the other declared that woman's primary role as housewife and mother made female employment not worth studying.

Several counseling psychologists, (e.g., Fitzgerald, Betz, Farmer, and Harmon) have been conducting and reviewing research that contradicts these assumptions. The housewife/mother is rapidly becoming the exception rather than the rule. Rush hour traffic and restaurants at noon in any American city attest to an abundance of women in the workplace. Data show 60 percent of all women eighteen to sixty-four are working; the odds of women working sometime in their lifetimes have risen to nine out of ten. In fact, women will work an average of 27.6 years of their lives. More than half of all mothers work. The reality of the changed world of work has made assumptions about woman's place archaic.

Similarly, the theories of career development that have helped in counseling men have proved disappointing for guiding women. Although the number and variety of careers for men fill books, the list of work options for women has been traditionally limited to a small group of occupations. Many women continue to be relegated to jobs that are low-level, low-status and low-pay. Career theories based on men cannot explain why this is so.

Many writers, both popular and scholarly, agree that the barriers to achievement for gifted women are both external and internal. Some barriers are society's; others are personal. External barriers include training subtly geared to lower status for girls, discrimination in education and the workplace, and lack of resources. The picture has been changing during the last twenty years because the women's movement has raised society's awareness of discriminatory practices against women and of cultural pressures they face.

Traditional child-rearing patterns that included teaching of rigid sex roles have been largely cast aside. Allowing children the freedom to define their identity without the fetters of sex-role stereotypes represents a more enlightened picture in the United States today. The subtle forces that inhibited women from equal opportunity to be educated and seeking work for which they qualified except for gender are gradually dissipating. But the final chapter is still being written as some external barriers have not fallen — barriers that continue to stifle gifted girls and women from fully using their intellectual gifts and potential.

Even when there is no discouragement or discrimination from our society, girls and women are prone to internal or personal barriers. These are psychological obstacles that trip many gifted girls and women who may be unaware of their own feelings of inferiority although they may be aware of sexism. The "Horner Effect," and "Cinderella Complex," and the "Imposter Syndrome" are all names given by the popular literature to the ways in which women sabotage their own successes. Each of these describes a specific set of self-defeating attitudes: toward success, toward independence and risk-taking, toward brilliance. These internal barriers obstruct gifted women far more seriously than they affect most average women, because gifted women can achieve so much more if they are not struggling with inner roadblocks. Ironically, psychological health — not psychological disability — seems to be another internal barrier for gifted girls.

All these barriers hinder gifted women in their development, and all gifted women must find ways of coping. Such adjustment surprisingly parallels adjustment to disability, disaster, or even dying. There are several explanations of how and why.

## External Barriers

### Shaping for Femininity

From the moment a baby is born, adults begin to shape either masculine or feminine behavior. Pink clothes and sex-typed nicknames come with girls, along with certain expectations. Few people know that there are also basic differences in infant and toddler handling (Fagot, 1977) for boys and girls. For example, parents generally respond to a newborn girl's cries more quickly than they do to a newborn boy's cries. Perhaps the girl is perceived to be in distress, while the boy is thought to be simply exercising his lungs! Girls are picked up; boys are left a while to howl. As babies grow, boys are permitted to express more aggression than girls. Parents allow boys to hit, poke, and throw things at them, while frowning on such aggressiveness by their daughters. Girls frequently receive praise for "prosocial" behaviors such as helping, cooperating, sharing; boys much less so. When girls in primary grades become frustrated with a task, parents are more likely to rush to help them than their brothers confronting a similar plight. Dependency is expected and even desired in girls, but frowned upon in boys (Hoffman, 1972).

By age seven, boys and girls themselves have learned sex-role stereotyping: They can clearly identify careers as male or female. First-, second-, and third-grade girls list notably fewer career options than boys do, and these are dominated by one or two choices. One researcher (Siegel, 1973) found that while thirty-two grade school boys listed twenty different occupations, 70 percent of the girls listed "nurse" or "teacher." In grade school, girls' dependency continues to be encouraged, often subtly undermining their confidence.

Why do some girls lose confidence in their abilities while so often continuing to receive high grades? Most teachers are unaware of the myriad ways in which they differentially train girls' and boys' attitudes toward their own achievements. However, it is clear that girls learn to view their successes as caused by luck and their failures as due to lack of ability; boys learn to attribute their successes to ability and their failures to bad breaks.

How does such a self-view develop? Two educational researchers (Dweck & Gillard, 1975) discovered that most teacher feedback to boys is negative and focuses mainly on conduct and social behavior. Lack of effort is the usual criticism of boys; teachers consistently tell boys that they are not trying hard enough. Teachers' feedback to girls most often is positive, and seldom refers to effort. When girls fail at a task, teachers seldom tell them they are not trying hard enough. Thus, girls do not learn to associate their effort with either failure or success. Boys learn from being told to "try harder" that they have control over the results of their work. Such shaping is not limited to elementary education; it continues throughout high school.

Even in college, where so many gifted women can be found, professors shape achievement behavior differently for men and women (Bernard, 1976). Men are called on in class more often than are women. Men are more frequently invited to become student assistants and to participate in research. It is not surprising that many women students increasingly feel left out as they progress through college. Bernard found that university professors respond to female students and even to female professors in two characteristic and negative ways: with put-downs and with avoidance. Put-downs include overt and subtle sexist comments in lectures, conversations, and recommendations. Even more common is avoidance; many male professors passively neglect and resist women's academic efforts. Higher education, according to Bernard, seriously shortchange women, and for many gifted women provides only a "null academic environment" without encouragement.

The differential encouragement of independence and achievement behavior in school and college seriously hinders gifted girls and women. It seems incredible that a girl who has received straight As would attribute *all* of them to luck; but many do. It is likewise extraordinary that a qualified woman does not recognize when she has been discriminated against in employment, but instead interprets the rejection to mean that she must be less qualified — but this too, happens.

Sexism and Discrimination

"A woman needs to work twice as hard for half the credit."
"A woman's formula for success: Act like a man. Dress like a lady. Work like a dog."
"A woman's worth on the job market is 62¢ for every $1 a male is worth."

These statements describe effects of sexism and discrimination on women's chances for success in a man's world. To be sure, the climate has improved. The women's movement has raised awareness of inequalities in education and work. Legislation has improved the chances of a girl in the United States growing up to reach her potential. Title IX has required that schools receiving federal funds make efforts to reduce disparate educational practices for boys and girls. Title VII's Affirmative Action legislation requires that qualified female candidates be considered for higher education admissions and for jobs. Nevertheless, damaging forms of discrimination still exist.

Discrimination in employment has been well documented. One researcher (Levinson, 1975), investigating sex-typing of careers and discrimination, asked a male and a female to inquire about 265 positions in classified ads for jobs that traditionally were male- or female-dominated. One partner would call about a "sex-inappropriate" job (e.g., the male would call about "hairdresser" or the female would inquire about "construction worker.") Then, the other partner would call about the same job. In 35 percent of the cases, clear-cut discrimination was evident even at this initial stage of inquiry: The sex-inappropriate applicant was told the job was filled and later the sex-appropriate caller was encouraged to apply. In another 27 percent of cases, the sex-inappropriate person was actively discouraged from applying.

Other studies have shown that employers viewing identical male and female resumes will more frequently choose the male. In some states, married women cannot yet receive credit, or own property alone; pregnant women may be denied maternity leave on the same terms as sick leave and cannot be assured of being reinstated to the same job if they do leave temporarily; and many forms of discrimination on the basis of gender exist in educational and occupational establishments that do not receive federal funding.

These conditions affect all women; however, except for women at poverty level, they seem to affect gifted women most adversely. Bright, achieving women are particularly likely to encounter a "ceiling effect" in career development; women nearing the top of the career ladder experience the boundaries. Every highly achieving professional woman recognizes when she has reached the "ceiling" in her ascent toward her career goal. Whether in business or academe, she had been accorded respect and has provided leadership in mixed-sex task groups and committees up to that point. She has risen to higher positions of responsibility and has encountered few setbacks attributable to her sex — at least few she could not overcome. As she advances she notes that the committee meetings and work groups number fewer women, minorities, and young professionals. Finally, one day she enters the board room, and finds only business suits and men's grey heads nodding to each other. She feels alone. She observes that when they speak, it is to each other. When they seek information from her, they ask her supervisor or a male colleague next to her: "Has Mary got the budget from the subcommittee?" They avoid eye contact with her. When she speaks, they look puzzled and resume their conversation with each other.

Mary feels dismayed and bewildered amid these undercurrents. It is apparent she will not rise higher. This is the ceiling effect, a phenomenon encountered only by women who are highly achieving, because in today's society, it is mainly at the very bottom and at the very top of the job prestige hierarchy that women receive such overtly unequal job treatment. Women in middle-prestige, moderate-salary jobs often are protected by affirmative action and other legislation and, more important, by the implicit agreement of employers and co-workers with new middle class values. Discrimination and negative attitudes toward women occur less often in middle management positions than they did a decade ago, according to recent studies of how women in management positions are perceived. At top levels, business executives and public administrators know how to circumvent affirmative action. Statistics confirm that they prefer to work with males. Since top-level personnel decisions are risky in many ways, they want to deal with known quantities, i.e., men. When a job opening occurs, they call their friends and ask about "good people." This has been called the "Old-Boy Network," or the male mentoring system; when the system acts consistently to exclude women, it is called discrimination.

Gifted women have been the most frequent subjects of such unobtrusive discrimination. Despite some enlightened changes, the fact of discrimination comes as a rude surprise to many women who do not expect it, especially since many barriers have been removed from higher education and from entry-level professional positions. But the discrimination is real. An elderly female professor, in speaking to a student women's group, remarked not long ago, "Bright young women entering their first highly-paid jobs often say, 'I've never been discriminated against!' I want to say, 'Just wait!'"

Lack of Resources

Another major external barrier to achievement by gifted women is a lack of resources — ranging from money for adequate schooling to neighborhood day care facilities. Lack of money is inevitably linked to discrimination and becomes the foremost missing resource. Women's lower earning power prevents them from earning adequately to pay for professional education. Historically, it has been more difficult for women to get loans for medical school, law school, and other professional programs. But money problems also nag at women from other sides. Often, women's quickest road to poverty is to become divorced. Exclusive care of the children, unaffordable home mortgage payments, and the immediate need for a job often impel her priorities, and, preclude training for higher level jobs. Women's opportunities to learn financial management skills have been generally lean — particularly long-term money planning for retirement and insurance programs. For mothers aspiring to careers, child care and help with household chores are indispensable, but reliable help tends to be hard to find and expensive. Thus, it is small wonder that women worry about jeopardizing safe, though lesser paying, traditional female roles.

## Internal Barriers

Internal barriers that women harbor are equally inhibiting and even more insidious. These are the beliefs, attitudes and self-fulfilling prophecies that highlight the axiom "We have met the enemy, and it is us!" More than one researcher has observed and labeled aspects of this phenomenon.

### The Horner Effect

I first encountered the Horner Effect in college in my general experimental psychology lab. Our professor gave us a "verbal learning experiment," in which he handed out to each student ten simple lists of words and ten M & M candies. He then paired us with a partner. As we sat facing each other, each student slowly read a list of words to the partner. The partner was to repeat as many words as he or she could remember. When the entire list was remembered, the partner won an M & M. This continued, the students taking turns reading and reciting, until all the lists were read. We were to count M & Ms afterwards and write our "score" on the board. My first partner was a polite, smiling, blonde girl. We laughed as we flubbed words and cheered each other as we gained M & Ms. I think I won the most M & Ms.

We entered our scores on the board, and our professor announced a second experiment for us in "Digital Dexterity." This time a set of tiddlywinks was given to each student, and he reassigned each student to a new partner. We were to play tiddlywinks for fifteen minutes, and then to record our scores on the board. Now my partner was a beefy hippie in overalls with a full beard surrounding his grin. We played tiddlywinks, at first laughing and then in mock seriousness. I thought I saw that my partner really wanted to win, so I didn't play very earnestly. Sure enough, I lost. Like a good sport, I went up to write our scores on the board.

Then came the surprise. This experiment was *not* about verbal learning and digital dexterity at all. Rather, it was a demonstration of male/female attitudes toward competition. He purposely had assigned us to an even number of mixed-sex and same-sex partnerships, and involved us in two competitive games, one intellectual and one physical. "Let's see what the scores look like when we put them in same-sex and mixed-sex columns," he said, and rearranged scores on the board. Even without calculations the trend in the results was clear. *Women's scores were much lower when they competed against men than when they competed against women.*

"It's the Horner Effect," he said. "It's happened in every class today." Matina Horner (1972), psychologist, discovered this predictable pattern in her experiments on achievement motivation like ones my professor had used. She observed that women characteristically under-achieved when competing with men. Despite exceptional ability, women would actually perform decidedly below their ability and, curiously, would usually be unable to explain the reason. The Horner Effect later was renamed the "Fear of Success" syndrome. It was reasoned that the typical woman feared success, because to win against a man in competition was actually to lose. What might she lose? Perhaps her "femininity" or his goodwill.

The Horner Effect, or Fear of Success syndrome, has been confirmed repeatedly in experiments since the 1970s. More recently, however, the Horner Effect has become less predictable. Some women — at least those young college women who are the most frequent research subjects — seem to be changing. Now not *all* women show fear of success. More recent research (Tresemer, 1977) suggests that the Fear of Success syndrome interferes most with the achievement of those women already traditionally "feminine" in interests and attitudes toward their sex roles. Women with nontraditional attitudes are less likely to be victims of the Horner Effect, the study shows.

What is the impact of the Horner Effect on gifted girls and women? Since they are astute, gifted girls become sensitive to the conflicts for women in competitive situations much earlier than average girls do. Their abilities in the classroom may have encouraged them to be competitive and achieving. Conversely, they often have been discouraged from being competitive in "boys'" activities, games, or sports they may enjoy. The Horner Effect involves holding back one's efforts and dampening one's enthusiasm. Alas, gifted girls have more ability than most to hide, making it more likely that they will have to work at hiding it. Hence, gifted girls are likely to be more aware of their underachievement, and even frustrated by it, although they may not know why they are underachieving. Terman's studies show the gifted girls and women have an even stronger need to please others than average women do. Even when a gifted woman understands how irrational or impractical it is to underachieve, she may continue to do so if she believes success will result in social disapproval.

Therefore, fear of success seems to have its most powerful effect on the very women most likely to be successful. Their fears increase as they approach achievement and success. How curious that a bright girl or woman who is keenly in touch with social norms, and who exhibits much potential should become progressively anxious as she nears the academic or career success for which she has yearned. As she anticipates the consequences of too much success, she slips to underachievement. She is puzzled by her underachieving, and usually feels intense, if undefinable, dissatisfaction with herself. This conflict is difficult and demeaning, requiring keen personal effort to cope, even with an understanding of the issues.

The Cinderella Complex

Colette Dowling (1981) observed how she and others avoided achieving. When she learned of the Horner Effect, she conceived a snappy title that included both fear of success and the desire to be cared for: The Cinderella Complex. She wrote a book by that title and advanced the theory that personal, psychological dependency is the chief force that suppresses today's women. The Cinderella Complex is a network of largely repressed attitudes and fears that detain women in a kind of half-light, retreating from the full use of their minds and creativity. "Like Cinderella, women today are still waiting for something external to transform their lives" (p. 31). Women caught up in the Cinderella Complex are "too angry to stay behind and too frightened to move ahead."

Though not based on a rigorous scientific study, Dowling's thought-provoking insights must not be ignored. Dowling observed in her interviewees (largely bright, middle-class women) most of the conflicts others have described as troubling gifted women. Being "overhelped" as children, women are crippled by a subsequent sense of dependence on others, says Dowling. In adolescence, she observes, many women who had been intellectually encouraged by their fathers, now felt particularly betrayed by them. Fathers abruptly changed their opinions as their bright daughters' career goals grew. Why? Were the fathers threatened by the achievements of daughters; did they feel a need to squelch their daughters' ambitions before they surpassed their own?

Dowling quotes Simone de Beauvoir's description of her adolescent relationship with her father:

"I was obeying his wishes to the letter, and that seemed to anger him. He had destined me to a life of study and yet I was being reproached with having my nose in a book all the time. To judge by his surly temper, you would think that I had gone against his wishes in embarking on a course of study he had actually chosen for me."

What about the mothers among Dowlings' interviewees? Most were rather faceless, passive women who had made small contribution to the lives of the daughters. Many were jealous of their daughters' lofty goals and attempted to curtail them by encouraging them to seek the "right" boyfriends.

Dowling found that most of the women she studied acquiesced to the expectations of their parents, and began to desire the total "fusion" of marriage. They learned to judge men by their competence to take care of them completely. Dowling describes single women who refused to commit themselves to permanent jobs or careers because they hoped that the "right man" would come along. Similarly, she describes married women whose dependency fed upon itself, so that with each passing year, they became less capable of pursuing their own goals; they seemed to base their self-worth on the man they had married. Often only crisis could shock these women out of the complacency of submerging themselves in marriage and family, Dowling felt. Determined self-exploration, even psychotherapy, were needed to help women uncover and work through what she believed were often unconscious and severely limiting fears of independence.

Many of the women Dowling observed had sought psychotherapy; they were especially unhappy with their prior life decisions. Perhaps their fears of independence were more extreme than those of women in general. They were not typical of all women.

Still, some other research supports Colette Dowling's ideas. Studies (e.g., Astin & Myint, 1971; Tangri, 1974) show that girls who choose nontraditional or "pioneer" careers are not likely to be pressured by parents to date and marry. In addition, the findings suggested that career-oriented women often come from homes that foster independence, achievement, and active exploration. These career-oriented girls generally have working mothers as models or mothers who are positive about careers, along with well-educated fathers who are proud of them.

It seems then that there is a Cinderella Complex at work when pressure to date is high, when independence, achievement, and exploration are discouraged, and when mothers and fathers are unsupportive about careers. Gifted women coming from such homes may be particularly "at risk" for experiencing the handicaps associated with the Cinderella Complex.

## The Imposter Phenomenon and Low Academic Self-Esteem

The Imposter Phenomenon offers yet another example of bright women's internal barriers to achievement. According to case studies by psychotherapists Pauline Clance and Suzanne Imes (1978) at Georgia State University, numerous bright female clients denied that they were intelligent despite significant successes and measurable accomplishments. The researchers describe the phenomenon this way: "Women who experienced the imposter phenomenon maintained a strong belief that they were not intelligent; in fact, they were convinced that they had fooled everyone." Such women believe that their high examination scores are attributable to luck, that some mistake must have been made when they were admitted to prestigious colleges and graduate programs, and that their successes on jobs are due to their work being overevaluated, the researchers found. The women they studied consequently feared that someone important would discover they were "intellectual impostors."

Clance and Imes point out the irony that since success for women is contrary both to social expectations and to their own self-concept, they need to explain away their accomplishments — in this case by believing that they have fooled other people. How peculiar it is that a bright woman can change her own self-image so that she denies her clear achievements and abilities even to herself.

Are there particular family dynamics that generate the imposter phenomenon? Clance and Imes identify two patterns. In one kind of family, one sibling has been labeled the intelligent one; the "imposter," who may be quite as intelligent, is given some other label, such as "the sensitive one." Nothing she undertakes will prove to her family that she is intelligent, even if she gets better grades than the "intelligent one." She begins to doubt her intellect and believes that her family is correct despite the evidence.

In the second family, a girl has been given her family's full support. She has been persuaded by family to believe that she is superior virtually unto perfection. As the girl matures, she realizes that some tasks are indeed difficult for her. She suddenly begins to distrust her parents' perceptions of her. She may hide the fact that she has to study because it would destroy the family myth that she can do everything with ease. Her difficulties now prompt her to believe that if she isn't a genius, she must actually be only average, or even dumb — and clearly an imposter.

Paradoxically, four common behaviors actually work to help these women maintain the believe that they are imposters. First is diligence; the "imposter" works hard believing she would otherwise be discovered. Her hard work leads to more praise and rewards, frightening her into working even harder!

Second is a feeling of being "phony" that, Clance and Imes think, is often based in reality; most of the women studied had tried to tell professors and supervisors what they wanted to hear, rather than what these women really believed or knew.

Third is the use of charm and perceptiveness to win approval from superiors. A woman exhibiting this behavior may seek a mentor from among superiors she respects, and enthusiastically pursue an intense relationship with that person; she hopes inwardly that this person might bring out her intellect and creativity. When the mentor does declare her to be superior to others, however, she cannot accept this fervently sought appraisal; the mentor's evaluation, she fears, is based entirely on her charm and not on her ability.

Finally, a woman can also maintain her belief that she is an imposter by avoiding any display of confidence in her abilities. She thus plays on the negative consequences of both fear of success and the Cinderella Complex: The imposter suspects that if she truly believes in her own intelligence and shows it, she will be rejected by others (especially men) and will be forced into a lonely life without being nurtured by others. Thus she convinces herself that she really is not that intelligent and so eludes risks.

Among the women in my own study, I found support for the imposter syndrome in women's and girls' negative views of their academic abilities, and in denying their giftedness. In general, women tend consistently to underestimate their abilities.

As a group, women also take few academic risks — especially in math, an area that has been perceived as reserved for men (Sells, 1980). Most girls and women deny entirely any ability in math and avoid courses that might prove or disprove this belief in their inability. This characteristic avoidance of math and math-related courses has a powerful impact on women's career development, particularly in today's modern technological society.

The "math filter," as it is called by Sells (1980), effectively prevents the majority of women from entering high-status, high-paying occupations. In a study at the University of California—Berkeley, only 8 percent of women versus 57 percent of men had four years of high school math. Yet, four years of math were required to be eligible for three-fourths of UC's academic majors. Thus, avoiding math locked 92 percent of college women out of most of the numerous academic options.

Fear of success, avoidance of academic risks, and the imposter phenomenon all erode academic and vocational self-concept, distorting women's views of their abilities, and inhibiting their career development. These frustrations form the hurdles that stifle women who aspire to high-level professional careers.

The Process of Adjustment

The Fear of Success, the Cinderella Complex, and the Impostor Phenomenon together might suggest that all gifted women are pathetic neurotics crippled by success paranoia, independence, and their own brilliance. Or, they are merely repressing unconscious fears and hiding their anxieties. Yet when all the evidence is in, it appears that no single theory accounts for gifted women's underachievment. All barriers are at work for some gifted women, none for others, a combination of certain ones at certain times for most. The fact is that many patterns of adjustment characterize being female and gifted.

The three internal barriers described here may be characterized as pathologies, implying that gifted women are tainted or maladjusted in some way. This may be because many who experienced these barriers were women who had sought psychotherapy, reflecting the impact of these barriers on their lives.

However, there is a fourth internal barrier to achievement that ironically is not related to any unhealthy psychological state, even though it, too, often results in underachievement. It combines a healthy psychological state with an accommodating personality. This barrier is psychological adjustment, the process of resourceful adaptation to the environment — compromising and adjusting in order to survive and to cope psychologically. Some people must make greater adjustments than others. Those who are different from the average often must make the greatest adjustments.

An enlightening analogy can be learned from "rehabilitation psychologists," who study and treat individuals coping with disability of various kinds. The adjustment to severe disability comes in stages much as adjustment to dying does: denial, bargaining, anger, and acceptance. Denial is the stage when patients refuse to believe there is anything seriously wrong. (Amputees may refuse to acknowledge the stump of a leg.) In bargaining, the patients believe they can make a few changes, compromise in some way, and all will be well. When frustration mounts to a breaking point, patients experience rage at the condition, and anger sets in. Finally, acceptance is the phase when patients are at peace, having finally reconciled the dilemma, having faced the impossibility of change, but having found positive, constructive ways of coping. Only when a patient has reached acceptance can he or she be considered ready for vocational/career rehabilitation. The amputee baseball player must willingly give up his dream of playing in the major leagues. The heart patient must decide against going for the more prestigious, more stressful administrative position that once would have been possible.

It may seem a peculiar comparison — adjustment to disability and career development of gifted women. However, when one examines the adjustment of gifted women to their often restrictive lifestyles as wives, mothers, teachers, and nurses, the similarities are strong. Gifted women often seem to be adjusting to the *disability of being female*. Denial is rampant in the teen years; nothing is wrong, there is no problem with being a female. The teenager says she will be a doctor, get married, and take off for eighteen years to raise children. Or, there is no problem with being gifted; it's perfectly all right when gifted women drop out of college to marry because their giftedness wasn't real.

Later comes the bargaining. The gifted woman will hold back on her education to put her husband through medical school if he will do the same for her. She will move to another city with him if he will move when she gets a big break. She will have a child if he will help out so she can finish her thesis.

The anger stage seldom reaches full flower in a gifted woman. More often, it is expressed in apathy, cynicism, or depression. After years of supporting her husband's education, she gives up on her own ambitions in mild irritation. It's too late; she couldn't cope with being a student. After moving from city to city in response to her husband's promotions, she professes at least slight resentment that it will be too costly to find a satisfying job for her. After realizing that she must take primary responsibility for her child at the expense of her interests, she may feel angry with her husband, but only for a while, and she attempts to convince herself that she is more fulfilled than she actually is.

Acceptance comes when the anger has passed. She understands that she is gifted and has not really fulfilled her potential; but she also understands that she is a female, and that her experiences are simply typical for women in American society. She strives to find satisfaction in her achievements whenever she can, and vicariously enjoys the accomplishments of those around her. She blames nobody and is generally able to feel good about who she is. She realizes that she has accomplished a lot within the limitations of her lifestyle. She is unlikely to make any major changes.

So, it is a healthy adjustment process that sometimes prevents achievement; it is admirable self-acceptance that sometimes prevents optimal self-actualization. Gifted women who have accepted the disability of being female are often happy women who enjoy their lives. Margaret Mead describes a scholar/mother who said she could not finish her research "because the baby cries so much." Mead felt she just as well might have said, "the baby smiles so much." For it is the *pleasure* of children that has so often deterred gifted women from other work, not always the *burden* of children. It is often the husband's love and not the husband's oppression that has drawn women away from accomplishment. The society that wastes female brilliance has made it the norm for gifted women to lead the comparatively simple life lived by average women; and gifted women have largely adapted to that norm.

The process of adjustment is probably more to blame for women's failure to achieve their potential than the other internal factors combined, though clearly all these forces interact. It seems imperative that psychologists study the process of adjustment in gifted women more closely. Do gifted women perceive their own development as researchers describe it? Are there any ways of intervening so that women don't give up too easily on pursuing their own goals? Can psychologists help gifted women to understand that accepting barriers too readily may lead to cheating themselves as well as society of the fruits of their talents?

## Bibliography

Clance, P. R. and Imes, S. A. "The Impostor Phenomenon in High Achieving Women: Dynamics and Therapeutic Intervention." *Psychotherapy: Theory, Research, and Practice*, Vol. 15, 1978, 241-45.
This article is popular reading for graduate and professional women's support groups. It helps them understand fears about their own gifts.

de Beauvoir, S. *Memoirs of a Dutiful Daughter.* New York: Harper & Row, 1959.
This autobiography recounts the childhood of one of France's most eminent philosophers. It describes the extraordinary intellectual influence of her father in her early years, an influence followed by later criticisms of her intellect; the book thus describes a classic case of betrayal of the gifted girl. This is the first in a series of autobiographical volumes, all translated into English.

Dowling, C. *The Cinderella Complex.* New York: Summit Books, 1981.
Although based on a small sample of women, the book advances a theory that may have interesting implications for any woman who has ever found herself wanting Prince Charming to take care of everything.

## Supplemental Bibliography

Astin, H. S. and Myint, T. "Career Development and Stability of Young Women During Post High-School Years." *Journal of Counseling Psychology*, Vol. 19, 1971, 369-94.

Bernard, J. "Where Are We Now? Some Thoughts on the Current Scene." *Psychology of Women Quarterly*, Vol. 1, 1976, 21-37.

Candry, J. C. and Dyer, S. L. "Behavioral and Fantasy Measures of Fear of Success in Children." *Child Development*, Vol. 48, 1975, 1417-25.

Dweck, C. & Gilliard, D. "Expectancy Statements as Determinants of Reac-

144

tions to Failure: Sex Differences in Persistence and Expectancy Change." *Journal of Personality and Social Psychology,* Vol. 32, 1975, 1077-84.

Fagot, B. J. "Sex-determined Parental Reinforcing Contingencies in Toddler Children." Paper presented at meeting of the Society for Research in Child Development, New Orleans, March, 1977.

Farmer, H. S. "Environmental, Background, and Psychological Variables Related to Optimizing Achievement and Career Motivation for High School Girls." *Journal of Vocational Behavior,* Vol. 17, 1980, 58-70.

Farmer, H. S. "What Inhibits Achievement and Career Motivation in Women?" *The Counseling Psychologist,* Vol. 6, 1976, 12-14.

Fitzgerald, L. and Betz, N. "Issues in the Vocational Psychology of Women." In W. B. Walsh and S. H. Osipow (eds.), *The Handbook of Vocational Psychology.* Hillsdale, NJ: Erlbaum, 1983.

Harmon, L. W. "Career Counseling for Women." In *Psychotherapy for Women,* E. Rawlings and D. Carter (eds.). Springfield, Ill.: Charles Thomas, 1977.

Hoffman, L. W. "Early Childhood Experiences and Women's Achievement Motives." *Journal of Social Issues,* Vol. 28, 1972, 129-56.

Horner, M. S. "Toward an Understanding of Achievement Related Conflicts in Women." *Journal of Social Issues,* Vol. 28, 1972.

Levinson, R. M. "Sex Discrimination and Employment Practices: An Experiment in Unconventional Job Inquiries." *Social Problems,* Vol. 22, 1975, 533-42.

Sells, L. W. "The Mathematics Filter and the Education of Women and Minorities." In *Women and the Mathematical Mystique,* L. H. Fox, L. Brody, and D. Tobin (eds.). Baltimore: Johns Hopkins University Press, 1980.

Siegel, C. L. E. "Sex Differences in the Occupational Choices of Second Graders." *Journal of Vocational Behavior,* Vol. 3, 1973, 15-19.

Tangri, S. S. "Role Innovation in Occupational Choice Among College Women." JSAS *Catalog of Selected Documents in Psychology,* Vol. 4, 1974 (MS. NO. 555).

Tresemer, D. *Fear of Success.* New York: Plenum, 1977.

# 9

# Guiding Gifted Girls: Preschool through Professional School

Chapter 7 pointed to evidence that, basically, gifted girls and women are psychologically healthy. Rather than treating them as victims of disorders that prevent them from achieving, society would do well to treat them as normal, whole individuals who are simply not functioning at the upper limits of their abilities and who live in a society that is not accustomed to their exceptional talents. Respecting their wholeness, those who would foster their growth must offer them guidance that focuses on identifying their talents, building their strengths, helping them feel confident, and challenging them with the potential for personal and professional excellence.

Most parents of gifted children underestimate their own abilities and fail to consider that their child may be gifted. It is as though they believe gifted is the same as genius. "Well, she's bright, but not gifted," parents will say. Since underestimation seems particularly likely with preschool girls, I would admonish such parents to reevaluate their notions — they may well have a gifted child.

Even after children are identified as gifted, many people continue to believe that such children need no special help and can make it on their own. In reality, gifted girls, in particular, need the guidance of parents, teachers, and counselors throughout childhood, adolescence, and young adulthood if they are to achieve maximum potential. But what sort of guidance is most beneficial? A number of helpful hints and specific recommendations can be offered.

Gifted girls in the upper 3 to 5 percent intellectually live in a world primarily oriented toward the other 95 percent, where mediocrity and conformity are more valued than achievement. Gifted children need special support despite the myth that bright minds will find their own way. The book, *Guiding the Gifted Child* (Webb, Meckstroth & Tolan, 1982), provides an excellent understanding of these issues and contains practical suggestions about handling such common problems as motivation, discipline, sibling rivalry, stress management and peer relationships. It also discusses areas such as depression, identification of gifted children, and tradition breaking. The advice contained in that book, and others like it, is basic and necessary. Recommendations specifically for gifted girls and women must go further, however.

The following suggestions, addressed to parents, are equally applicable to teachers and counselors. These guidelines are divided by age-group: preschool, primary, junior high, senior, college, and post graduate.

### Preschool

An important principle for parents of preschool gifted girls to remember: If you don't want people to treat your girl like a fragile little flower, don't dress her like a doll in a nursery. Lace dresses that are difficult to keep clean prevent children from running, jumping, and climbing, and teachers moan when tears and stains inevitably appear. For school, dress your daughter for active play, rather than for inactivity on the sidelines. There are times and places for wispy materials and clever designs, but not at school — you wouldn't wear your evening gown to the hardware store! Dress your daughter in bold, bright, washable colors, not pallid pastels.

Choose nonsexist toys, or at least a broad array of toys, so that your daughter is not limited to dolls. Encourage her interest in toys that allow manipulation of objects and active solution of problems. She needs practice to develop a sense of mastery and self-worth. Don't discourage nurturant and quiet play, however! Simply make sure that other options are available and reinforced.

Choose child care cautiously; avoid day care centers or preschools that segregate girls and boys. Determine the attitudes of the child care workers toward sex roles. Look for child care facilities with men as well as women teachers. Often it will not be enough just to ask; you will need to observe how the teachers actually handle sex-role issues.

Be sure that day care centers/preschools do not rigidly enforce sleeping at nap time. Find a school that has "quiet time" instead, when children may lie quietly on cots and look at books or picture cards if they are not sleepy. Gifted girls seem to need afternoon alone-time more than sleep, and certainly they vary widely in the amount and types of limits and structure they need. You want a school that allows for individual differences.

Be sure that day care centers/preschools have plenty of books and that time for looking at books is encouraged. Many gifted girls will want to begin learning their alphabet or to try writing. This should not be discouraged since these children are often indeed ready for such adventures. It is also important that some individual time with puzzles, mechanical toys, musical instruments, and art work is allowed, especially when the child seems interested.

Take your preschool girl to your place of work and explain your job to her. Explain the work of all the people she sees while shopping, traveling, and/or attending to household needs. Particularly help her see women in leadership positions and in various occupations.

At about age four or five, have her take tests of intellectual ability, such as the WPPSI, the Kaufman ABC, or the Stanford-Binet. These may be required for early admission to kindergarten or special preschool gifted programs. Even if they are not, such tests will give you reasonable objective benchmarks for comparing your daughter's abilities with those of other children. However, remember that scores are only moderately meaningful at this age. (These tests are more helpful in identifying children with deficiencies than they are in pinpointing children with superior abilities.) No test for preschoolers can adequately predict superior academic achievement in primary or later school although school districts and educational programs persist in their use for this purpose. To administer the test, select your own psychologist, one who seems to have rapport with your daughter and who takes the time to develop it. Then interpret the results cautiously and perhaps even as an underestimate of true ability.

Take advantage of any preschool programs that may satisfy your gifted girl's hunger for intellectual stimulation or for an opportunity to exercise her abilities. As long as your daughter wants these activities and enjoys them, you're not "pushing." Try anything once, and see if she likes it — Suzuki lessons, karate, story hours, whatever sounds interesting.

Be alert to television programming. Sex role stereotypes in most children's and adult programming are worse than ever. Always discuss the meaning of girls' and boys' roles as seen on T.V., and your feelings about what you are watching. Your comments can help inoculate your child against the pressures to conform to the average.

Take time to answer her questions. It is easy to let yourself become so busy that you have little left to give her, particularly when she seems to ask so many questions that your ears feel tired. Build in a few minutes of special time each day when she has your individual attention. This will help her feel that her curiosity is appreciated.

### Primary

Gifted girls are usually reading by kindergarten, and their interest in reading grows rapidly. Many parents notice that their gifted daughters seem to be teaching themselves. Find books, books, and more books for her. Choose books that portray women in many roles. Let her read all she wants, and help her when she asks. If her reading skills cause her to finish tasks well ahead of classmates, insist that she be allowed to read quietly until the others are done.

Girls who are gifted in mathematical/logical reasoning often want math puzzles and problems to work with; seek them out. Often school supply stores in the community can be a treasure trove for games like these. A home computer may be a necessity, rather than a luxury, for the mathematically talented girl.

Girls with special talents such as visual arts and music need to understand and hone their abilities, but can do so only if they have the implements and instruments of their art. Individual lessons are usually valuable investments. How much do you push practice? There is no single answer except to say don't force practice to the point that it seriously jeopardizes your relationship with your daughter.

Gifted primary school girls typically thrive on adventure and novelty. Camping, exploring, museum-hopping, and traveling all broaden the child's exposure to what is possible in today's world. If you have to take a short business trip, take her with you and then stop in a museum on the way back home.

Don't over-schedule so that every waking moment is programmed. Gifted young girls need a private, special place: an attic, a basement room, a playhouse, or a treehouse. Fantasy and imagination develop well in such settings.

Don't push social relationships. For six-to-ten-year olds, books and play at one's own level are sometimes more interesting than other children are. Intellectual peer groups are useful, especially if you live in an area that has a gifted/parent group; but don't insist on participation. Chances are your daughter has the ability but not a great need to form close social relationships. Her friendships may become few and carefully selected, but quite intense.

If your girl is in a regular classroom, watch for signs of boredom and/or withdrawal: unwillingness to go to school, poor class participation, daydreaming, and sadness. These signs suggest she needs more stimulation and opportunity through mentoring, individualized instruction, or acceleration. She may not complain or act out as a boy might.

Role models are important. Even in baby sitters, try to find an older girl or woman who is intellectually oriented, self-confident, and assertive to be a sometime companion.

Support your child emotionally even when she is "thorny." A characteristic of gifted girls is their intensity, although usually it takes time and support for them to learn how to harness this intensity. Show that you will love her even if she is not just like the other girls. Chances are that she doesn't find herself likable right then either and needs your special support and encouragement.

Help her feel special and unique. Let her know you are delighted by her gifts and talents. Always be honest about what you know about her abilities, and don't hide her giftedness from her, although you may call it by various other names, such as "bright," "curious," etc. Gifted children are almost always aware that they are different, but often don't understand how or why or whether the difference is good or bad. To open this area for discussion is important and, despite parents' worries, is not likely to give her an oversized ego.

## Junior High

Try to conceal your astonishment when your uniquely gifted offspring suddenly wants to be like every other girl in her class. Pressures to conform are intense at this age. Try not to protest about her sudden desire to be "normal." Let her buy the faddish clothes and strange records. Within limits, let her go to the parties she wants to attend and try to avoid useless power struggles — particularly those you can't win.

Refuse, however, to cooperate in her attempts to evaluate herself primarily in terms of her attractiveness or her relationships. While you should be tolerant of her fluctuating self-image, continue to encourage her "self-actualizing" efforts — school work, activities, career planning. Though at times you may feel your efforts are useless, your continued support will help her develop a sense of personal worth and integrity independent of evaluations from others.

Insist that your daughter continue taking math and science courses if those have become optional. Whether she performs outstanding work in such courses is not the issue. Basic knowledge in these subjects preserves her options for choices later in her life.

She may go through periods of being exceedingly self-critical, particularly as she becomes aware of the conflict between "fitting in" and developing herself as an independent person. Receptive listening and gentle advice are needed. Perhaps she can talk also with some bright high school and college women about these issues.

Help keep her career aspirations high by encouraging continuing exploration of careers. Biographies are helpful reading. Volunteer work in the right settings can provide experience-based career education.

## Senior High

With most gifted girls, your efforts will begin to have positive resuls, although you may still have many days when you feel that these efforts have been useless. You can expect at least brief episodes of a rekindled interest in academics and careers. When they happen, be ready to reinforce them lavishly; support and encourage these spurts in growth.

Help your daughter find college and scholarship guides, as well as good career information. The family's clear interest and expectation that she will attend college is of inestimable value. Talk about colleges and postgraduate education at the dinner table. Accompany her to college social and sports functions, and to the college guidance and placement services.

Seek competent, nonsexist career guidance that includes assessment of vocational interests, personality, and values. Take advantage if there is a high school or college counselor with a special interest in gifted girls. Otherwise, find a career guidance specialist in private practice through your state gifted association.

Senior high gifted girls need to complete four full years of math in order to assure all career options. If four years of math are not available through the high school, try to find evening courses at a local commuity college.

The need for a mentor continues; if your daughter has become especially talented in a specific area, find a coach or instructor in her area. A female may not be available in some male-dominated areas; but a man can also be an appropriate mentor. So, seek the best available instructor without regard to gender.

Your gifted daughter will particularly need to understand the implications of her giftedness on her relationships at this time in life. Help her to understand that she has choices in romantic feelings, that she can deliberately choose boyfriends with whom she can communicate easily. Sometimes gifted girls find they have relatively few boys from which to choose. As parents, you too must be realistic about her narrow range of choices for relationships with men, and help her develop patience.

The pitfalls of pregnancy and early childbirth and marriage may be avoided by providing accurate sex education and discussions about marriage. Just because she is gifted, don't expect your daughter to know all about sex. Sex is a very powerful urge in high school and is embedded within rapidly changing relationships. Also, help her make the difficult, future educational decisions that are likely to be independent of relationship decisions.

Gifted girls are full of activity and intensity. When possible, prevent her from spreading herself too thin and becoming an exhausted teenager. Encourage her to focus on excellence in a few areas rather than trying to be perfect in everything.

A particularly helpful technique for promoting perspective is to ask her to imagine her life ten years from now. What would be the perfect future day for her? Then, help her to examine what barriers she sees that might prevent such a day, and how she might overcome those barriers.

## College

Try to find an all-women's college or a serious, academically oriented coed institution with a decent proportion of female faculty. Evidence indicates that women's colleges and campuses with high proportions of women faculty members produce more women scholars and leaders, apparently because they are better able to provide role models.

Encourage your daughter to seek career counseling early in her college program so that she can avoid the frequent changes of major common to "multipotential" students. Suggest that she find a mentor even if she must begin as an unpaid assistant to a potential mentor; perhaps she can find such sponsorship in her academic advisor.

Help her to understand the internal and external reasons that women's grades slip in college. In all likelihood she is quite able, but is she willing to compete with male students? Are her professors nonsexist, or do they seem to favor male students? Suggest assertiveness training if she needs it in order to speak up in class. She will want to be sure her professors notice and respect her, but she can only accomplish this if she is reasonably assertive. Share with her some of your successes in being assertive.

Help her keep problems with relationships in perspective. She will need to understand that the traditional college dating system is not likely to lead her to satisfying relationships with men since the emphasis is typically on popularity, "good looks" and conformity. Suggest that she seek men and women friends in those campus organizations that have goals more closely in tune with her own.

If she becomes involved in unusual campus groups, don't panic. Gifted young women are often very idealistic or even iconoclastic; membership in slightly fringe groups provides them an opportunity for intellectual independence and testing values. Most eminent women needed to pass through this stage.

Initiate values-centered discussions. In what way is she seeking meaning and purpose in life? How is she planning to make a difference?

Her ideas often will be awkward, incomplete or unrealistic. Nonetheless, it is important that you indicate your confidence in her growing ability to contribute importantly to society.

Make your home a safe haven. With their intensity, gifted young women often overextend themselves and have intellectual or emotional crises. Sometimes college can be lonely and frightening, especially if your daughter is younger than most, or farther from home than others. A home base to return to is extremely reassuring and helpful.

## Postgraduation/Professional School

By now your gifted daughter's education may extend beyond that of both parents. Her interests may be esoteric and far from your area of expertise; this could become a barrier between you. Maintain your curiosity and interest in her work. She still needs your emotional support.

She may be feeling a need for financial independence; many of her peers are now working at full-time jobs, making more money than she. Help her out as much as she will let you, and discourage her from passing up educational opportunities because of the cost. What may seem like a large amount of money to her now — for special lessons, for tuition to a prestigious graduate school — will be well worth the investment.

Discuss with her the possibilities of being underemployed and underpaid, and encourage her to familiarize herself with what she rightfully can expect in various positions. She may need to learn new on-the-job interpersonal skills to prevent others from placing barriers in her path, or to prevent herself from hindering herself by her own behaviors.

Her self-doubts may recur. Having set high standards for herself, she may fall short, causing her to feel inadequate, even depressed. Believe in her even at times when she doesn't believe in herself. You have raised a person with a fine intellect and extraordinary talents, who also happens to have the cultural "disability" of being female. If you continue to be a supportive parent with high expectations for your daughter, you can help her maintain her aspirations even in a society that discourages her achievements.

After reading part of the first manuscript for *Smart Girls, Gifted Women*, Big Mary wrote me this epilogue.

It ain't easy being gifted . . . you see more, hear more, feel and understand more. I'm confident ignorance is bliss. Being gifted is enormously beneficial . . . providing thorough, serious, logical work habits and arming one with the rather obvious advantage applicable to getting through life. Standards are higher. The old competitiveness of the gifted classroom favorably influences future success.

However, it has also contributed shamefully to my smug, elitist, impatient frustration with the large mass of mediocrity. After all, a respectable chunk of my school years were spent surrounded by those who met and kept up that demanding grade. During some extensive dental work, I experienced a laughing gas-induced hallucination that revealed a "master plan." Part of the plan was based on the revelation that a large mass of society was actually composed of "filler people." Not real people . . . automations like the slobby neighbors, half the drivers on the road, all Republicans. The subconscious demonstration of elitism.

I really don't have much call for my "gift" these days . . . I'm a homemaker and mother of a gifted 8 year-old daughter. See how I maneuvered that into the conversation? I'm not above maneuvering either of our giftedness into conversation, like a trump card — to be used only and modestly and legitimately at its exact hour. Even though my gift is temporarily atrophying, when called into action, it sometimes even impresses me.

I can truthfully proclaim it to be the single most important, consistent, valuable factor through this trip we're all on. At times my giftedness has been the only (and fortunately most valuable) asset that either literally or in my mind could not be stolen, stripped, denied or diminished. During many torrid periods, I clung to the value of my brain like many people find solace in their God.

As will be increasingly useful in the future, I can presently look in the mirror and see the effects of a lot of mileage on the old appearance, laugh at how athletic I was, regret the neglected art talent, but rejoice at what's still there in the brain department . . . "Oh no, they can't take that away from me."

Perhaps if there is any rhyme, reason, forethought or plan to life on earth, my 'gift' was a necessity to me, a formerly docile, shrinking, discounted sufferer of acutely reduced self-image. My brains gave me courage and self-confidence to question, act, progress, accomplish where it might have been easier to ignore.

# 10

# Helping Gifted Girls
# Aim Higher:
# Programs That Work

Parent groups and schools interested in developing guidance programs based on gifted girls' special needs often search in vain for models. They know that bringing gifted girls together to share their feelings about their educational and vocational plans, to be exposed to role models, and to gain college and career information is important in overcoming psychological barriers to achievement and in raising aspirations. Models do exist, however, and their programs are outstanding in helping gifted girls make challenging academic choices and raising career aspirations: the diagnostic-prescriptive program of Project CHOICE; Lynn Fox's "Changing Attitudes" program for gifted girls; and the Raising Career Aspirations project at the Guidance Laboratory for Gifted and Talented at the University of Nebraska.

## Project CHOICE

In 1979, Case Western Reserve University in Cleveland sponsored Project CHOICE: Creating Her Options in Career Education, a diagnostic-prescriptive program for talented adolescent women. The counselors' functions were to diagnose barriers that stood in the way of gifted girls' achievement and to prescribe a series of activities to overcome those barriers. The program broadened the career options for participants by pointing out personal and cultural barriers likely to interfere with their realization of potential. Project CHOICE was field tested with gifted eleventh grade girls screened by counselors using a talent inventory and school records.

An initial diagnostic approach centered around a student questionnaire and an assessment of internal barriers. The questionnaire sought information about possible external barriers such as family structure, parents' occupation and education, parental aspirations for the child's exposure to role models, financial resources, and sex discriminatory practices. Internal barriers were examined through various measures of self-esteem, achievement motivation, assertiveness, and fear of success. The level of each student's career development was measured by the degree to which the student's career ideas were crystallized and by the appropriateness of these ideas.

A prescriptive plan resulted for each participant, indicating possible treatment of or solutions to internal or external barriers. Sometimes these strategies were individual, such as providing a student with a role model in the community; other times they were group strategies, such as referral to a "self-esteem" group.

The overall fourteen-week career development experience contained three career information workshops, student-selected role model experiences, and eleven group sessions in which the core curriculum was modified to meet the needs of each group member.

While it was one of the most comprehensive programs on record for guiding gifted girls, Project CHOICE was limited because evaluation information was not available to measure long-term success.

Such a program treats the gifted girl as a whole person while at the same time assisting in reducing barriers. It serves as a model for those who wish to improve a gifted girl's chances for achievement.

## Changing Attitudes for Gifted Girls

At Johns Hopkins University, Lynn Fox developed a program to change junior high girls' attitudes and course-taking behaviors toward careers in science and mathematics. Normally, girls drop out of math courses early in their education, thereby closing off many options. The program provided special social stimulation to motivate girls in math and science. Twenty-six Baltimore-area seventh grade girls were selected because they had scored extremely well on the SAT-M test, a mathematics achievement test for high school seniors.

The three-month course, taught by women instructors, was exclusively for girls. The informal structure stressed small group and individualized instruction, and cooperative rather than competitive activities. Since girls generally focus on social careers, teachers emphasized the ways in which mathematics could be used to solve social problems. Individual and family counseling encouraged girls to view themselves as competent in mathematics, and to overcome any "math anxiety."

To help researchers assess the program's effectiveness, two control groups were used, one female and one male. These groups were pretested on knowledge of algebra, values, and career interests; boys were already more predisposed than girls to consider mathematics and science careers.

Only eighteen of the twenty-six girls attended the class on a regular basis, and eleven enrolled for Algebra II the following year. At the end of the first year, ten girls and no boys were accelerated by one year, girls in the control group as well as all girls participating in the experiment were more advanced in math knowledge than boys in the control group. Two years later, 48 percent of the girls in the experiment were accelerated by one or more years, compared to 9 percent of control girls. Control boys were accelerated at about the same rate as girls in the experiment.

The program was successful in challenging the girls to higher achievement in math. However, during that same three-year period the career interests of these girls in math rose initially, but then dropped off. Gains from the experimental treatment faded as time passed without any further encouragement from female role models.

## The Guidance Laboratory for Gifted and Talented

Soon after the high school reunion that stimulated my interest in the career development of gifted women, the University of Nebraska–Lincoln agreed to support a new Guidance Laboratory for Gifted and Talented. The Guidance Lab, which would provide counseling services and a setting for research, was modeled on the successful Guidance Institute for Talented Students at the University of Wisconsin–Madison. Each Friday, ten to fifteen high school students from Nebraska came for day-long career guidance through vocational, personality, and values inventories, visits to university classes, career information, and individual and group counseling.

From the beginning, counselors noticed that the girls had lower career aspirations than boys; statistical analyses of the prestige scores of their most preferred careers confirmed this observation. How could the Guidance Lab personnel change gifted girls' attitudes? The ambiguous results of previous studies and programs were discouraging. Too many sex equity/career education programs had attempted and failed to interest young women in nontraditional careers and lifestyles. At an early session of the Guidance Lab, one counselor suggested tactfully but determinedly that "secretary" was perhaps not appropriate as a career aspiration for a straight-A student. The young woman to whom he spoke brushed a hand through her curls, straightened the cameo at her lacy neck, smiled winningly at the counselor and said, "Oh no! I would *like* working with people in an office. Besides, my mom is really into Women's Lib but I'm *not!*" What seemed to be happening was that the gifted girls with low aspirations had heard feminist arguments for higher achievement and hadn't bought them. They regarded the counselor's suggestion as women's liberation rhetoric; and a gifted sixteen-year-old can be one of the most narrowly focused and stubborn of all beings.

The sermons of feminism generally don't work with today's gifted adolescent girls for several reasons. First, members of their generation recognize and reject rhetoric, even when they believe in the basic value of the points being made. Second, a feminist argument for higher aspirations is simply too abstract and too alien for young women; they want concrete information about alternatives, and are too young to be interested in political or philosophical implications of career decisions.

Beside using feminist arguments, counselors also often make the mistake of suggesting arbitrary high-paying, high-status careers as alternatives to girls' more traditional choices. For the girl who wants to be a teacher, a counselor is remiss to suggest engineering simply on the basis of the better salary. If a girl chooses nursing, the counselor might suggest "doctor." The alternatives must not be offered without first exploring what draws the young woman to nursing; it may be the study of medicine, but it could also be the opportunity to nurture, or the smaller investment in higher education, or many other motives.

In the end, it became clear that our lab at Nebraska needed to try new approaches that involved neither rhetoric nor arbitrary suggestions of high-level careers. Perhaps if young women could raise their aspirations from within their current personality structure and personal values, they might be more lastingly interested in change.

The Career Aspirations program was designed as an intensive career education workshop for gifted girls who were juniors in high school. Many of these girls are rural gifted, and drove as far as 400 miles to spend a day at the Guidance Laboratory for Gifted and Talented. In addition to the variety of vocational, personality, and values tests, the campus tour of university classes in their interest areas, each girl met with an individual counselor who helped her set goals using the "Personal Map of the Future." In addition, a group counseling session encouraged the girls to fantasize their "Perfect Future Day," and then to discuss the barriers to attaining such a perfect day.

The major strategy of the individual counselor in raising aspirations is to establish clearly what the girl's personality traits and values are, then to raise her aspirations to higher-status careers that are appropriate within those traits and values. Thus, the gifted girl with a great need to provide nurturance and who loves to work with children is encouraged to elevate her aspirations from child-care worker to child psychologist. The bright and enterprising girl who expresses a need for order and convention is encouraged to raise her aspirations from secretary to business woman.

The group counselors then provide information about the long-term consequences of current lifestyle decisions. Information based on research outlined in this book is described during the course of the discussion: Girls learn about the success of integrators, the greater satisfaction of Terman's professional women, and the negative effects of early marriage and childbirth on career achievement. The counselors do not preach; they simply share their knowledge about the lives of gifted women to help girls make their decisions.

The Guidance Lab techniques seem to work. When we compared the girls' aspirations before the Guidance Laboratory experience with their aspirations six to nine months later, we found significant change. Girls had changed their career choices from "teacher" to "lawyer"; from "designer" to "architect"; from "X-ray technician" to "physician"; from "youth counselor" to "administrator for juvenile services." We were overjoyed! It was, to our knowledge, the first time that gifted girls' attitudes to their own futures had been altered. A comparable group of gifted girls, who had not attended the Guidance Laboratory, had experienced no change over the same period of time. Will the change last? We don't know, but we hope so. It would be unusual for a one-day experience to have a lifelong impact. However, if the girls found other sources of encouragment, and their changed aspirations led them to seek better educational opportunities, we may have started a snowball rolling. We will be following this group for some time, and hope to see continued high aspirations and achievements.

## Individual Counseling and Guidance

Individual counseling and guidance can help gifted girls and women change negative attitudes toward themselves and to raise their career goals. Few psychologists or counselors specialize in the gifted and talented. Hopefully, the number of mental health providers who understand the needs of gifted and talented will grow as our society's interest about this population develops.

A few major centers for individual counseling of gifted and talented do exist. Notable among these are: the Guidance Laboratory for Gifted and Talented in Lincoln, Nebraska; SENG (Supporting the Emotional Needs of Gifted) at Wright State University in Dayton, Ohio; and the Guidance Institute for Talented Students in Madison, Wisconsin. A gifted resources institute at Purdue University does not focus on psychological needs of gifted, but does provide counseling. Similarly, various talent search programs such as the Talented Identification Program at Duke University and the Study for Mathematically/Verbally Precocious Youth at Johns Hopkins University will consult and make appropriate referrals for counseling.

## Bibliography

Case Western University. *Project Choice: Creating New Options in Career Education*. Cleveland, OH: Case Western Reserve University, 1979. (ERIC Document Reproduction Service No. ED 185 321).

Fox, L. H. *Changing Behaviors and Attitudes of Gifted Girls*. Papers presented at the American Psychological Association, September, 176b, Washington, DC (ERIC Document Reproduction Service No. ED 183 088).

Kerr, B. A. "Raising aspirations of gifted girls." *Vocational Guidance Quarterly, Fall, 1983*.

Dr. Frances Cordova, astrophysicist at Los Alamos National Laboratories, voted one of the 100 most distinguished young scientists by *Discovery* magazine says of her career:

You're never too old to get into something new. It's never too late. I started out in English literature; I thought all I could do was teaching — teaching of English. I was discouraged by nonscientists from pursuing science. At 23 I started over in science. Until I tried these things, until I made my own decisions, I let myself be discouraged. It's remarkable I could have been so discouraged!

I had a good model — my mom started law school at 40.

Being a woman hasn't affected me in any way but positively. I'm really happy with how I've been treated. With science, people are egalitarian: anybody in the lab who is capable is wanted there. Even in school I was treated equally — that is — I was treated as poorly as the rest of the students.

My work is inherently interesting. I don't mind putting in the work needed — there's a big reward: the satisfaction of finding something new in the sky.

# 11

# Conclusion

So what became of the little girls I remembered from my school, who were to be the leaders of tomorrow, and who were so scrupulously trained for that destiny? Nearly a decade has passed now since Mary asked me that question at our ten-year reunion. Now I can offer some answers.

Most of these women had not fulfilled the promise of their girlhood. Their childhood dreams flickered, their hopes for achievement dimmed; their lives at twenty-nine differed little from women of average intelligence. Most were homemakers or in "disposable" careers such as teachers and nurses; only a few were professionals. They were still decidedly easy to identify as gifted people. Their articulate, introspective letters and comments told both of their special qualities and the unfulfilled hopes, the vacuum that now permeated their lives.

Although bright and talented, all but a few of my former classmates were careful to deny their giftedness and to minimize its importance. Only a few claimed to be unhappy with their current situation; most were positive and cheerful about their lives. They portrayed themselves as self-assured, self-accepting women despite evaporated childhood visions.

My review of the research confirmed that my St. Louis classmates were quite representative of gifted women generally. They had been more adventurous and curious than was characteristic of less gifted girls; within the interests they professed, they were more like boys than other girls. As other studies had shown, my classmates, too, had excelled in elementary and secondary schools, usually surpassing boys in academic achievement. Adolescence struck this group harshly as giftedness, careers and dreams were swept aside — not unlike findings involving gifted adolescents in other studies; the girls redirected their energies into such traditional achievement as finding boyfriends and showing concern about their popularity. Although they had shown they were good at math and science, these young women typically chose the more standard feminine humanities and social science courses. Those who did attend college entered traditional women's fields, such as teaching and nursing. Ten years after high school, the proportion of my Sputnik school group in homemaking and traditional occupations matched Terman's group of gifted women almost exactly. Would the homemakers in my group be as dissatisfied fifty years hence as so many in the Terman group at age sixty-two? Would the working women have as pathetic an earning record as the underpaid Terman women?

Underachievement among gifted women is fact. I looked to my classmates and to the literature for explanations. The attitudes and overt discrimination of our culture had created an environment that was fairly hostile to feminine achievement; my classmates and others knew that employment usually translated into underemployment. The Horner Effect or Fear of Success may have prompted the most feminine of the group to underachieve in competition with men. The Cinderella Complex may have affected the most dependent of the group, sending them into a determined search for someone to take care of them. And the Imposter Phenomenon may have drained the success of a few high achievers who doubted themselves. However, most women in our group, as most gifted women, did not suffer from psychological disabilities; paradoxically, most of them were hurt by their tendencies to be well adjusted, easy going and accommodating. They adjusted to the disadvantage of being female, accepting fractured aspirations much as a patient caught in a no-choice predicament accepts fractured limbs.

What about the very few in our group who are realizing their potential — the doctor, lawyer and university professor? Characteristics that distinguish them from their peers also are similar to those found among eminent women. Those who achieved had stubbornly held to their dreams. They probably received more intellectual nourishment as children and more time alone to digest knowledge. They were not as conforming or popular as others. Being at the rim of the social ladder may actually have helped them maintain both independence and some sense of their aspirations. They had mentors and counselors who helped them. They stayed single, chose a lesbian lifestyle, or married men who supported their achievements. Most important, they fell in love with an idea, took responsibility for themselves, and thus derived strength.

It is a national tragedy that a mere handful of gifted women have attained eminence while the remainder accept obscurity. How long can society continue to squander the brilliance of gifted women? How long will gifted women stand on the threshold of self-actualization, not taking steps that would fulfill their dreams because they might inconvenience someone?

Gifted women in general, despite a characteristically composed appearance, know they owe the world and themselves more than cheerfulness, compliance, and children. While all that pent-up potential may be dormant, it is still alive and its intensity can resurface.

For gifted women to fulfill their potential and their responsibilities to society is a two-way street. On the one hand, the woman must be willing; but society also must take substantial responsibility for guidance of gifted girls and for creating situations that would nurture, direct and inspire intellect among gifted girls.

What then must be done for gifted girls? First, gifted girls must be discovered. The field of gifted education offers old and new techniques for identifying gifted and talented students. I.Q. tests, creativity tests, musical auditions, art competition — all help lead to the discovery of the gifted. With their social camouflage, gifted girls are not always easy to identify. No matter, they need to be found.

Second, they must be *nourished,* by providing as much reading and computer time or music as they crave. For them, it may mean skipping a grade or accelerating within subject areas or, if these are not possible, seeking enrichment opportunities in the regular classroom. Individualized instruction through tutoring or coaching can provide the stimulation the gifted girl needs.

Third, they must be *guided.* The most striking feature of the education of my group of gifted peers was the total lack of guidance. Gifted girls will not get by on their own. Ideally, they should have access to skilled counselors who will provide them with the emotional support, with comprehensive information about career education, and with the specialized strategies that can help raise and maintain high aspirations. Parents and teachers can also augment gifted girls' needs for personal and career guidance by shaping their adventurousness, seeking information about future alternatives in their areas of interest, and always challenging them to be more and do more than they thought they could.

And, they need to be *loved.* Being smarter, more sarcastic or cynical and sensitive to the point of tears make a gifted girl hard to love. But such qualities also make great love all the more necessary. A gifted girl whose intelligence places her into a miniscule percentile will feel alone easily, and should never be treated as a "walking head." The thorns of some gifted girls are largely reactions to the lack of friendliness and absence of love they sense from others. When the gifted girl's cynicism melts it is because of a warm and caring relationship. Unusual sensitivity of gifted girls means they need more reassurance to help them through times of sadness; and if such reassurance takes place, they are capable of great compassion toward others.

Finally, they need *room.* Whether it is "a room of one's own" or a job of one's own, gifted girls and women need the opportunity to do what they love to do — to learn and to work. In so many families, the intellectual and emotional needs of gifted girls go unmet because the family has other priorities, and because gifted girls are so accepting of their families' other priorities. Everywhere gifted women are under-employed, taking the jobs they can get and hoping one day for a chance to prove what they can do.

Gifted women have revitalized the arts, humanized the sciences, and changed our history. Our daughters can shape the future if only we challenge them, guide them, and preserve their hope.

# 12

# Appendix A

## Questions and Answers

As director of the Guidance Laboratory at the University of Nebraska, I have counseled hundreds of gifted girls, gifted women, and parents of gifted girls. Much of the content of this book has grown out of my counseling and research work at the Guidance Laboratory. Many problems recur, and I have collected the most common questions to address here; they are grouped into problems of childhood, adolescence, and adulthood.

## Problems of Childhood

**Q. Our three-year-old daughter shows signs of giftedness; she is verbally far ahead of her peers; she has many creative ideas, and her energy level is very high. Even though we have been very careful about bringing her up in an egalitarian home, our concern is that she is so very feminine — she plays only with girls and seems only interested in girls' toys. We want her to develop all her talents, not just traditionally feminine ones.**

A. It is natural for preschoolers to gravitate to their own sex, and it is inevitable that they will learn sex-role behavior of the dominant culture from the peer group. The T.V. advertisements during children's programming promote dogmatic sex-role stereotypes; media images of women continue to portray them as weak, silly, passive, and compliant. You cannot completely protect your child from these stereotypes and images because they are everywhere.

You can, however, help her develop an independent mind and the strength to refute cultural stereotypes. Be openly critical of sexist advertising and programming; explain in simple terms why they are wrong: "Those police are all men, but women are police too." Soon she will pick up the habit. A three-year-old I know well said of the popular cartoon series, "Hey, Mommy, where are all the women smurfs?" However, never be critical of her desire to play with dolls, dress up, play house, etc.; you would only make her ashamed of her femininity, which is precisely what you want to avoid! Instead, provide her additionally with alternative games and toys she may choose if and when she desires. Deirdre Lovecky (1983), who reported on gifted females at the National Association for Gifted Children in 1983, suggests that types of toys given to gifted girls may also be important in their developing mastery skills. Toys that have multiple functions, use different levels of skill over time, and encourage use of strategy and imagination are those to which gifted boys tend to devote much time and energy: Legos, erector sets, building sets, trains, puzzles, games with elaborate rules or use of strategy, science kits, and arts and crafts projects. If girls are also given such toys, one important outcome can be their development of the types of visual-perceptual-motor skills, problem-solving skills, alternate strategies, risk taking abilities, and persistence behaviors that underlie successful perform-ance in math, the sciences, and other traditionally male roles.

Finally, continue to encourage your daughter's independence by helping her see that her successes result from her efforts and not from luck; always praise "trying." Teach her that her ideas count by listening to them and by putting her suggestions into effect. Make it clear that *you* know she has important things to say, and show her how to get others' attention through polite but firm assertion.

In this way, you will add to those important qualities of nurturing, cooperation, and even temperedness, the equally important qualities of independence, achievement-orientation, and assertiveness.

**Q. My gifted nine-year-old girl doesn't want to do anything but read. She sits inside even in the summer and reads all day. What can we do to get her outside?**

A. First, it's important to understand that the period between seven — when most high-I.Q. children become capable of reading really interesting books — and eleven — when adolescence be-gins — is a time when gifted girls are most likely to enjoy being alone and to enjoy reading more than any other leisure time activity. This doesn't mean that your daughter is going to be a cloistered bookworm when she grows up; it most likely means that she is feeding an intellectual curiosity that is as yet unblemished by social anxiety. For her, reading most of the time is probably okay.

If you're worried about her getting fresh air and exercise, you might try two strategies. Build a tree-house (really!) where she can read outside. Suggest nature books and stories about people exploring the outdoors or enjoying sporting adventures to encourage her participation in such active events.

**Q. Our third grade girl hasn't had any close friends since kindergarten; she plays alone even at recess at her school. We don't think it's by choice, but she won't talk about it. If we try to force the subject, the discussion ends in tears. We wish she could be in gifted classes, but our school doesn't have any at her grade level.**

A. Gifted girls often do prefer to play alone, but it sounds as if your daughter is unhappy about her situation. She may be ashamed to talk with you about it because she knows her isolation makes you unhappy. Many possible reasons can explain the social isolation of gifted girls: others may resent their good grades; they may be dissimilar in appearance and behavior at a time when conformity is very important; they may lack "friendship skills" such as ability to listen and to give compliments and share toys and treats; they may pick the wrong kids to approach; they may talk about topics or suggest play that is too advanced for other children. Sometimes gifted children try to organize or boss the other children, or with their intensity will attempt to be the center of activity through making up complicated games, rules, etc. Talk with her about friendship skills, empathy, sharing, and tolerance. Role playing is often particularly helpful for promoting understanding of how others see her.

You may never be able to identify the causes. What you can do is this: If she seems to feel pressure to make friends, take the pressure off. Let her know that you don't consider friendships to be achievements that she must attain. Let her know that bright girls do sometimes have periods of loneliness, but that these periods don't last forever; a time will come when she will find friends like herself.

Continue your search for intellectual peers — boys or girls — and try to arrange for them to meet. Many parents of gifted groups exist, even in small cities, though they may be identified as Friends of the Museum or the Inventors' Council. Try to find out where the nearest group is and see if they have a children's play group.

Do help your daughter develop similarities to other children. Make sure she has clothes and toys like the other girls if she wants them. Many parents dislike kids' fads and refuse to allow them to participate; I think this may hurt gifted children more than it protects them from the crassness of consumerism. You don't need to go overboard; just ask her if there are any things she would like, and mildly go along with choices.

Help her learn friendship skills by allowing her to bring small treats or toys for friends and to give gifts of compliments. Many parents of gifted children feel that this is "buying friendship." It may very well be that, but it happens to be how friendships are formed in children's culture.

Make sure that all of these strategies are not unilaterally announced and instituted by you; instead, suggest them to your daughter objectively and allow her to choose to try them if she wishes.

**Q. As a homemaker, how can I possibly help my highly gifted daughter? At ten years old, she already seems to have read more than I have. I feel I am not a good role model for her. I was not able to pursue my education because of family responsibilities.**

A. There is no reason for you to believe that you must be an exact role model for your daughter, and there is no evidence that gifted girls with professional mothers are any more accomplished than those whose mothers are homemakers. A mother can be a role model, or she can be a supporter of her daughter's ambitions. If you are willing to show interest in your daughter's enthusiasms, to help her find special tutoring and role models she might need, and to show her your love and acceptance when she feels different and alone, then you will have been a very great help to her indeed.

Q. Our eight-year-old gifted daughter loved school at first, but now she says she doesn't like it "because there's nothing to do." She is often sick before school and sometimes has to leave school feeling ill when there is apparently nothing physically wrong. She also has nightmares at night. Her home life is happy, her teachers like her, and she has nice friends; I'm puzzled.

A. Boredom is the single most common school problem of gifted and talented students in the regular classroom. Boys will show their boredom by disruptive behavior and disorderly work. Girls, on the other hand, often show no overt sign. They continue to smile and participate even when they are irritated by the repetitiveness of it all. Their anger comes out in daydreaming, psychosomatic illnesses, bad dreams, and nervous habits. Investigate the possibility that your daughter must have a chance for more challenge. Consider moving her up a grade or more, getting tutoring for part of the day, or better still, attending a school with special classes for the gifted. If you aren't sure how bright she is, have her tested by a competent child psychologist.

Q. What is the effect of acceleration and grade-skipping on gifted girls? Can these practices be harmful?

A. Grade-skipping and acceleration are far less harmful than the alternative — staying in the regular classroom. In fact, at both our Guidance Laboratory and Wright State University's SENG, acceleration often has been found to be a treatment of choice for gifted children with certain kinds of emotional problems. Gifted girls, who mature earlier than boys, probably adjust to grade-skipping more easily than boys. Acceleration or early entrance into school, when applied appropriately, can hardly be anything but helpful.

Q. My little girl has such wild and crazy ideas. She wants to talk about space travel, ESP, and fantasy tales. She dresses like a nut, and experiments with talking in foreign accents. Every day she's into something new and strange. I hate to say this, but I *do* wish she'd be a little more normal, especially in social situations.

A. My first impulse is to tell you to enjoy your delightful little eccentric while you can, because, sadly, what puberty doesn't accomplish, peer pressure will to make your daughter less "different." Your daughter's interests are not unusual among gifted children. Think of it this way: Certain subjects allow gifted kids intellectual sensations they crave. For instance, an interest in space travel and ESP gives a gifted child the sense of wonder and possibility that is nearly impossible to achieve in a world where there are no new geographical frontiers. An interest in funny clothes and accents allows a gifted child to "try on" personalities and so to explore human nature and potential. So what seems like wild and crazy ideas actually serve the important function of training your girl's intellectual curiosity and sharpening her empathy.

On the other hand, gifted girls who are smart enough to impersonate cockneys and cowgirls also are smart enough to impersonate nice little girls. So when you have those few situations in which you need an imaginary nice little girl (reunions with aged, wealthy relatives, for instance) you might ask your daughter to trot out her "Pollyanna" role for an afternoon.

**Q. My daughter is such a perfectionist it scares me. Won't this lead her to put too much stress on herself?**

A. Perfectionism is a common characteristic of gifted children; it's a trait many of them seem to be born with. At the Guidance Laboratory we have seen casual, easygoing parents who are amazed that they have raised a child who is obsessed with neatness and order, "doing things right," and obtaining 100% scores on all school tasks. Unfortunately, I've heard educators blaming this on parents, driving their kids too hard and expecting too much of them. Often this just isn't the case — instead, most parents of gifted perfectionists would be relieved if their children would just relax a little. Although some perfectionistic parents may "infect" their children, I believe that most of the time perfectionism in gifted children begins with a predisposition for fastidiousness coupled with a learned fear of failure. Fear of failure is the result of lack of experience with failure. Many gifted children who have been unchallenged in school become addicted to the As that come so easily. As the years go by with straight-As piling up, many gifted children become more and more personally invested in maintaining these grades; this has become a part of their identity. These children will eventually avoid taking any course or participate in any activity in which they can't shine. The life of the perfectionist, who must go on obtaining imaginary As long after the days of report cards are over, is really a very stressful one.

What can you as a parent do? First of all, you can work with your girl's inflexible and fastidious personality by helping her to enjoy or at least tolerate imperfection. You can do this by modeling humorous, tolerant responses to your own and others' mistakes and messes; by encouraging her to be a slob once in a while (camping out is a good occasion for this); and by teaching her compassion for all of these who couldn't possibly attain perfection even if they wanted to. Second, you can help her to overcome her fear of failure by allowing her opportunities to fail — or at least, not be the best. This may mean encouraging art, music, or sports activities — whatever doesn't guarantee an A, and then showing her how to enjoy an activity for its own sake, and not for the final result. Noncompetitive games, such as "New Games," cooperative 4-H group projects, and creative hobbies all can be helpful in overcoming perfectionism.

**Q. Our daughter is depressed and always puts herself down. She says she's tired of being weird and different.**

A. Depression happens when people feel that nothing they do can improve their situation — when they feel helpless and ineffectual. It sounds as though social isolation is the key to your daughter's depression; she feels trapped by her role as a "weirdo" and doesn't want to try any more to be like the others. And the more intelligent she is, the harder she has had to try. Talk with your daughter to be sure that she, too, believes her isolation is the root of her sadness. If so, she may benefit from the special programs that have helped many gifted children to feel better about themselves and to overcome isolation. Summer camps for gifted, summer enrichment programs, scholars' academics, and Saturday schools all provide gifted children with opportunities to interact with their intellectual peers and to be with adults who don't expect them to "act normal!" I like to see how gifted girls who have felt weird and unloved can blossom in these special environments. It's also comforting to know that from even such a temporary environment of support many gifted children can reenter their old environment with the confidence and strength they need to "tough it out" for the rest of their time in school. Summer friends make great penpals, too.

**Q. Our daughter tries to cram twenty-eight hours into each day. I'm worried she'll end up with nervous exhaustion.**

A. The activity level of most gifted chlidren is usually more exhausting for the parents than for the children themselves. Gifted children often sleep less, play harder, and demand more parental attention than average children do. The major concern I have about gifted girls is the frequency with which they lack focus for all of their activities. Most junior highs and high schools seem to encourage the blind accumulation of in-school and out-of-school activities as a sign of female popularity and success. Gifted girls will often become overinvolved, participating in so many school activities that they become ill from lack of sleep and good eating habits or from the stress resulting from spreading themselves too thin. Whereas boys will blow up or just quit what they're doing when overloaded, I've observed that gifted girls will go until they are felled by mononucleosis, pneumonia, or other exhaustion-related disorders. You can prevent this by insisting that your daughter try to focus and limit her interests. I think that enormous energy directed toward a few cherished goals is always less stressful than energy that is indiscriminately spread out over a variety of unrelated activities. I think it would be unwise to try to enforce rest periods or quell all that energy; simply help your daughter to channel it more effectively.

## Problems of Adolescence

**Q. We were pleased when our daughter's high school began to offer calculus this year because she has been identified as mathematically gifted and has excelled in this area. The course is offered as a final period elective, which falls at the same time as her cheerleading practice. As a result, she doesn't want the course. What can we do?**

A. Your daughter attends a high school that seems to assume that cheerleaders don't take calculus. You should take issue with this assumption, but it probably won't change the schedule. Give your daughter the best possible information about her loss if she were to discontinue mathematics. Mathematics is the key to numerous high paying, prestigious careers. Even careers in journalism, psychology, and law require substantial mathematics. Medicine, engineering, life sciences, and natural sciences are closed to people without high-school, undergraduate, and graduate math courses.

Second, it is always unwise to "drop out" even for a year from mathematics; it is too easy *not* to go back to math.

Third, a course in calculus will have a much greater impact on your daughter's chances for admission to a first-class college/university than participation in cheerleading. Without being overly critical of this enjoyable activity, try to point out that, in this case, it may be an investment in time that will not pay off. If persuasion fails, you have two other choices: You can refuse to give permission for her to attend cheerleading, or you can locate a night course or summer course in calculus.

**Q. We are horrified by our daughter's choice of boyfriends. She is about to enter college, and we don't like to think about**

the types she'll bring home. All of her boyfriends are either troublemakers or weirdos. One of them is involved with drugs, one has been in trouble with the law, and one shaves his head and plays in a band. She is a good girl, always pleasant and easy to be with. We can't understand her attraction to these boys.

A. Gifted girls often enjoy dating odd, nonconforming, or down-and-out types, for the simple reason that they are more interesting. Gifted girls are usually aware that they are not yet seeking a lifemate, and are mainly interested in challenging and stimulating relationships. Gifted girls like to "reform" drunks, encourage creative companions, and egg on daredevils.

However, it is important to assure yourself that her boyfriends are not abusive, pathological, or serious violators of the law, so talk with her straightforwardly about them. Once you are assured, she is happy in and about these relationships, you can probably relax; as she matures, she will naturally select more appropriate partners. Try to avoid making her choose between you and her friends, or to criticize her so that she avoids talking with you. Your relationship with her is extremely important and should be the most long-lasting. If you find, however, that the relationships make her troubled and unhappy, she needs your help. If they put her in physical or legal jeopardy, she needs your guidance. Share your fears and your understanding of her feelings about her friends. Let her know you understand how frustrating friends can be when they show so much promise but can't measure up to our expectations. Offer your continuing help.

Q. Our thirteen-year-old is hanging around with a terrible bunch of girls. She has friends her own age and ability in her grade, but she has become enchanted with some older girls who think of nothing but boys, who overdress, and who wear hideous makeup. We're afraid her school work will suffer since these girls are not interested in academics at all.

A. If her school work isn't suffering yet, it may not at all. Gifted girls are often perfectly able to associate with "nonacademic" friends and continue to do well in school. The early teen years often find gifted girls seized with a sudden desire to be incredibly "normal," and their intellectual peers of the same age may not be "normal" enough.

You do need to be prepared for the possibility of her lowering her career aspirations as a result of peer pressure. If she suddenly develops a desire to be a beautician, you may need to do a little at-home career education! Simply remind her always that you have confidence in her ability to realize her potential, and have a counselor or teacher explain her potential to her.

**Q. Our daughter has switched college majors at least three times; we're beginning to worry that at seventeen she wasn't ready for college.**

A. It is more likely that *multipotentiality,* and not immaturity is the problem. Many gifted students have problems with multipotentiality — that is, the ability to select and develop any number of career goals. People are always telling them "You can be anything you want to be," but that is precisely the problem. Most gifted college students who play "musical majors" are struggling with multipotentiality. For gifted women, it is a special problem because then they are more likely to experience self-doubt and to give up on ever finding a career goal. Self-doubt, lack of clear focus, and criticism by others make it more likely that they will then drop out.

We must deal with gifted girls' multipotentiality early in life by teaching them focusing, values clarification, and goal-setting skills in junior high and high school. If multipotentiality is a problem in college, good career counseling with a professional can help her to narrow her interests and weigh the pros and cons of her goals. As a parent, make sure you show understanding of your daughter's embarrassment over her intellectual riches.

## Problems of Gifted Women

**Q. What kinds of relationship problems are related to gifted-**

**ness in women? It seems that gifted women have more trouble finding the right kind of men.**

A. The most frequent relationship problems we see at the Guidance Laboratory are related to romantic expectations. Often a gifted woman's intellectual maturity far outstrips her maturity about feelings and relationships.

Just because women are intellectually mature and gifted doesn't mean that they haven't bought the American romantic myth lock, stock, and barrel. The myth goes something like this: "When the right man comes along, he will sweep you off your feet. You and he will be intensely attracted to one another and will not be able to bear to be apart. You will agree on everything, and you will share all your deepest feelings with one another. Neither of you will ever need anybody else ever again. He will be strong and protective, and you will be nurturing and supportive. You will both be completely faithful to one another in all ways. You will marry in a perfect wedding, have perfect children, and have a happy home life. You will continue to be madly in love with one another. You will grow old together, sharing every experience. You will both die on the same day, in each other's arms."

Every sentence of this myth is wildly untrue; but every sentence has been believed sincerely by many gifted women. As long as gifted women wait for the "right men" to come along, they will be alone. As long as gifted women assume that they must be physically attracted to a man in order for love to occur, they will lose a great many opportunities for true intimacy based on friendship. If gifted women decide they like less intelligent men because many gifted men may be sarcastic and argumentative, then they may be condemning themselves to a lifetime of boredom. If a gifted woman opts for a man who will take care of her instead of a man who will demand her strength and independence, then she is forging her own chains. If she expects the kind of perfection in her marriage and family that she has been able to attain in her work, she will be disappointed. If she does not first and finally learn to live on her own as a separate individual, defining herself through her own values, goals and career, she will be nothing if he is not there.

The romantic myth has done incalculable damage to gifted women because no matter how hard they try, they cannot live it; and being unable to fulfill the expectations of the myth, they live in constant anxiety and frustration. The research and accounts of eminent women clearly show that gifted women must often temper their intensely idealistic relationships, and should attempt at least somewhat to rationally and pragmatically consider their decisions about relationships.

**Q. As a gifted woman, how can I find a suitable partner?**

A. Love through work and ideas has been the key for eminent women, and it is appropriate for most gifted women. To find the right mate, stop looking. Find the dream, the movement, the work to which you can commit yourself wholeheartedly. Strive for excellence in your chosen field, and associate with others who share your passion and are committed to excellence. Explore your idea or serve your people. When you no longer feel you *need* a partner — when your work and your community created by your work are enough — then you will be ready for true intimacy.

**Q. Why do gifted women want romantic relationships so much? Why aren't they happy with collegial or companionable relationships with men?**

A. Gifted women sometimes confuse intimacy with achievement. Gifted women are often very achievement-oriented; they want to be the best and have the best. They have often bought into society's belief that a woman's highest achievement is a relationship with a man. They also have astutely determined the kind of man who, in the eyes of society, is best to possess: one who is handsome, strong, masterful, and aggressive. They do this figuring much in the way they used to psych out what they needed to do in class to get an A; only now they are trying to get an A from society for catching the "right kind of guy."

But the right kind of guy in society's eyes is exactly the wrong kind of guy for most gifted women. Gifted women seem happiest when partnered with supportive, easy-going men — men who seem definitely unromantic to women brought up on a diet of *Cosmopolitan*, best selling novels, and Burt Reynolds movies. Such men are less threatened by gifted women's achievements and more willing to share domestic responsibilities so that a combination of career and family becomes manageable. They are also more likely to place more emphasis on their partner's ideas and values than on their physical attractiveness, and are more likely to see women as their equals. In the friendly, interdependent relationship of equals, a gifted woman can attain true intimacy, not in the hollow achievement of landing "the perfect man."

**Q. I have had the odd experience all through college of having professors call me in "just to talk" or making extra time to discuss my work. I really used to think they were making a pass at me, having read enough about sexual harassment to be very wary. Nothing like this has happened, and I find these relationships very stimulating — but strange.**

A. Gifted women often seem to be drawn to, and drawn into, "intellectual affairs." Brilliant men, often married to less than brilliant women, may find themselves starved for cognitive conversation; a female student who is well read and articulate is a delight and a discovery. This is especially true for male academics and intellectuals who are sometimes threatened by other gifted males. In college, these "intellectual affairs," if engaged in thoughtfully and carefully, can blossom into the kind of mentorships that enrich one's education immeasurably. Later, among professional equals, these kinds of relationships can lead to satisfying collegial marriages.

One final note relative to several of the questions and answers about relationships: I cannot emphasize too strongly the fact that marriage and having children are not required for gifted women to have satisfying lives. Single, childless, gifted women are among the happiest of this population. A community of friends, a life of one's own, a sisterhood of independent women are reasonable possibilities, and can hold promise of a satisfying single lifestyle for gifted women.

**Q. As a homemaker, I resent the emphasis on steering gifted girls away from the traditional woman's role of wife and mother. Surely we need gifted mothers at home if there are to be gifted children. This is the road I've taken, and I'm proud of it.**

A. This question embodies so many similar concerns of women who have found life satisfaction in the traditional women's roles. However, I also find many problems in this comment. First, as the biographies of gifted women have shown, there is no evidence that gifted children are the product of, or must be raised by, gifted mothers. Second, we do not discourage girls from marriage and family at the Guidance Laboratory; we point out that they can have a career *and* a family. Most professional positions such as college professor, physician, and lawyer, allow the freedom to take time off and to arrange a flexible schedule. So, if girls have high aspirations, they are more likely to have time for family later than if they are forced to work in lower level jobs to supplement family income. Finally, it is important for you to understand the resentment you feel. It is hard not to want our daughters to make the same choices we did. But a gifted girl who is deciding to be primarily a homemaker is probably making a choice that will not lead to great satisfaction; the research is unequivocal about this. Homemakers feel under attack right now, and many feel defensive about their own lifestyle. It is important to leave the options open for your daughter, even if you didn't have those options for yourself.

**Q. At thirty, I am dead-ended in my career. I work as a sales representative for a film distributor. I hate my work. It is a family-owned business, and I have no chance for promotion. I am paid so poorly I can hardly keep up with my rent. Worst, I feel humiliated to be working in a job a high school graduate could do; I have a masters degree in art history. There are no jobs in art history, the only thing I really care about.**

A. These are very harsh times for gifted young adults — especially gifted young women. Underemployment is a bitter and exasperating condition; it robs even the strongest individuals of self-esteem and creates an inner rage that feeds on itself. It is hard not to be angry at everyone: your employer for taking advantage of you, your friends and family for not understanding why you are so unhappy ("You have a job, don't you?"), and your society for ignoring and wasting your gifts.

If you give in to your despair and settle for this life, you will join the people who are selling you short. It is important for you to reconsider your situation, and then act. First, rethink: You must learn to distinguish between your job and your career. Sales is your job; art history is your career. A job is something someone gives you to do in return for money; a career is something only you can give yourself. *It is a rare gifted woman whose job really matches her career.*

Of course, you will want to continue to seek a job that more closely approximates your career. Until that time, you should be spending your limited free time in building your career in art history. What question or problems in art history fascinate you? What needs to be done in the field of art history? What about art history do you care about?

Then act: If you cannot afford to be formally enrolled in a research program, do your own research. Seek people who are interested in the same problems as you are. You don't have to have a job in art history to attend art history conferences and to associate with art historians socially. You don't have to have a job in art history to do committee work for a professional association. Your knowledge, rather than your job title, are the most important career credentials.

Nobody can take away your career as an art historian, because it is your basic identity. However, fatigue from a forty-hour job can rob you of energy you need to actualize your ideas. Conserve your energy! Work competently at your job, but don't exhaust yourself — it is a bad investment of your time. Don't feel that you must involve yourself intensely in social relationships at work, because you need to save yourself for friends who have interests more like yours. If you use your spare time for involvement with your career, you will find that you have more energy than you thought, and you will begin to feel better about who you are.

## Bibliography

Lovecky, D. "The prodigies were never female." Paper presented at National Association for Gifted Children Confrence, Philadelphia, 1983.

# 13

# Associations and Advocacy
# Groups for Bright Girls
# and Gifted Women

- American Association of University Women
  2401 Virginia Ave., NW
  Washington, DC 20037

- American Psychological Association
  Division 35 (Women)
  1200 17th St., NW
  Washington, DC 20036

- The Association for the Gifted (TAG)
  Council for Exceptional Children
  1920 Association Drive
  Reston, VA 22091

- Mensa, Gifted Children Program
  % Roxanne H. Cramer
  5304 1st Pl., N.
  Arlington, VA 22203

- The National Association for Creative Children and Adults
  8080 Springvalley Drive
  Cincinnati, OH 45236

- National Association for Gifted Children
  1155 15th St., NW, #1002
  Washington, DC 20005

- National Association of State Boards of Education
  Council of State Directors of Programs for the Gifted
  Suite 340
  701 N. Fairfax St.
  Alexandria, VA 22314

- National Association for Women Deans, Administrators
    and Counselors
  1325 18th St., NW #210
  Washington, DC 20036

- National Career Development Association
  Status of Women Commission
  % Jan Deeds
  5002 Adams
  Lincoln, NE 68503

- National Coalition for Women and Girls in Education
  % National Education Association
  1201 16th St., NW
  Washington, DC 20036

- National Organization for Women
  1401 New York Ave., NW Suite 800
  Washington, DC 20005

- National/State Leadership Training Institute on the Gifted
  and the Talented
  316 West Second Street, PH-C
  Los Angeles, CA 90012

- National Women's Political Caucus
  1275 N. St., NW Suite 750
  Washington, DC 20005

- National Women's Studies Association
  % Caryn McTighe Musil
  University of Maryland
  College Park, MD 20742

- Women's Equity Action League
  1250 Eye St., NW Suite 305
  Washington, DC 20005

- The World Council for Gifted and Talented Children, Inc.
  Dorothy Sisk, Executive Secretary
  Room 414
  University of South Florida
  Tampa, FL 33620

# INDEX

193

194

*Disciplines of the Christian Life*

# Disciplines of the Christian Life

GEORGIA HARKNESS

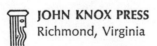 **JOHN KNOX PRESS**
Richmond, Virginia

Unless otherwise indicated, Scripture
quotations are from the *Revised Standard Version of the Bible,*
copyrighted 1946 and 1952.

LIBRARY OF CONGRESS CATALOG CARD NUMBER: 67-10344
© M. E. BRATCHER 1967
PRINTED IN THE UNITED STATES OF AMERICA
J. 4022

# Preface

This book on the disciplines of the Christian life is presented
with some trepidation, for who can presume to tell another how
to be a Christian? Yet in some measure every Christian leader
must attempt to do this even though, like Paul, he must feel
the need always to be on guard "lest after preaching to others
I myself should be disqualified."

From time to time I have written articles for various periodicals on this or that aspect of the Christian life. The editors of
John Knox Press have suggested that I arrange some of these
in a sequence for publication in book form. In every instance
revisions have been made, sometimes for updating, sometimes
simply to try to say it better. In some of the articles the incorpora-
tion of new material and deletion of the old has been rather
extensive. However, in each case the main substance of the article has been preserved.

The book is in two sections. The first part deals with the
foundations of the Christian life. Here the reader will find some
observations on the meaning and inclusive scope of the disciplined
life, the need and possibility of such disciplines in our day, and
the basic elements of Christian faith on which they are grounded.
Without such foundations, especially those in relation to our faith,
any suggestions as to method would be simply one person's individual opinions. While at best no authoritarian claims can be
made, the chapters devoted to foundations will, I trust, afford
some objective basis for what counsels may then be given.

The second section is mainly methodological. It begins with
a chapter on how to become a Christian; that is, with how to

find God as the undergirding and directing Presence in one's life. God takes the initiative in finding us, but how do we respond to him? Chapters then follow on hearing God speak through the Bible and of the place of the church and of corporate worship in the Christian life. A chapter on common obstacles to both public and private prayer is followed by two on the moods and procedures of personal prayer. The two concluding chapters aim to direct the disciplines of Christian living outward into the world of work and of service to human need, yet from the focus of the individual's obedient response to God's call and in grateful rejoicing in God's good gifts.

How is the book to be read? As the reader chooses, of course. It can be read straight through at a sitting, but that is not my recommendation. The chapters have purposely been kept short enough so that they may be read one at a time and thought about as the Holy Spirit may lead, either in private consideration or group discussion. The reader is invited to go afield from the book in thoughtful and prayerful pondering as to whether his own experience is, or may not be, in keeping with what is presented. Such departure from the book might well prove to be its greatest value.

I wish gratefully to acknowledge my indebtedness to the following periodicals for permission to republish with revisions material which originally appeared in their pages: to the Woman's Division of the Board of Missions of The Methodist Church, Program Book for 1964-65, for "The Disciplined Life," "Hearing God Speak Through the Bible," and "We Would See Jesus"; to *The Christian Home* for "Creative Insecurity"; to *motive* for "Life on the Cross"; to *The Christian Advocate* for "The Holy Catholic Church," "The Mechanics of Prayer," and "What Is Regeneration?"; to *The Wesley Quarterly* for "If a Man Die, Shall He Live Again?"; to *The Christian Century* for "Discovery of God"; to *The Intercollegian* for "Prayer and Life"; to *Child Guidance in Christian Living* for "Teach Us to Pray" and "Give Thanks Unto the Lord"; and to the *United Church Herald* for "Vocation and Work in Protestant Perspective."

# Contents

PART ONE

---

*Foundations*

# I. THE DISCIPLINED LIFE

This is a book about the spiritual life of the Christian, not in any narrow connotation but in the widest sense in which this term can be used. Perhaps I should explain why I have chosen to use the more austere term—"the disciplined life."

The primary reason is the ambiguity of "the spiritual life," a term so easily bandied about that it results in meaning quite different things to different people. In one setting—and that a very common one—it means simply "devotions." Thus, the Spiritual Life Chairman of a woman's organization in the church is responsible for the Scripture, devotional thoughts, and prayers with which the meeting is opened or closed. Such devotions or similar ones for the cultivation of the spiritual life may, of course, be engaged in privately, and while no statistics are available they doubtless still are used by more than a few in spite of the rush of modern life. A central task of the churches through the Sunday services of worship is the nourishing of the worshiper in his spiritual life. All of these uses of the term refer to legitimate and important procedures, and I do not wish to disparage any of them. If this book should prove helpful in these directions, the author would rejoice.

Nevertheless, such inner vitalization, even when the procedures are really vital and not as perfunctory as they too often are, is not all there is of the spiritual life. They have been known to defeat God's larger purposes by cultivating an ingrown withdrawal into a self-centered enjoyment of one's own spirituality. The spiritual life in its fullest sense means "life in the Spirit,"

the linkage of the totality of life with the endeavor to discover
and to do the will of God through the guidance and strengthening
of the Holy Spirit.

It is in this wider context that we shall be thinking about
the spiritual life in these pages. Therefore, to avoid misunderstanding it seems wiser to speak of the disciplined life. The word
"discipline," of course, implies effort—something that one does
not simply drift into. And, let it be said clearly and firmly at the out-
set, *there is no authentic spiritual life without effort.* God imparts
his spiritual gifts; we do not earn them by our merit. Yet he imparts them to those who care enough to be active recipients of
these gifts and participants in the work he sets before us to do.

The trouble with many of us is that, even with the best of
intentions, we are still so undisciplined that being a Christian
makes very little difference in our living. We are "nice people"—
we hope!—but this is quite different from being the kind of
Christian whose life is a witness to what God in Christ has done
for us.

What is discipline? The word comes from the same stem as
"disciple," which means a "learner." By discipline we learn—
and whether as children or adults, without it we cannot grow
into the kind of persons we ought to be. The word has come to
mean the formation of habits and patterns of life, usually by
repetition until they become a part of us.

There is external discipline, which may range all the way from
the most dictatorial control to the gentle but firm "You must"
of the wise parent whose word is authority for the growing child.
There is self-discipline, which both children and adults need to
acquire in order to achieve maturity.

As we consider Christian disciplines we shall be dealing mainly
with self-discipline. Disciplines have to become inward, or they
are unreal. Yet, in the sense that God requires of us such self-
discipline, it is never a wholly subjective, psychological adventure.
Though few of us wear boots, "lifting ourselves by our own boot-
straps" has become a familiar phrase. This we are definitely
*not* concerned with, though occasionally one finds prayer groups
that seem almost to fall into this category.

We perhaps shrink from the thought of discipline because it sounds like legalistic "do's" and "don'ts." At times in the past the church has imposed too many of these. Today, however, in the churches as in society as a whole there is so much freedom that it tends to be tyranny—not life that is "free and easy" but life that is difficult because we have so little that is solid to tie to.

God has made us with freedom of choice and decision—that is the most distinguishing mark of the human spirit. God has also set before us in Jesus Christ the example of a life completely obedient to his will and the love commandment which embodies it. Whatever the changes in social conditions, it is always required of us that we love one another. Nothing changes *that*. Nor does anything ever change the fact that God not only demands obedience to the love commandment but stands ready to help us to fulfill it. This situation of being both bound and free in our daily living is admirably stated by Samuel Longfellow in one of our familiar hymns:

> Holy Spirit, Right divine,
> King within my conscience reign;
> Be my Lord, and I shall be
> Firmly bound, forever free.

Spiritual discipline requires effort and determination. This is why we tend to shrink from it, and let the pressures of our own egos and the things and people around us pre-empt our attention and determine our actions. Yet it can be joyous also, especially when it has become part of one's personality. Said the psalmist, "Blessed is the man . . . [whose] *delight* is in the law of the LORD" (Ps. 1:1, 2). If the delight were sought for its own sake, the search would not be spiritual discipline, but an emotional luxury. It is God's gift to one who will pay the price.

Spiritual discipline, we have said, must extend outward into the whole life. This is why we shall turn our attention to some areas which concern us all, and in which our Christian living is tested. Discipline affects our attitudes and behavior in little things as in great ones; in fact, it is in what may seem like little things that we are most apt to slip. Hence, I shall speak of some quite everyday things and suggest some queries for self-examination.

(1) *The personal devotional life.* Let us begin by asking ourselves these questions:

> Do you have a definite time of prayer each day? If not, why not?
> Do you read a passage in the Bible every day? If not, why not?
> Do you say grace at meals? If not, why not?
> What does Christ mean to you?

Do not hesitate to ask yourself these questions, and to answer them thoughtfully, prayerfully, unhurriedly. God will show you what you ought to do if you will let him speak to you.

God has said to us through the words of Paul: "whatever is true, whatever is honorable, whatever is just, whatever is pure, whatever is lovely, whatever is gracious, if there is any excellence, if there is anything worthy of praise, think about these things" (Phil. 4:8). Our personal devotions may well become the center of our thinking about these things of greatest worth.

(2) *The church.* Since most of those who will read this book are members of churches, some questions in this field may also be relevant.

> If you attend church regularly, why do you do so? Are these motives thoroughly Christian?
> When you joined the church, you promised to support it by your prayers, your presence, your gifts, and your service. Are you keeping these vows as fully as is possible?
> Granted that the service of worship is not conducted perfectly, what changes *in you* would make it a more meaningful time of worship?
> Are your words about your minister and other people always understanding and kind? No gossip or mean remarks?

It is often said today that secularism has invaded the churches, making them not much more than social clubs of congenial, well-mannered but often self-centered people. To the extent that this is true, it is not surprising that the churches seem irrelevant to the world outside of them. Our Master put it in words which have not lost their sharpness when he said, "For if you love those who love you, what reward have you? . . . And if you salute only your brethren, what more are you doing than others? Do not even the Gentiles do the same?" (Matt. 5:46, 47).

(3) *Your family.* The family is the most intimate circle, and the place which is the surest test of the disciplined life. Outside, we can put up a good front; in the home, we show what we are.

> Are you able to control your tongue and your temper, speaking firmly when necessary but always in love?
> When tensions emerge in the home, are you able to judge fairly whose fault it is? And ask forgiveness if it is yours?
> What do you want most for your family? How do these desires square with the things which Jesus put first?
> Are you helping your family in their Christian growth without trying to dominate them? They are persons, too!

There is no place where we need to watch our tongues more than in our own households. "How great a forest is set ablaze by a small fire! And the tongue is a fire," said James (James 3:5-6). It is on this reef that our spiritual disciplines are often shipwrecked. Most of us could repeat 1 Corinthians 13, but can we live it? Especially the lines which say: "Love is patient and kind; love is not jealous or boastful; it is not arrogant or rude. Love does not insist on its own way; it is not irritable or resentful . . ."?

(4) *The job.* More and more women are working outside the home. Thus for both men and women one's work becomes an important sphere for the exercise of spiritual disciplines.

> Do you think of your job as a Christian calling and channel of service?
> Granted that there are things about it that are unpleasant (monotony, hurry, nerve strain, unpleasant people to deal with), is there something *about you* that makes it irksome?
> Do you try to feel God's presence in your work?

One of the most important recent developments in the church is the recognition of the laity as the church within the world. Both in the making of ethical decisions in the light of Christian principles and in the unobtrusive but vital witness of Christian living on the job, the gospel must be carried to office and marketplace, factory and farm.

We cannot all be Brother Lawrences thinking about God continually in our work, though his *Practice of the Presence of God* has much to teach us. Far more often than we do, we can turn toward God in the midst of other activities with brief, inward, silent prayers of thanksgiving, petition, or commitment. If we have not been doing so, let us begin.

(5) *The community*. Let us think now about the place where we live.

> What are you doing for racial equality and justice in your community?
>
> What are you doing to help secure better schools, medical care for all, wholesome recreation, clean morals?
>
> Do your friendships include people of other races and religions, or only "our kind of folks"?
>
> Do you drive like a Christian, with due consideration for others in parking and on the road?

A Christian must decide how to make a fair distribution of time between family and job responsibilities, church work, and community agencies. There is no simple rule to follow. Yet two things are certain: we ought not to be indifferent to any channel of helpfulness within our reach, and if we live in close touch with God, he will help us to decide what is most important.

(6) *The larger society*. There are great problems in our time— wars both hot and cold, the advance of Communism, racial tensions, the population explosion, and much else. There is poverty even in the most opulent society in all history. There are millions of hungry people in the world, and new nations that cry out for bread, freedom, and dignity. What is a Christian to do about these complex issues? But let us get personal.

> What have you done to inform yourself about these crucial public issues?
>
> Have you expressed your views to your Congressmen?
>
> Have you used your voice and influence to keep down hysteria, hatred, and ill will and to build up the spirit of understanding and reconciliation?

The tongue can do a great deal of harm. So, too, it can do a great deal of good. It is in speaking to one another, and speaking clearly enough to "stand up and be counted," that attitudes are molded. In a democracy, every citizen is responsible. Such acceptance of Christian responsibility is a very important part of the disciplined life.

In short, we need to find God in the whole of our living.

> God be in my head, and in my understanding;
> God be in mine eyes, and in my looking;
> God be in my mouth, and in my speaking;
> God be in my heart, and in my thinking;
> God be at mine end, and at my departing.

So speaks the old *Sarum Missal*. And so shall we live in God's presence and bear fruit for him.

# II. CREATIVE INSECURITY[1]

At first glance the ideas expressed by the two words of this title may seem to contradict each other. Can one be creative or find creativity in the circumstances surrounding one, when he is insecure? Does not the fear that accompanies insecurity tend to make one withdraw into safe harbors of conformity instead of launching out into stormy seas? Is it not good sense to handle one's family responsibilities, one's job, and one's community relations as the people around us do, and not risk causing trouble? In an uneasy time, every natural impulse counsels caution.

This *is* an uneasy time, though it is by no means the darkest day in history. To think no further back than the present century, those persons now living who remember the Second World War, if not the First, with the great depression that came between them can never forget the anxiety of those days. Yet our time, though less filled with immediate sources of insecurity, is the most endangered of any in the world's history, for the threat of atomic destruction hangs over us like the traditional sword of Damocles. Add to this the grim realities of war; racial tensions too often erupting into violence; insidious attacks of numerous extremist groups, both left and right; the economic insecurity precipitated by automation; and the rapidly shifting moral standards that become evident in much drinking and gambling, theft of all sorts, easy divorce, juvenile delinquency, and the loosening of restraints in matters of sex—and it becomes certain that this is a day of alarming insecurity.

---

1. Reprinted from *The Christian Home.* Copyright © 1965 by Graded Press.

Shall we then try to "ride out the storm" by finding as safe a corner as we can? And as we wait for better times, half hoping and half despairing, shall we let the people around us set our standards?

This is how millions of persons are responding to insecurity. But instead of less insecurity, they are finding more of it. This is true both in the outward social scene and in the inner life. Because those who ought to be concerned about the prevalent social conditions will not "stick their necks out," conditions get worse. When "moderates" withdraw from action, extremists take over, and violence whether of words or physical attack breaks out.

This could be illustrated from many fields but I shall speak of but one, the race situation. To the degree that "liberty and justice for all" is denied, whether by prevailing social patterns or by vote, we contradict by action what we affirm in words every time we salute our nation's flag. Those on the receiving end of the injustice can scarcely avoid the feeling that democracy is being flouted, and the temptation to flout it in return is strong. As tensions mount, extremist groups both white and colored resort to violence, and everybody loses.

This has its effect on souls as well as on social conditions. Recent events have brought vividly to my mind something I heard Dr. Benjamin Mays, eminent Negro President of Morehouse College, say at the Assembly of the World Council of Churches in Evanston, Illinois, in 1954. Said he:

> Usually the question is: What does discrimination or segregation do to the person segregated, to the disadvantaged person? . . . But we seldom realize what discrimination does to the person who practices it. It scars not only the soul of the segregated but the soul of the segregator as well. When we build fences to keep others out, erect barriers to keep others down, deny to them freedom which we ourselves enjoy and cherish most, we keep ourselves in, hold ourselves down, and the barriers we erect against others become prison bars to our own souls.

This, of course, is not the only way in which we mar our souls by trying to escape insecurity through conformity. As the elements of disorder in our culture increase, so does the sense of meaninglessness and frustration in individual lives. The novels, drama, and other art forms of today reflect this very clearly. So do the gigantic sales of tranquilizers and the prevalence of nervous breakdowns, to say nothing of the increasing vogue of going to psychiatrists in a desperate hope of finding some inner peace, and the fact that nearly half of the hospital beds in America are occupied by mental patients.

The effects of an insecurity that is conformist but not creative appear everywhere in the intertwining of social disturbance with inner instability. Excessive drinking, broken homes, sexual looseness, dishonesty, adolescent lawlessness—are these cause or effect of the lack of inner moorings? They are so often *both cause and effect* that we get off base if we do not look at the problem from both sides.

Yet as we go to the Bible and note the panorama of developing religious insight and obedience in faith, we discover that the greatest moments seldom occurred in good times. It was in times of insecurity that the vision of God became clearest. It was during the bondage of the Hebrew people in Egypt that Moses, who could have remained in the safe seclusion of tending his father-in-law's flocks in Midian, felt called by God to challenge Pharoah with the demand: "Let my people go." It was under God's protection, yet still with danger and difficulty, that he brought them out and led them in spite of their complaining until he had made a nation out of this band of serfs and nomads. As these same people were tempted later to seek security and the fertility of their flocks and fields by worshiping the gods of their Canaanite neighbors, Joshua put the challenge squarely with the words: "Choose this day whom you will serve" (Joshua 24:15). It was in "the year that King Uzziah died" and the political situation was uncertain that Isaiah had his great vision in the Temple.

> "Holy, holy, holy is the LORD of hosts;
> the whole earth is full of his glory."

These great words of adoration became the incentive to the moral obedience expressed in the words "Here am I! Send me" (Isa. 6: 3, 8).

In fact, the greatest utterances of the Old Testament prophets, from Amos to Ezekiel, were either in a time of troubles before the Exile or after the blow had fallen and the nation was in shambles. It seemed to be insecurity that brought out their greatest creative insights. Had the prophets been simply conformists, they would have left no message. Yet God still speaks to us today through their words.

Turn to the New Testament and we find a similar situation, though on a higher level, in the experience of our Lord himself. From the moment when Jesus preached his first sermon in the Nazareth synagogue and the people at first marveled and "enjoyed" his sermon, then wanted to throw him over a precipice when they saw that it applied to them, Jesus lived in creative insecurity (Luke 4:16-30). It led him to die on a cross between two thieves, viewed by the populace and the ruling powers as a disturber of the peace. Yet we are bidden by Paul as he gives counsel to the early Christians, "Have this mind among yourselves, which you have in Christ Jesus" (Phil. 2:5).

It is not always easy to know just what we ought to do in an age of controversy and rapidly changing circumstances. There is no simple rule. Yet there is a guideline which is dependable—to seek to have "the mind of Christ." An honest and serious answer to the question "What would Jesus do if he were here in my place?" will point us in the right direction. It will tell us that we ought to feel goodwill toward those who injure us, treat fairly those who do not reciprocate this treatment, and view with love and pity those whose conduct we cannot approve. Yet it will tell us also not to be silent before evil. If we take this guideline seriously, we shall not hesitate to stand up and be counted on a controversial issue, or to throw the weight of our influence on the side we believe to be the more Christian even when it takes courage to do so.

This is what the early church did in the power of the Holy Spirit. If they had not done so, we should not have the church today. In the first chapter of Acts we read the promise of the

risen Christ: "But you shall receive power when the Holy Spirit
has come upon you; and you shall be my witnesses . . ." (Acts 1:
8). In the second chapter we read of the Holy Spirit's coming, and
the difference this made in the disciples. Those first Christians were
not daunted by the opposition to their witness, whether it meant
false charges, being thrown out of cities, riots, imprisonment, or
martyrdom. Whether in Peter's "We must obey God rather than
men" (Acts 5:29), Stephen's great sermon and then his martyrdom (Acts 7), or Paul's breathtaking list of hardships as they are
enumerated in 2 Cor. 11:23-28, it becomes clear that the church
was founded in creative insecurity.

We live today in different times. Yet we have the same gospel. We have it today because men and women of the past,
aflame with a divine urgency before social injustice and aglow
with a faith that gave them power, were not afraid to speak.
Were they "well-adjusted personalities"? Perhaps not in the
sense in which we often use the term. Yet they had no time—
and apparently no desire—to engage in the luxury of self-pity,
and the record reads as if they had "the peace of God, which
passes all understanding."

There have been prophetic, Christ-filled souls for many centuries whose names live on in history. The reader can make
his own list of them, and in doing so one is prompted to a
prayer of gratitude for such great living. It is not likely that
many of us will be accorded lasting fame. Nor is it necessary.
What is needful is that in our time and place we shall be faithful to the call of God, and do this work, however humble, that
he sets before us. If we are faithful, both our words and our
deeds will be a witness for him in our communities and churches,
at work, and in our families.

We shall not always see direct results. A considerable part of
the requirement of fidelity is to keep speaking and acting for
the right when we do not see results. Yet little by little those
around us, whether of the family or those less close, are shaped
by the contagion of person-to-person relationships. God can use
the gifts we bring in love to further his purposes even when we
do not see the outcome.

As we go forward in the difficult but imperative task of living creatively in the midst of insecurity, we do well to remember a word spoken long ago in an upper room. It still speaks to us today, and perhaps with a fresh poignancy, "Peace I leave with you; my peace I give to you; not as the world gives do I give to you. Let not your hearts be troubled, neither let them be afraid."

# III. WHAT IT MEANS TO BELIEVE IN GOD

At the center of Christian faith lies belief in God—not just any object of devotion but "the God and Father of our Lord Jesus Christ," as Paul repeatedly speaks of him. Belief that God exists is not enough; we must also worship and serve him in obedient love. Yet without some foundations in belief, God will mean nothing to us.

This does not mean that we must all be theologians, or be able to answer all the questions that arise. In fact, the theologians cannot probe all the mysteries of God, and if they are wise they will not pretend to do so. Yet some sure foundations we must have, and we *can* have, if we are to be disciplined and fruitful Christians.

There are some today who are saying that "God is dead." By this they may mean only that God is no longer appealed to much in our society to answer our intellectual or emotional problems, though sometimes they seem to say that God does not exist. It is, of course, true that with marvelous advances in sciences and technology, but along with these the persistence of human suffering, we are apt to rely on the various sciences to take care of the ills that beset us. Yet this does not mean that God is out of the picture, or that we can do as well without him.

In this chapter I shall state some reasons why I believe in God. At the same time I shall try to indicate how this makes a difference in our living if we hold this belief seriously. Dr. John Baillie has spoken of the difference between believing "with the top of our minds" and "in the bottom of our hearts."[1] He says that

---

1. *Our Knowledge of God,* pp. 52, 54.

some people who call themelves atheists believe in God in their hearts though they deny him with their minds. This is probably true, but the reverse is also true and apparently more common.

One reason for believing in God is the religious experience of humanity. The idea is one that must be *lived* rather than proved by argument, and belief in God is a characteristic human experience. This is not to say that it is instinctive, that every person has it, or even that all societies have it. I mean rather that it is natural and normal to seek after God, and that the person who does not do so is abnormal—just as it is the normal thing to be able to distinguish colors, while here and there is a person who is color-blind. There seems to be an upwelling urge in the human heart to find God—a tendency which made the French philosopher Sabatier say that man is "incurably religious." St. Augustine expressed this very beautifully centuries ago when he said, "Thou madest us for Thyself, and our heart is restless until it repose in Thee."[2] This may be why the Communists, with all their propaganda, have been unable to stamp out religion in the countries they dominate.

I do not claim that this deep-seated religious impulse gives positive proof of God. Nevertheless, it affords a very strong evidence. Everywhere else in our experience where there is a strong impulse within us, there is something outside of us corresponding to it. We have an organic hunger impulse—and there is food; a sex impulse—and there are mates; a yearning for friendship—and there are friends.

But it is not alone man's impulse to worship which leads me to believe in God; it is the kind of life which flowers from it. The best and finest people I know are religious-minded folk. There is, of course, the common argument about church-goers who do not act in a very Christian way and atheists who are altruistic and noble-minded, and there are certainly some of each. But the people I know who bear suffering most bravely, who are most serene and poised in the face of difficulties, who are most sympathetic and helpful toward others, and who live the most genuinely happy lives, are people to whom faith in God is a vital reality.

A saint in the usual meaning of this term is a rare occurrence.

2. *Confessions,* I, 1.

Yet there are many unheralded Christian saints, known only to the limited circle of those whose lives have touched theirs, who by their fidelity to God have left life the richer. My life has been blest by some of them. To illustrate, I will speak of but one, a simple country woman though something of an artist in an amateur fashion. At ninety-one she had lost her family and her property and had almost lost her sight. When I last saw her she told me she had tried to paint a picture and had found she could not see to do it. She began to cry, then stopped and said to herself, "Hannah Annis, aren't you ashamed of yourself for not being thankful to God for all the years you have had eyes, instead of mourning now because you haven't?" In her last letter to me, written in a scrawling hand, she not only told me that she thought the newer times were better than the old (a bit unusual for a person in her nineties!) but she summed up her faith in these words: "God never fails. When He takes away one thing, He always gives another."

It is simple, triumphant faith like that, observable again and again in human living, which makes one believe in God. In more poetic language the famous chaplain of the First World War, G. A. Studdert-Kennedy, expressed it thus:

> Peace does not mean the end of all striving;
> Joy does not mean the drying of our tears.
> Peace is the power that comes to souls arriving
> Up to the light where God Himself appears.[3]

To turn to another angle of the matter, the discoveries of science —far from eliminating belief in God—support it very strongly. This does not mean that they support *every idea of God* that has been held by Christians, such as creation of the world in six days or that upon our entreaty God will change his orderly ways of working to suit our desires. Of these things we must say more later in the chapters on the Bible and prayer. Yet that God is "the Father Almighty, Maker of heaven and earth" is reinforced by every fresh discovery of the nature of our world.

We all have rightly marveled at the exploits in space of our

---

3. From "The Suffering God" in *The Unutterable Beauty.*

astronauts within recent years. They merit our admiration. Yet neither these expeditions into space nor the minute calculations which have charted every part of their journeys would be possible except for a dependable order in the universe which man discovers but did not make. When I consider, as a novice may, what astronomers tell us of magnificent distances in the skies— of spiral nebulae and island universes millions of light years away—I find new meaning in the psalmist's exclamation: "The heavens are telling the glory of God." When I understand (though incompletely) something of the marvelous union of intricacy with simplicity in the inner world of the atom, I am sure that "the firmament proclaims his handiwork." Everywhere in God's physical universe there is a remarkable order, and this speaks to us of an ordering, unifying Creator who brought these worlds into being.

The splitting of the atom, which ushered in the nuclear age to release almost unlimited power for human betterment or for destruction, is a good example of the mixed character of our human situation. There are plenty of things in the world that ought not to be as they are. Some of them are caused by man's sin or carelessness or ignorance, some through the forces of nature not yet brought under control in response to God's ancient injunction to "fill the earth and subdue it" (Gen. 1:28). We can well believe that God desires us to work with him to eliminate suffering and everything else that keeps men from their fullest and highest living. But as we wrestle, either intellectually or practically, with the problem of evil, we must not forget that if we did not live in an orderly universe, conducive on the whole to good, we should be plunged into chaos and unspeakable misery.

When one thinks today of the immensity of the physical universe one is apt to feel as a certain psalmist did, long before modern science had arisen to astonish us with its findings:

> When I look at thy heavens, the work of thy fingers,
>     the moon and the stars which thou hast established;
> what is man that thou art mindful of him,
>     and the son of man that thou dost care for him? (Ps. 8:3-4).

Our reaction to this question tends to move in either of two directions. One may feel either humble or proud, and it seems to be the contemporary mood either to belittle man as a creature of sordid impulses or to exalt man's technological prowess. The psalmist's answer is truer, for it sees in man a greatness that is the gift of God.

> Yet thou hast made him little less than God,
>   and dost crown him with glory and honor.
> Thou hast given him dominion over the works of thy hands;
>   thou hast put all things under his feet (Ps. 8:5-6).

Man's thirst for knowledge, his power to do reflective thinking, his aspiration toward moral ideals, his appreciation of beauty, his quest for God—these are traits which put man above and outside of everything in the subhuman world. In fact, man's highest traits, the capacity for love and goodness, wisdom and creativity, are the very traits that Christian faith ascribes to God, though in God these attributes are infinite and in ours very obviously limited. This likeness of man to God should not surprise us, for we are told that God made man in his own spiritual image (Gen. 1: 27).

It is these qualities in the nature of God, as we find them reflected in the Bible and supremely in Jesus, that justify us in speaking of a personal God. This does not mean that God is a magnified man, with a body like ours or with our petty and sinful impulses. To say that God is personal is not to make him human. Yet it does mean that he is the Mind above all minds, infinite in creative power and ordering wisdom. Furthermore, he is our Companion whom we may trust in any circumstance, however dark, for while the outward situation may or may not change, he will see us through it. He requires love and goodness from us because he gives them to us in unlimited degree.

This we know from the Bible and our long tradition of Christian faith. Yet we know it most surely, in a form which must be freshly understood from age to age but never changes in its essence, from God's disclosure of himself in Jesus. This seems to be what Paul meant when he spoke so often of "the God and Father of our Lord Jesus Christ." In Jesus we have the world's supreme revelation of God. Jesus lived like God; prayed to God;

triumphed over temptation and pain in Godlike victory; died in love and suffering for men. The cross is the eternal symbol of the union of love with suffering—of love and suffering at the heart of the universe. It is no accident that people find the way to God most readily, not by speculation which can neither prove nor disprove God's existence, but through devotion to the Christ in whom God has revealed himself so clearly.

And if we believe in God, not merely with intellectual assent but with a personal appropriation of this great experience, it will do something to our living. We cannot afford to live cheaply or carelessly in the presence of supreme realities.

We shall find ourselves growing in richness and fullness of life. We shall find our horizons broadened and our sympathies deepened. We shall care more about other people and be more eager to be helpful to them. New goals appear as life takes on deeper meaning, and courage is given to meet life's daily demands. In short, the "abundant life" of which Jesus spoke becomes an increasing reality.

Since the remainder of this book deals with the roots and fruits of God-centered living, not much more need be said of it at this point. However, I shall end the chapter with two quotations which converge in their witness though from very different settings. One is from a little poem that I came across years ago. It is by Jessie Wiseman Gibbs, though I know nothing of the author except her name.

> If we believed in God, there would be light
> Upon our pathway in the darkest night.
>
> If we believed in God, there would be peace
> In this world's warfare, ever to increase.
>
> If we believed in God, there would be joy
> Even in tears, that nothing could destroy.
>
> If we believed in God, there would be love
> To heal all wounds and lift the world above.
>
> Lord Christ, be near us, that beholding Thee
> We may believe in God and be set free!

The other quotation is from a very famous figure, Dag Hammarskjöld. From his *Markings,* a spiritual diary of reflections on many themes, one catches a sense of loneliness and personal struggle in spite of great outward success. After he was able to say Yes to God, he says, "from that hour I was certain that existence is meaningful and that, therefore, my life, in self-surrender, had a goal." Whence came this assurance? He leaves us in no doubt. "As I continued along the Way, I learned, step by step, word by word, that behind every saying in the Gospels stands *one* man and *one* man's experience."[4]

To this one Man we now turn.

---

4. *Markings* (New York: Knopf, 1964), p. 205.

# IV. LIFE ON THE CROSS

Since infancy most of us have heard or said prayers which ended "Through Jesus Christ our Lord." Since the beginning of Christianity, Jesus has been called Lord; we have in some way equated him with God. In Jesus, the Christian sees the revealer of God and the Redeemer of men. We must ask what these terms mean for us today.

Let us think first about Jesus as the revealer of God. Jesus is not our only avenue to the discovery of God. In the beauty and bounty and orderliness of nature, in the best of human insights and strivings of the ages, in the upward climb of man, and even in the thwarting of human desire when we sin against God, are revelations of God. But gleaming high above them all, is the manifestation of God in human life that Jesus presents. When we see Jesus, we know what God is, and what he requires of us.

The Christian doctrine of the incarnation means that in Jesus we see God "in the flesh." As Paul put it, we see the glory of God in the face of Jesus Christ. When we ask what this light of God's glory is that we see in the face of Jesus, we must do what the first disciples did—get acquainted with him. And the more we read the story, and let the mysterious radiance and beauty, the gentleness and valiant strength of his personality capture us, the more plausible it appears to say that the glory of God shines in his face.

We do not have in the Gospels a biography of Jesus, but a portrait drawn by the first-century Christians. Read one of the Gospels through at a sitting, and see what it says to you. The best Gospel for this purpose is Mark's—the earliest and most dependable account of Jesus' life. However, Matthew contains the epitome of his teachings in the Sermon on the Mount.

It is apparent that here is a man who had a remarkable power over people, and that this power was joined to sympathy with and concern for everybody. He was never too busy to heal and help the multitudes of people who needed him. Others might give a wide berth to lepers and poor insane folk thought to be possessed of devils, but not he. Other "respectable" people condemned him for eating and chatting with tax-gatherers and sinners, but he saw that they too had souls that needed help. He had time to play with children and to talk with women—two things common enough now as a result of centuries of Christian influence, but not then. When a Roman centurion's son or a Syrophoenician woman's daughter needed help, he broke across racial lines to give it; and one of his greatest parables is of the neighborly act of a despised Samaritan.

Wherever Jesus went he healed the sick, encouraged the fearful, gave new life to the weak and the sinful whose faith reached out to him for deliverance. He did for men, in outgoing, inclusive love for all, what in our best insights we know God is seeking to do for us. In such acts of Jesus we see the glory of the Father, "full of grace and truth."

Though Jesus was not a systematic theologian it is not difficult to sift from his words the primary things that he taught. About God, he taught that like a father, God loves all men and is concerned that all his sons live in goodwill and brotherhood with one another. About man, he taught that we are weak and sinful at best, ever prone to sin against God and our neighbor, but nevertheless creatures of supreme worth and dignity in God's sight. About the nature of the good life, he taught that the greatest virtues are not those of outward obedience to the law but of inner purity of motive, and that a life of sincerity, humility, mercy, and forgiveness is the blessed life. Regarding the things to be prized, he counseled simplicity and the placing of spiritual above material possessions. Regarding the sources of power for our salvation, he taught that through faith in God, not through any merit of our own, our broken lives can be made whole.

Regarding our destiny, he spoke few words, but great comforting ones that promise eternal life. As his central message, many times repeated, he placed before men the great ideal of the righteous rule of God in human lives, the coming of God's Kingdom on earth as it is in heaven.

Put together what Jesus did and what he said, and we have a clue to undestanding what is meant by Jesus Christ as the supreme revelation of God. At three points this stands out. First, Jesus practiced what he preached. Second, his religion and ethics, like his life and his words, are all of one piece. Third, Jesus had a sure, unerring sense of what was important. He took the best in the Old Testament and lifted it to a place of central importance. In whatever human situation he touched, he saw to the heart of the issue. He gave no precise rules or codes of conduct, but by his discernment of what God puts first, he has been enabling men ever since to "seek first his kingdom and his righteousness."

But what of Jesus Christ as our Savior and Redeemer? The word "redemption" sounds old-fashioned and meaningless to many people. It means literally to be "bought back," and it came into use originally from the idea that a person who had become a slave to sin could be restored to freedom only when a price was paid. In spite of the outmoded metaphor, there is a deep meaning here, for the Christian believes that Jesus in love for men did something for us which we could not do for ourselves. However, we shall understand it better if we change the word a little and say that Christ has brought us back to God. Redemption means salvation, and salvation means healing, health, wholeness of living. To say that "Jesus saves" is to say that when we have strayed from our true home in God, when our souls are sick and at loose ends, he brings us back and heals and unifies us for strong and victorious living.

How does this happen? No better account has ever been given than in Jesus' own story of the prodigal son—the boy who, wishing to enjoy himself and have things his own way, left home only to become very unhappy when he got his own way. "But when he came to himself he said, '. . . I will arise and go to my father,' " and returning he found salvation, for in spite of his badness the father had not ceased to love him. This is a parable that

applies to ourselves, and to human nature in every age. Not that we
must literally come *back* to God, for in our self-seeking we have
never been really at home with him! What the story means is that
when we try to run our lives and have what we want, however well
we may meet the requirements of ordinary decency, we fall a long
way short both of the goodness and of the inner satisfaction that
come from being in fellowship with God. Only as we stop trying
to depend on our own merits and "with hearty repentance and
true faith" turn to God, can his forgiving mercy receive us and
give us his strength and joy.

This is what has been happening all through the centuries
by the power of Christ. One thinks of Saul of Tarsus persecuting
the Christians until God blinded him on the Damascus Road to
open his eyes; of Augustine wrestling futilely with sexual temptation until God said to him, "Put ye on the Lord Jesus Christ,
and make not provision for the flesh to fulfill the lusts thereof";
of St. Francis of Assisi renouncing his father's wealth to serve
the poor in utter simplicity and humility; of George Fox cured
of the depression that was ruining his life until he heard a voice
which said, "There is One, even Christ Jesus, that can speak to thy
condition"; of John Wesley having his heart "strangely warmed"
until he was empowered to revitalize the faith of many thousands.
As one thinks of such famous Christians, one must not forget to be
grateful for the millions of humble, nameless ordinary folk of all
ages and all lands who have mastered overwhelming difficulties
to live greatly through the power of Christ. The life of Jesus gives
us a supreme center of loyalty. In it we see God, and by its power
we are lifted.

But it lies at the center of Christian belief that Christ died for
our sins. What, then, is the special place of Christ's death in our
salvation?

It is not by accident that the cross is the central symbol of
the Christian religion. The cross symbolizes God's way of dealing
with men. The cross means the meeting-point of suffering with
love, and God's way of conquering evil through suffering love. If
we ask how the cross came to mean this union of suffering with love
as God's way of delivering us from evil, we are taken back to

what Jesus was and what he did. That the cross is our symbol because Jesus died on the cross is obvious. But just how did his death make it our pattern and source of power?

This question is not easy to answer, for into the saving death of Christ are compressed the mystery and the miracle of God's saving love. To grasp it fully we should need, as Paul said, to "understand all mysteries," and instead of trying to make it appear entirely resonable we had better say gratefully as Paul did, "Thanks be to God for his inexpressible gift!"

Yet this does not mean that we should refuse to think. Down through the ages Christians have given this subject much thought. Many theories coming down to us still possess great truths though often not in the form in which they were originally held. At their time, for many Christians they seemed satisfactory, but for many of us today, they are inadequate. We are driven to look deeper for the meaning of the cross and for a doctrine concerning the saving death of Christ.

The view that seems to me the truest centers both in the incarnation and in human experience. It takes radically the belief that "God was in Christ reconciling the world to himself," and that in Christ we not only see the nature but find the power of God for our salvation.

What happened on the first Good Friday is what always happens when evil men thwart God's will—the innocent suffer. But the heart of Good Friday does not lie simply in what his enemies did to Jesus. When Jesus died, God gave himself—freely, fully, to the uttermost in love of men. The meaning of what God is always doing for us is focused here, and into the climactic moment in history are compressed both the pattern and the power of God's eternal work with men.

I have nowhere seen this better put than in a book that was written many years ago:

"I know something of the arguments whereby we seek to keep our faith in the divine goodness in the presence of the world's pain and sorrow and the manifold sinister aspects of existence. I do not disparage them; upon occasion I use them; but I always feel that at best they are only palliatives and leave the great depths of the problem untouched. There is only one argument that touches the bottom, and that is Paul's question: 'He that spared not his own Son, but delivered him up for us all, how shall he not with him also freely give us all things?' We look on the woes of the world. We hear the whole creation, to use Paul's language, groaning and laboring in pain. We see a few good men vainly striving to help the world into life and light; and in our sense of the awful magnitude of the problem and of our inability to do much, we cry out: 'Where is God? How can he bear this? Why doesn't he do something?' And there is but one answer that satisfies: and that is the Incarnation and the Cross. God could not bear it. He has done something. He has done the utmost compatible with moral wisdom. He has entered into the fellowship of our suffering and misery and at infinite cost has taken the world upon his heart that he might raise it to himself."[1]

What this means for us is that there is a Cross (with a capital "C") which shows us God's way as clearly as human eye can see it, a Cross on which the purest of all men suffered with and for guilty men like ourselves, a Cross from which comes assurance of God's forgiving love as we seek to do his commandments. From this Cross, as we make it the center of faith and loyalty, comes new power for living. What we must do then is "to take up our cross daily"—our little crosses that seem so petty by comparison —and out of them, by God's strength, make a Christ-centered, loving, and victorious life.

---

1. Borden P. Bowne, *Studies in Christianity*, pp. 98 f.

# V. WHAT IS REGENERATION?[1]

In previous chapters we have considered both the need and the possibility of disciplined Christian living in an age of inner and outer insecurity. We have looked also at the basic foundations of Christian living in Christain belief—belief in God and in Jesus Christ as God's Son and our Lord.

We are ready now to look further at what it means to be a Christian in our own personal experience. To focus thinking in this direction I shall use an old word which is out of fashion in some circles—"regeneration." One could as well say "conversion," but this word too seems to some people to suggest a revival meeting in which emotional enthusiasm may run high for the moment but soon cools off. These are good words, and we ought not to lose sight of what they stand for.

Regeneration means, according to its derivation, being "born again." In the third chapter of the Gospel of John we read of a man named Nicodemus, a Pharisee and ruler of the Jews, who came to Jesus by night with a searching and restive sense that Jesus "had something." The words of Jesus to him on that occasion are as challenging now as they were in the first century if we take them seriously, "Truly, truly, I say to you, unless one is born anew, he cannot see the kingdom of God."

A little later in the account of this incident Jesus says again, "Truly, truly, I say to you, unless one is born of water and the Spirit, he cannot enter the kingdom of God." The reference to water indicates that by the time this Gospel was written, around

---

1. "What Is Regeneration?" Coypright 1952 Pierce and Smith.

the end of the first century A.D., baptism had become a common
practice in the churches. However, the main thrust of the story is
not about baptism, but about the need to be born of the Spirit and
thus to feel the presence and power of God in one's life.

Nicodemus did not understand, as many of our time do not, what
it could mean to be "born of the Spirit." But Jesus knew, as did
those whose lives were transformed by him, and such newness of
life lies at the heart of the Christian gospel.

This incident—let us not forget—is introductory to the immortal words "For God so loved the world that he gave his only
Son, that whoever believes in him should not perish but have eternal life." On God's part regeneration means the free gift of his Son
for our salvation. On our part it means accepting this gift with responsive wills to enter into the experience of being "in Christ," as
Paul puts it, and hence "a new creation."

"Therefore, if any one is in Christ, he is a new creation; the
old has passed away, behold, the new has come." These words
from Paul's Second Letter to the Corinthians were written before
John's Gospel, and together they describe the great, life-transform-
ing experience of having outlooks changed and personalities made
over from the foundations by the touch of Christ. What happened in the first century has happened in every century since,
and happens today.

Other great words for the experience of Christian regeneration,
besides "conversion," are "salvation" and "redemption." Conversion stresses the turning about from a self-centered to a God-
centered life, and thus the new orientation by which life is governed.
Salvation means being delivered from sin, worry, weakness, and
futility to moral victory through Christ's mastery of the springs of
feeling and action. Redemption is what God in his love and mercy
does to bring us to forgiveness and new life in Christ.

Today we are perhaps more likely to speak of this great experience simply as "accepting Christ" or "becoming a Christian."
Indeed, we often do not quite know what to call it. However, if the
experience is genuine it means being "born again" in the center
of one's being and hence having a new outlook and approach to
life. From the time when this happens, if the regeneration is

deep-going, one's choices and decisions are different. Feelings and words and acts take on a different tenor. "He seems like a new person" or "I feel like a new man" is a commonplace but accurate description of the change that has thus been wrought.

Sometimes the change is so radical as to seem miraculous. Again, there is a gradual, and at times almost imperceptible, change in values, motives, feelings, modes of responding to situations. If there is no difference at all, regeneration has not occurred.

Several problems are apt to confront us. How does a regenerated person differ from a decently moral, well-behaved, public-spirited citizen who is not a Christian? If a person has been brought up in a Christian community, a Christian home, and a Christian church, does he need to be "born again"?

It is both the blessing and the curse of our society that is has in it so many "good people" who are not Christians. It is obviously a blessing in that we can be glad of their kindness, generosity, self-control, and other forms of responsible action. The bad side of it comes in the fact that when one is a respectable person and a decent citizen one is likely to assume that he is good enough. This too often happens in churches as well as outside.

This is no new phenomenon. The rich young ruler who came to Jesus asking what he should do to inherit eternal life had kept the commandments from his youth, and very likely Nicodemus had also. To this situation several things can be said.

1. We ought never to decry real goodness, but rejoice in it wherever it is found.

2. We ought not to suppose that being a kind neighbor or a "well-adjusted personality" is a true equivalent for that life in the Kingdom of God of which Jesus spoke.

3. We must start with people where they are—whether serene and kindly or tragically upset and wrong in their actions—if we are either to find Christian regeneration for ourselves or help others to find it.

It is important to realize what we are to be saved *from* if we are to think about being saved by Christ. Traditionally, salvation has meant being saved from sin, and while we are apt not to talk or think about sin as much as our forefathers did, this is still our basic need. Sin is present wherever we are self-centered, thoughtless of the feelings or needs of others, indifferent or rebellious toward God and his will. All of us are sinners, even the best of men as social standards go. Salvation is available when in penitence we ask forgiveness of God and the persons we have sinned against; then press forward in the awareness that God's mercy and grace, however undeserved, are undergirding our lives.

However, there is another need which Jesus was always ministering to. This is for peace of mind and soul, conquest of fear, strength in weakness, the ability to "be of good cheer" and to "be faithful unto death."

Today we recognize that not only sin but "nerves" are very disturbing to personality. Our generation is probably no more sinful than any in the past, but it is more jittery. Many persons to whom the whole idea of Christian regeneration seems quaintly out of date are inwardly crying out for exactly what it has given to Christians through many centuries—courage and inner peace.

Thus our message, if we are to witness faithfully to the Christian gospel, must always have two sides. On the one hand, we must uncover the sin of which most people are so largely unconscious— the all-too-prevalent sins of pettiness, harshness, jealousy, self-pity, and self-will—along with the great social sins of ill will and indifference to the needs of others. We must call men to repentance as the basic requirement of transformation into the new life in Christ. Yet we must also with understanding and sympathy mediate to unhappy, anxious, turbulent lives the gift of the peace of God which passes all understanding.

But if a person has "grown up a Christian" does he still need regeneration? Are not the influences of a Christian home and church enough to make him a Christian without having to be "born again"?

Certainly not everybody must have the dramatic about-face experience of Paul on the Damascus Road. But the experience of Martin Luther and of John Wesley, to cite but two famous examples among many, is significant. Both of them as young men were Christians in a secondhand sort of way. They had grown up in a Christian environment and were servants of the church, but without great vitality until a personal experience gripped and transformed their lives.

Christian nurture in homes, church schools, and the steady impact of the worship and activities of churches is very important. It is the channel through which most Christians today grow into their Christian experience. Yet to become a committed Christian is not something that happens automatically. Personal decision, somewhere along the way, is essential. Such a decision may be overwhelming in its emotional effect and may change radically the currents of one's vocational, domestic, and community relations. On the other hand, it may be made so quietly that its effects are the deepening rather than the discarding of previously formed ideals and goals. Such a decision may, or it may not, be dated at a precise moment. Yet personal decision there must be, or Christian experience remains marginal and inert.

This brings us to another question, a large one which can only be touched on briefly here. Granted that we have ourselves become committed and concerned Christians, how shall we attempt to win others to personal regeneration? Certainly we must not override their freedom, and at times much harm has been done by an intolerant pressure. Yet the gospel means "good news," and such life-enriching good news we ought to share, in whatever ways are open to us.

Christian experience normally emerges and is nourished within a fellowship. Preferably, this fellowship begins in a Christian home, but lacking this, it can develop in a student group, a work group, a place of recreation, or anywhere else where persons mingle and Christians are present. The church exists to be a carrier of the gospel within a Christian fellowship. Whatever other forms of fellowship may be involved, it is important for individuals to be connected with the worship, the sustaining companionship, and the service of the church if they are to grow in the Christian life.

Joining a church is not identical with becoming a Christian. Yet when this step is taken seriously, and not perfunctorily as it too often is, it is both a public affirmation of one's desire to be a Christian and an entrance into a fellowship which can enable one to grow in the Christian life. To put it in the classic language of

2 Peter 3:18, the church is the primary channel by which we are enabled to "grow in the grace and knowledge of our Lord and Savior Jesus Christ."

From the first century onward, Christian experience has been spread through witness. In this witness the spoken word, whether from pulpits or in personal conversation, has had a large place. But never the only place. How Christians have *lived,* whether in going to the lions under Nero's sadistic mania or simply being Christian in the ordinary events of ordinary living, has been an indisputable witness. A truly regenerate Christian is one about whom there is never any doubt as to which side he will be on in a critical moral issue, or how he will meet a crisis that might shake another from his moorings.

This is not to say that Christians will always agree on the right course of action to take. Life is too complex for that. Yet the committed Christian will have the stamina not only to state but to live by his convictions after having tried earnestly and prayerfully to discover the will of God. In the vast range of human problems, he will take seriously the injunction to love God and one's neighbor, and to view as one's neighbor the people of all races and nations, all classes and creeds. With this commitment he will "speak the truth in love," yet refuse to be complacent before the injustice, the evil-doing, or the suffering of others.

"Truly, truly, I say to you, unless one is born anew, he cannot see the kingdom of God." A large order, that! Too great for us, in both our comprehension and our power. But not too great for God, "who has shone in our hearts to give the light of the knowledge of the glory of God in the face of Christ."

# VI. "IF A MAN DIE, SHALL HE LIVE AGAIN?"[1]

This question which Job asks wistfully in the midst of his pain is the perennial cry of the human heart. Death is the one fixed, irrevocable fact of life. Its coming may be long delayed by better medical facilities, amazing feats of surgery, hygienic living, or a naturally strong body; it comes eventually to all. Even those who claim not to care about eternal life for themselves are forced to think seriously about death and what may lie beyond it when their loved ones are taken from them.

For centuries regeneration or salvation, of which we were thinking in the preceding chapter, meant preparation for heaven. While the mood has shifted in our time, there are still many people to whom being saved means the assurance of heaven for those who have accepted Christ while others will be cast into hell or outer darkness.

Perhaps it may seem unnecessary to include a chapter on death in a book on the disciplines of living. I hope I have made it clear that to live as a Christian here and now is vitally important. This would be true even if there were no promise of heaven or threat of hell. Yet the picture would be incomplete without the longer vista, and that is the reason for this chapter. What a person believes about eternal life makes a difference in his living now, for it affects his total perspective on human existence.

1. "If a Man Die, Shall He Live Again?" Copyright 1961 by The Methodist Publishing House.

Yet for several reasons, this subject is often bypassed. In the first place, it touches our emotions so deeply that we shrink from thinking about it until we have to. Then many feel that we do not know enough about it to make very positive statements, while others are too dogmatic. Since we do not have access on this side of the veil to what lies beyond it, there are many shades of opinion. It is a sphere in which we must walk by faith and not by sight.

Nevertheless, it is so vital a subject, so close to where our deepest feelings lie when death comes near us, that it ought not to be bypassed. When a person is in good health and neither he nor anyone that he cares deeply about seems to be in any special danger, he usually does not think much about death. Let the situation change, as it can in a moment through an accident or a serious illness, and it becomes a matter of great importance.

It is not surprising that there should be differences of opinion as to what lies beyond death. In fact, though the Bible gives us great words of assurance about the reality of eternal life, it does not tell us much about its nature. These words are mainly in the New Testament, for the belief in personal survival beyond death does not appear until late in Hebrew history. In the fourteenth chapter of Job, where we find the poignant cry "If a man die, shall he live again?" the answer appears to be negative. In the nineteenth chapter there is a more affirmative mood in these words, though scholars differ in their interpretation:

> For I know that my Redeemer lives,
>     and at last he will stand upon the earth;
> and after my skin has been thus destroyed,
>     then without my flesh I shall see God.

For our conclusions we must look to the message of Jesus about the love, the goodness, and the power of God. To this we must add the fact that he has not only promised eternal life but has led the way. Nowhere is this more clearly stated than in the great comforting words of assurance as Jesus talked with his disciples on the night of the Last Supper:

Let not your hearts be troubled; believe in God, believe also in me. In my Father's house are many rooms; if it were not so, would I have told you that I go to prepare a place for you? And when I go and prepare a place for you, I will come again and will take you to myself, that where I am you may be also. . . . because I live, you will live also (John 14:1-3, 19).

These promises must be seen in the light of Jesus' own resurrection. The Easter message is the vindication of the power and goodness of God, victorious over sin and pain and death. While it does not give any scientific proof of eternal life, since such matters lie outside the realm of science, it does afford a great assurance that accords with the promise "because I live, you will live also."

So the early church believed, and it gave them a faith and a hope that carried them through every obstacle. This is reflected throughout the book of Acts, in Paul's letters, and in that cryptic but faith-filled book of Revelation with which the Bible comes to an end.

Many passages could be cited which would show that the resurrection faith of the disciples made them dauntless and flaming witnesses. Less is said of their own personal destiny, for this was apparently not their main concern. However, in the fifteenth chapter of First Corinthians, Paul tells us as much as anyone can say about the "physical body" and the "spiritual body," and the imperishable nature of the latter. He comes to a magnificent climax as he quotes first from the prophets Isaiah and Hosea and then adds his own affirmation of faith:

"Death is swallowed up in victory."
"O death, where is thy victory?
O death, where is thy sting?"
The sting of death is sin, and the power of sin is the law. But thanks be to God, who gives us the victory through our Lord Jesus Christ.
Therefore, my beloved brethren, be steadfast, immovable, always abounding in the work of the Lord, knowing that in the Lord your labor is not in vain.

So may it be with us, as we pursue our labors in the work of the Lord, knowing that death is God's inevitable but not his final word. But what may we know of the nature of the new life that awaits us? It is true that we "see in a mirror dimly" on this side of the great transition. Yet God has given us all the knowledge we really need to have.

First, we know that eternal life is not solely a matter of endless time; it is a quality of life. This thought is brought out repeatedly in the Gospel of John, where stress is laid on the fact that it begins here and now. It is a certain kind of life to which Jesus calls us, a life of loving obedience and trust. Eternal life is not bare, endless duration, such as we might not wish to have if we could; it is a life of love and of service in God's nearer presence.

Second, eternal life is a life of joy. Traditional thought has placed this first. I do not subordinate it because joy is unimportant, but because joy is found best through loving service and a soul-enriching fellowship. There is great meaning in the word of Jesus to the woman at the well in Samaria, "whoever drinks of the water that I shall give him will never thirst; the water that I shall give him will become in him a spring of water welling up to eternal life."

Some persons may ask, "What of the crowns, the harps, the golden streets, and the pearly gates by which heaven has been described?" This is simply an imaginative way of saying what cannot be said in prosaic terms. Of such symbolism Dr. Robert J. McCracken has written:

> It is all a picture; it is an attempt to express the inexpressible. White robes are symbols of stainless purity, crowns of moral victory, harps of abounding happiness, gold of the timelessness of heaven—gold does not rust—and of the preciousness of it. Stainless purity, moral victory, abounding happiness, infinity— the Easter faith is the promise of something we all want, and never cease to want, something for which our hearts crave, something not to be had in this world, but to be found in heaven.[2]

A third great boon of eternal life is fellowship. Christians often ask wistfully, "Shall I know my loved ones over there?" There is good reason to believe that the answer is Yes. A good

---

2. In "Who Wants to Live Forever? An Easter Meditation," *The Churchman* (April 1958), p. 7.

and loving God has made us to love one another. Can we suppose that he abruptly blots out this fellowship in the larger life? Bodily sight and touch just like the present we cannot expect to have, but the bodies we know here need not be God's only instrument. Something we are now too earthbound to describe may well be the instrument by which our personalities meet and enrich one another in the life beyond our present sight.

Above all, there will be that great gift of a closer fellowship with God, earthly barriers of pain and limitation laid aside in a new freedom of the spirit. Though the references to angels' wings may be taken as poetic and symbolic rather than literal descriptions, shall not our spirits take wings in this larger and more glorious freedom? And shall not "the grace of the Lord Jesus Christ and the love of God and the fellowship of the Holy Spirit" have new meaning for us in this final benediction?

What has been said is not mere speculation; it is inference from what the Bible tells us of the goodness and power of God as he has come to us in Christ. Nor is it something *proved* in the usual meaning of this term. For more than fifty years now studies have been made in the field of psychic research to try to ascertain if the dead can communicate with the living. Some highly regarded persons, such as the philosopher William James and Sir Oliver Lodge in an earlier day and Dr. Leslie Weatherhead and Professor Ralph Harlow today, believe this has occurred in well-authenticated cases. Though the results fall short of proof, we do well to keep our minds open to the possibility.

The Christian's belief in a larger, more beautiful, and more meaningful life beyond bodily death needs no proof, for this faith rests on the firmest of all grounds—the love and the goodness of God. Although there is much that we should like to know and do not know, we still can say with Paul,

> "What no eye has seen, nor ear heard,
> nor the heart of man conceived,
> what God has prepared for those who love him,"
> God has revealed to us through the Spirit. For the Spirit searches
> everything, even the depths of God (1 Cor. 2:9-10).

So, as we ask Job's question of long ago, we are able through

Christ to give the firm and assured Yes before which he hesitated. In this faith we can go forward with firmness and assurance in that quality of disciplined and committed life that begins right here, right now.

Yet there are those who do not make make such a commitment in this life. Some appear to be grossly self-centered and sinful; others are kindly disposed and "good people" in the usual meaning of this term but not Christians. Some are, while many are not, adherents of some other form of religious faith. With the increasing secularization of society, the number of such persons increases. We all know some of them. And what of their destiny after death?

In the past, it was customary to believe that all such persons were consigned to hell. This has often been placed in the forefront of the effort to win others to Christ. Yet sometimes more compassionately it has been believed that their existence simply stopped at death.

Here we must move carefully, for we must not claim to know more than we do. Yet again, if the love and the goodness of God are the foundation of our faith, must we not believe that he loves these persons also? Even you or I can care enough for these persons not to wish them consigned to hell or to annihilation; can we suppose that God cares less than we do?

That divine judgment is a reality is certainly true for this life, and presumably for the next. The commitments we make and the kind of life we lead here must certainly make a difference beyond death. The joy of eternal life—we have been saying—begins in the joy of Christian living now, and it is reasonable that the opposite be true. God is never indifferent to sin, and our rebellion against him and his holy will or our indifference to him is never a trivial matter.

But does this justify belief in hell? That those who reject God cut themselves off from his best gifts seems credible enough. It is not difficult to believe that a hell of alienation, loneliness, and self-induced separation from God is in store for those who persistently reject fellowship with him and obedience to him. These may be the "spirits in prison" to whom we are told Jesus went to preach (1 Peter 3:19). But that God ceases to love such persons does not accord with anything that Jesus tells us of God. It is more credible that he does continue to love them, and seeks to win them, and asks us to love them too. To be sure, there are passages in the Bible which speak of a burning lake of fire and of perpetual weeping and gnashing of teeth; yet such passages seem more likely to reflect the thought of the biblical writers of the first century than the mind of Christ.

So, let us leave this matter, as well as those we love, in the hands of a just and loving God, and know that in his good keeping all is well. For ourselves, let us fix attention mainly on the affirmative side of the picture, whether we call it heaven, or personal immortality, or resurrection, or simply the life eternal. For others, let our judgment be both understanding and charitable, and trust our loving God to do with them and for them what is right.

Eternal life, whether now or in the next life, is God's gift. We do not earn it; he gives it. Yet it requires of us the meeting of certain conditions. What these are and how we may best meet them will be our next concern.

# PART TWO

*Procedures*

# VII. DISCOVERY OF GOD

In the preceding chapters, attention has been given mainly to foundations in faith on which a disciplined Christian life can be built. Along the way, the bearing of Christian belief on the demands of Christian living has been suggested. Yet the main focus thus far has been on faith as belief in the great essentials rather than on what we must do to become disciplined Christians.

I trust the reason for such foundations is clear. Yet a further word of explanation may be in order. Faith has a double meaning. It means belief and it means commitment. The center of the disciplined life is commitment. Yet there is not apt to be a very deep commitment of one's life to God or to the love commandments of Jesus unless there is a sufficiently well-grounded belief to make such a commitment seem realistic. There is a legitimate place in Christian experience for honest doubt, and a continuing search for truth should be a lifetime enterprise. Faith as commitment can be greatly strengthened by such a quest. Yet a faith that rests simply on traditional notions that no longer seem persuasive, or on wishful thinking, soon disintegrates under strain.

In Chapter Three some reasons were given for believing in the God of Christian faith. In this chapter our concern will be the discovery of this same God in our living, that is, how to make God seem real and vital in personal experience. This is almost equivalent to saying "how to become a Christian."

"O that I knew where I might find him" has voiced the aspiration of serious-minded, earnest-hearted people in all generations. Sometimes in a contentious mood, like Job who wanted to argue with God about his suffering, sometimes in a quest rooted in the conviction that in God alone is our true security, it is the heart-cry of the ages. So it is today, even though there are a few theologians—a small minority—who say that God is dead and there are many secularists to whom God seems to make little difference in their lives. Complex as our time is with its many interests, God is still what the late Professor Paul Tillich called man's Ultimate Concern.

Let us see, then, by what steps we may find our way to a personal discovery of the God of Christian faith, and thereby be enabled to live as Christians. There is, of course, no single specific route, but there are great general guidelines.

### 1. Awareness of Need

The first step in the personal discovery of God is awareness of need. God does not thrust himself on anybody. We have to want what God offers and stands ready to give, or his gift of new life and spiritual vigor will pass us by. It was when the prodigal son said, "I will arise and go to my father," that his redemption began.

The awareness of need which is essential to the finding of God comes oftenest, if not always, through a human stimulus. Through the ages corporate worship has been its main channel, and it still is. This is why the church, often criticized today as a barren institutional structure, needs to be revitalized without being so much disparaged.

The sermon certainly ought to awaken a sense of the need of God as well as give assurance and direction to the worshiper. The liturgy in a more formal way has this same function. So do the often unconscious influences of the music, the fellowship of other Christians at prayer, and the total atmosphere of the house of worship. Likewise, the personal contacts involved and the responsibilities assumed in various church activities serve to deepen interest and they ought to awaken an awareness of the need and the possibility of "a closer walk with God." Without question, both the clergy and the laity could do more in this direction. Yet churches are and doubtless will continue to be the main channel for this vital witness.

Churches are by no means the only channel. The quickening of our sense of need of God comes also in our daily living, at work, at home, at leisure, in community relations. This is why the church in recent years has come to a fresh sense of the mission of the laity as the church within the world. The witness we give there may be in words, but this is not the only form of witness. Often the most effective kind is such personal integrity and outgoing Christian concern for the needs and feelings of others that "actions speak louder than words."

There are manifold sources of awakening. The stimulus that stirs one may come through a casual conversation that turns to the deeper issues of life. It may come through a counselor who is both Christian and understanding. It can come through an address that strikes home in a new way. It can come through reading a book, and if this book should have some such effect it would be the author's best reward.

The darker aspects of life have also their contribution to make. Even our darkest experiences can be reminders that we are not so self-sufficient as we thought we were. Suffering can either embitter us or send us to God for victory over it. We cannot rightly say that God sends suffering as his purpose for his children; we can say that suffering rightly used can be God's messenger to our too complacent selves.

## 2. Surrender of Will

The second step, growing out of the first without clear separation, is surrender of will. The term "surrender" sounds strange to modern ears, for it reflects a mood at variance with the prevailing mental climate. Not only in victory in warfare, but in the space race, in man's conquest of nature, of his competitors, and theoretically of himself, power is the great desideratum. The idea of surrendering to anybody or any thing suggests servility, and nobody wants to be servile.

Until we can shake ourselves out of this self-willed mood no great advances in religion, either personal or corporate, are likely to take place. The distinctive characteristic of religion is not human fellowship, important though it is. Fellowship is promoted through service clubs, schools, Boy Scouts, and numerous other character-building agencies. What makes religion *religion* is willingness to worship, to bow in humility before an utterly holy deity and subordinate self to the leadership of that deity. Then, if our religion is vital, it will prompt us to greater love for other persons and to deeds of service without trying to dominate them.

This has a bearing too on our conquest of self for a better personal adjustment. As long as religion is used as a means to an end—even a worthy end like peace of mind and more gracious relations with those about us—it eludes us. *Using religion* means trying to make God do what men want done, and this is not religion but magic. *Being religious* means subjecting man's will to the will of God.

How to know what God wills is often not easy. We cannot safely trust either tradition or intuition. The will of God is a matter to be discerned in the light of our most sensitive judgments and most reasoned insights within the circumstances. Prayer is certainly needed; so is the weighing of the probable consequences of any proposed action. Neither is a substitute for the other, and the attempt to make one do duty for the other is neither good sense nor good religion.

To decide what is right to do is important; to be willing to do it is indispensable. Without it, the discovery of God gets mired in self-will. With it, self-will does not wholly disappear, for none of us is sinless. Yet the self is enlarged and sweetened by the inclusion within it of many interests hitherto dormant or rejected. Persons and causes to be served move from the outer circle to the center of attention; and with these and God in the center, life gains a new stability and strength. It is not inappropriate that such a reorientation has long been called "conversion," the turning about from a self-centered to a God-centered life.

Such surrender of will involves repentance for sin as well as the upward and the forward look. Sin is not a very popular term today, but it is by no means an outmoded fact. It is the most persistent fact of human experience, and there is more in it than departure from conventional standards of decent living. Sin is rebellion against God and disobedience to his love commandments. Repentance means facing our sins squarely, without morbidness and without self-delusion. It means earnest self-searching, sincere contrition, and, so far as possible, restitution to any person sinned against. Repentance is not all that is required, for without deliverance also from fear, loneliness, despair, and confusion of spirit, life will not be all that God wills it to be. Yet without sincere and honest repentance and such self-cleansing as is within our power, we shall get no farther.

### 3. Deliverance

The third step has already been suggested. This is deliverance. It is wrought by God, yet not without our co-operation. From divine forgiveness no magical perfection ensues, but a new sense of the "clean heart" and the "right spirit" for which the psalmist prayed (Ps. 51:10). With it comes an increase in poise and power. There is a paradoxical freedom here, for by the surrender of self-will one gains a higher freedom. Paul expressed it perfectly when he wrote, "For freedom Christ has set us free; stand fast therefore, and do not submit again to a yoke of slavery" (Gal. 5:1).

While the grace of God in imparting this new freedom beyond our deserving has been rightly stressed by traditional theology, it is important to recognize that this third step, like all the others, is one in which receptivity must be joined with active effort. God delivers, but delivers only those who will accept his gift of grace. God saves the person who is "lost"—bewildered and unable to find the way—as well as the repentant sinner, but God saves only him who is willing to try to find the way.

Such deliverance means far more than a comfortable emotional glow. When it is only this it soon cools and disappears. It means reorganization of life from the inside out, and from the bottom up. Failure to recognize this fact has sometimes led to the gruesome practice of counting the number of souls saved in meetings, and it has helped to fill church rosters with only nominal Christians whose lives are indistinguishable from those outside the churches.

Acceptance of deliverance means earnest, persistent grappling with the habitual sins that hold us in their grip, not always flagrant

offenses against the moral code, but the more insidious and therefore more dangerous sins of bad temper, censoriousness, jealousy,
arrogance, irresponsibility, laziness, self-delusion, petty-minded-
ness, complacency before the agony of the world. To overcome
these is both to take up one's cross daily and to rejoice in such
victory as God enables us to have.

## 4. Growth

The fourth step is progressive spiritual growth. It can begin
any time, but ought never to end. It does not mean "sanctification" in any sense that would imply either a sudden or a final
sinlessness. It does mean in the committed Christian the ongoing
achievement of an active saintliness or holiness of living, for
that is what sanctification really means. It means increasing spiritual sensitivity and increasing moral earnestness, joined with a
deep humility as to one's own achievement. It is fed by the life
of worship and energized by, as well as for, the doing of constructive tasks of human service. Without such expression any
incipient religious vitality fades away.

The person who achieves most fully the experience of personal discovery of God described in this chapter will be the last
to boast of being a Christian. But others will know him to be one,
seeing in him a living witness to the Christ who is "the pioneer
and perfecter of our faith."

Putting from us spiritual arrogance and indifference, we must
sense our need of God, surrender our wills in repentance and
trust, accept the divine deliverance, and live the life of progressive
soul-making in victory over sin and the chaos of disordered personality. There need be no spectacular fireworks about this. But
it does not happen by accident. These are the steps, as I see them,
which the great religious spirits have always taken. They are as
much needed today if we are to find power in God to grapple with
the problems of ourselves and of our time.

# VIII. HEARING GOD SPEAK
## THROUGH THE BIBLE

In this and several succeeding chapters we shall be thinking about the ways in which God speaks to the earnest listener who desires to live a disciplined Christian life. Attention will be given both to public worship and to the personal life of prayer. This chapter is related to both spheres, for the Bible is our primary source both of Christian wisdom and of the inspiration and empowering to follow what the early Christians so graphically called simply "the Way."

The Bible continues to be read in virtually every service of public worship. Yet this is not to say that it is always heard. In the story of the boy Samuel there stands a suggestive verse: "And Samuel grew, and the LORD was with him and let none of his words fall to the ground" (1 Sam. 3:19). This can scarcely be said of the reading of Scripture in the churches, where the words fall to the ground too often. As for personal reading and study of the Bible, there appears to be more interest in group study than formerly, yet in many homes the Bible is rarely if ever opened.

The Bible does not hesitate to regard God as speaking to man, his supreme creation made in his own image. All the way from the first chapter of Genesis with its recurrent "and God said . . ." to the final words of the book of Revelation, God speaks. He continues to speak today through the Bible to those who listen with understanding minds and responsive hearts.

## 1. The Bible as God's Word

Jesus began his public ministry by reading from the Scriptures. His mind and spirit had been nourished on the sacred writings of the past. They spoke to him, and they can speak to us.

The Bible has long been called the Word of God. This it is. Yet it is not his only Word, or even his primary Word. Let us not forget that the Gospel of John begins with the great affirmation "In the beginning was the Word, and the Word was with God, and the Word was God." A few verses further on we read, "And the Word became flesh and dwelt among us, full of grace and truth; we have beheld his glory, glory as of the only Son from the Father. . . . And from his fulness have we all received, grace upon grace" (John 1:14, 16). It is Jesus Christ who is God's supreme Word, his highest and most authentic channel of self-disclosure.

This great fact we need to keep in mind as we seek to understand the often obscure passages of the Bible. The inspiration of the Bible does not mean that God dictated it, word for word, and therefore that its truth is unmistakable. The word "inspiration" means "inbreathing," and in the Bible we find the breath of God's Spirit for man's invigoration as it comes through its human writers. Those who wrote the various portions of the Bible had a great sense of the importance of what God was doing in human life and history; yet they had their own prejudices and points of view as well. Inevitably, these crept into the record, so that we have in the Bible what Paul called heavenly "treasure in earthen vessels." The one sure test of whether in the words of these writers we find the Word of God is whether the writing accords with the spirit of Jesus, the supreme channel of God's revelation.

The Bible is a whole library, for in its sixty-six books are to be found many kinds of literature—history, prophecy, law, poetry, philosophy, short stories, sermons, letters, familiar proverbs, and cryptic symbolism. There is no science, for science had not yet appeared, and it is a mistake to read, for example, the story of creation as if it were science instead of the great prose poem that it is.

The Bible was written by many authors over a period of about a thousand years, and the events it tells about go back much earlier. Naturally, it reflects the social conditions and ways of thinking of the times when it was written. Those times were quite different from ours, and we often have to look beneath the surface to discover its permanent message.

Yet, in spite of these difficulties, it does have a great message from God. If not, Jesus would not have loved the Old Testament as he did, and the Bible would not have been read, as it has been, by many millions of Christians since. It has permeated the culture, the literature, and the speech of the whole Western world, and no other book in existence has ever been read so widely or exerted so much influence.

The one great theme that runs through all the varied literary forms and epochs of the Bible is the goodness and love of God and his yearning to save his sinful and erring human children. The Old Testament has its focus in the promise of a Redeemer; the New Testament reveals the coming of this Savior in Jesus Christ. Thus, Christ is the central Word in the Bible even where the words do not specifically speak of him.

So, if we find passages that seem somewhat dull and even boring, as we may in Leviticus and Numbers, or passages that seem a bit shocking by present standards, as in the polygamy of the Old Testament patriarchs or the cruelty of the wars of conquest, these things need not bother us. They reflect the human element in the Bible. What is divine about it is the message that comes to its climax in Jesus. Using him as our standard, we can look at the rest with a fresh perspective. What accords with the way Jesus lived and taught about God, wherever we find it in the Bible, is God's Word. This we must seek to hear.

## 2. Hearing the Word

Since our main concern at this point is how to live disciplined lives at the call of God and in his presence, let us think now about what we must do to hear God speak through the Bible.

Speaking and hearing are the principal ways we come into relation with one another. Yet unless there is some relationship to begin with which makes one want to hear, the speaking falls on deaf ears. Who has not tried to talk to somebody who simply would not listen?

This is an analogy of our relationship to God. He is always seeking to speak to us, whether through the Bible, the church, other Christian people, the events that befall us, or the inner promptings of our own spirits. But do we listen? A one-way conversation does not get through unless there is response. Response implies responsibility—the two words have a common source.) Go to p932

There are several things we need to do if we would hear God speak through the Bible. One is to learn all we can about how its various parts came to be written, what their literary forms are, what these passages meant to those who wrote them and to those for whom they were originally written. Such understanding often throws a flood of light on the meaning. In part we get this through study, but it also requires sympathetic imagination to put ourselves into these scenes.

Biblical scholars for over a hundred years have been doing much work in getting not only at the original text of the Bible but at the historical and social context through which to understand it better. Fortunately, there are simple books available which give the principal results of these studies, though the studies themselves are highly technical. God has a message for us through the Bible at every level of our understanding; yet the better we understand the Bible, the less likely we are to miss the basic message.

Much help may be obtained from such Bible study in church school classes. Children and young people should be taught in such a way that they will not later have errors to unlearn. It is a most fruitful study for adult groups, provided there is recognition that God has given us the freedom to have honest differences of interpretation.

As the Scripture is read in services of public worship, a brief explanation of the setting can throw much light on its meaning. In such reading, the way in which it is read is important. What the Bible says about the reading of Ezra and his colleagues from the book of the law might well be observed today: "And they read from the book, from the law of God, clearly; and they gave the sense, so that the people understood the reading" (Neh. 8:8).

All this is a large field. Many persons are hungry for a knowledge of the Bible that makes it meaningful in the modern day. This is available if we will seek it. But let us turn now to its devotional use.

If we are to read the Bible primarily for its nourishing of the inner life, a few suggestions of things not to do may be in order. (1) Don't feel obligated to read the whole Bible through in a year, or in a fixed sequence. Our fathers, or more likely our grandfathers, did this and often failed to understand or get perspective on what they read. (2) Don't open it at random, expecting in this way to receive a direct message from God. What your eye lights on *may* bring you such a message but it is as likely not to. This is too hit-or-miss for what God asks of us in a serious quest. (3) Don't try to find a text in the Bible to justify what you would like to do, or to prove what you already believe for other reasons. To do this is to try to use God for one's own advantage, not to hear him speak. As was stated earlier, such using rather than listening savors more of magic than of Christian faith.

Avoiding these pitfalls, how shall we go about it? The most important requirement is to be willing to hear what God is saying to us, that is, to be spiritually eager and alert, and at the same time to be willing to do whatever we feel God is asking of us. When Jesus' authority was questioned he answered, "My teaching is not mine, but his who sent me; if any man's will is to do his will, he shall know whether the teaching is from God . . ." (John 7:16-17) Such willingness to do God's will is a basic requirement if we are to disentangle our own selfish desires and thoughts enough to hear God speak.

And now a few practical suggestions. The translation you use is of considerable importance. The King James Version of 1611 contains beautiful Elizabethan English but many of its renderings are obscure today. It is fortunate that we have the Revised Standard Version and the New English Bible (thus far this is in the New Testament only). Both of these are careful translations

into modern English by highly competent scholars. If we prefer
a somewhat freer translation to bring the meaning home to us
more forcefully, there are the Phillips, the Moffatt, the Weymouth,
and various others.

In selecting what to read, one had better follow a system rather
than read at random. This may mean a book at a time, and within
it a chapter or a section of a chapter—not too long to be read
thoughtfully and prayerfully. Or it may mean following some such
system as the Bible readings suggested by a devotional manual or
the listings issued each month by the American Bible Society.
If a group is studying the Bible together or meeting periodically as
a prayer group, a common set of readings used by all the members
is very helpful. Then as you meet, you can share what these
passages have said to you.

The reading of the Bible may well be combined with a time
of private or family prayer, about which more will be said in
a later chapter. In any case, it is best to have a fixed time for it
when one is not too hurried. The strain and pressure of other
duties should be eliminated during this period. This may mean that
the time will have to be brief, but it ought never to be *crowded.*

Then read quietly and slowly, not as you would race through
the newspaper. Give God a chance to speak to you! Ask yourself such questions as "Why was this written in the first place?"
or "What difference would it make if this were lived up to today?"
But most of all, "What does this say *to me?*"

If you strike a snag, don't let it bother you too much. Straighten
it out if you can to see the meaning more clearly. But if not, go on
and the meaning of the passage as a whole will likely become clear.
We get letters from friends with words occasionally that are hard
to make out, but if one is sensible one does not for this reason
discard the letter.

To sum this all up, when God commands, prepare to obey.
When God condemns you, be penitent. When he offers you
assurance, stop being discouraged and fearful. When he shows
you some light—even a slender gleam—along life's way, follow it.

Not every question will be answered. Some mystery will always
remain, both because God expects us to use our own best thinking

and acting, and because we can never fathom fully the mind of the all-wise God. Isaiah wrote with great insight:

> For my thoughts are not your thoughts,
>   neither are your ways my ways, says the LORD.
> For as the heavens are higher than the earth,
>   so are my ways higher than your ways
>   and my thoughts than your thoughts (Isa. 55:8-9).

Yet the Bible can teach us much—more than any other book that was ever written—about God and man, about sin and salvation, about our duty and our destiny. Reading the Bible will not automatically make us disciplined Christians. Yet not to read it with the response of mind and heart is to cut ourselves off from a great source of illumination from God and invigoration for living.

Recently I found this expressed very movingly in *The Eternal Promise,* a collection of essays and addresses written some thirty years ago by Thomas Kelly and now published long after his death, as a sequel to his *Testament of Devotion.* He says, "The Book points beyond itself, to Him who has been found by its writers. And because He is already in the deeps of your own souls, these words of the Bible are made living and vivid to you. Read your Bibles, but *that isn't being religious.* Read your Bibles, and feel your way back into that Source and Spring of Life which bubbled up in the Bible-writers. And you'll find that Source and Spring of Life bubbling up *within you also.* And you'll find yourself in deep fellowship with these writers, because your life and theirs go back into the same Living Spring."[1]

So may it be with all of us.

---

1. Thomas R. Kelly, *The Eternal Promise* (New York: Harper and Row, 1966), p. 103.

# IX. WHY THE CHURCH?

Some things were said in Chapter Seven about the importance of the church in awakening an awareness of the need for a personal discovery of God. In this chapter the emphasis will not be mainly on what we can get from the church, as if our own concerns were uppermost, but on what the church is and does that makes it worthy of our loyalty. In spite of its shortcomings from the human angle, since human beings comprise it, we may still believe that God has established it as the principal channel for carrying the Christian gospel to all times and places. And if this be true, we ought certainly to support it by our prayers, our presence, our gifts, and our service.

First, then, let us think about what the church is in its essential nature. Many people see it as a respectable and ancient institution housed in a building where people gather for weddings and funerals, where a considerable number though by no means all of its members assemble more or less regularly on Sundays, and where words of moral exhortation from the Bible and the mind of the preacher are commonly spoken. But is this all? We must now take a look at some ancient and familiar but often obscure words about its nature; then ask what the church has done and is doing today to make it an indispensable channel for the Christian gospel and for Christian service to God and humanity.

## 1. The Holy Catholic Church[1]

"I believe in the holy catholic church, the communion of saints."

1. "The Holy Catholic Church" Copyright 1947 Stone and Pierce.

These words, repeated times without number by Christians throughout the centuries, have often brought more confusion than clarification to those who spoke them. What, then, do they mean?

It may be helpful to begin with the second of these two phrases.
The second term is explanatory of the first. In short, the holy
catholic church *is* the communion of saints. But this may sound
like explaining the unknown by the more unknown! So what is
the communion of saints?

Communion means fellowship; literally, a "strengthening together" of one another. A saint in Protestant thought is not a
person canonized by the church. Nor is he the long-suffering
martyr or the well-nigh perfect person that he is often assumed
to be. A saint in the New Testament sense is a faithful follower
of Jesus Christ, a redeemed person who has found new life in
Christ. A saint therefore means a Christian, but with special
emphasis on the Christian's fidelity to Christ. Paul's greetings to
"the saints in Caesar's household" or "to the church of God which
is at Corinth, with all the saints who are in the whole of Achaia"
are sent to his fellow Christians who in spite of difficulty have
managed by God's help to remain faithful.

Though we had better not tinker with the wording of this
time-honored creed, we are perfectly justified in substituting
mentally "the fellowship of the faithful." The communion of
saints is that great company of Christian believers, past and present,
living and dead, who have fought a good fight for Christ and in
loyalty of devotion to him have kept the faith. Some of these are
still living; the greater number have entered into the higher,
heavenly kingdom. Whether they are still in this life or have
gone to God's nearer presence, they strengthen us; and in our
flagging efforts to serve Christ we are spurred on by the thought
of being "surrounded by so great a cloud of witnesses."

There is a connection, not commonly realized, between the
communion of saints and Hallowe'en. Traditionally a time for
pranks and "tricks or treats," this children's festival has of late
acquired fresh meaning from the UNICEF collections. It falls
on the eve of All-Hallows Day, that is, the night before All Saints'
Day. While Protestants often observe the Sunday nearest to

October 31—the day that Martin Luther nailed his 95 theses on the door of the church at Wittenberg—as Reformation Sunday, we might well connect this with the first of November to call to mind with gratitude the great debt we owe to the fellowship of faithful Christians in all ages.

We must now ask what this has to do with the holy catholic church. There are differences of opinion as to what the church really is. We cannot here go into these disagreements. Most Christians, however, believe that the church is the community of Christ's followers, that in spite of its many weaknesses there is something of God's Spirit in it, and that it is meant by God to be universal and world-embracing. If one believes this, he believes in the holy catholic church.

To call the church "holy" does not, of course, mean that it is flawless, or wholly divine, or something to be worshiped as God is. It is composed of people, and all people—even the most faithful Christians—have shortcomings. The church is composed of people of varying degrees of faithfulness to Christ, and by no means are all saints! Nevertheless, the church is the carrier of a divine gospel. Its effectiveness is to be judged, not by the strength of its organization or even by its numbers, but by its fidelity to this gospel.

Paul's great description of the church as the body of Christ (1 Cor. 12) is a very suggestive figure of speech. It means that the church is a whole which needs all its parts, just as the foot needs the hand, as the ear the eye. But it suggests also that what the body is to the soul, that is, the carrier and vehicle of spirit and meaning, so the church is to the gospel that Christ has entrusted to it. In what the church has been given by God for the salvation of men, the church today as in every age has something divine and holy.

The word "catholic" in the creed is written with a small "c" and does not mean Roman Catholic. It means something far more inclusive, the universal church of Christ of all denominations around the world. In a sense this is an ideal rather than an actual description of the churches, for Christ's body is broken by many divisions. A cynic is said to have remarked, "I believe in the church universal and regret that it does not exist." Yet in another sense it is a very potent reality.

The catholicity, or inclusiveness, of Christ's church is an affirmation that it is intended to be world-embracing. The missionary outreach of the Christian gospel is implied in it. In our day for the first time in its history, the church has literally encircled the globe. This does not mean that the gospel has yet been "preached to every creature," but there is no major part of the earth's surface where it has not in some measure been taken. From this it follows that we actually have a church far more catholic than the early creed-makers could possibly imagine.

Another matter of great importance is implied in the word "catholic." This is the fact that the church is designed by God to be inclusive enough to embrace not only the people of all parts of the earth, but persons of every race, color, nation, economic or social class, age, sex, culture, language, station in life. Though the churches have never fully lived up to this ideal and have often sadly departed from it, the Christian gospel has always been a rebuke to race prejudice, national or class conflict, and every other form of man-made division. Some of the issues in which "the fellowship of the faithful" have most been called upon to resist the world, at personal cost and even death, lie exactly at this point.

During recent years the term "ecumenical" has come into use to describe this inclusive unity or catholicity of the church of Christ. The word means "from the inhabited world." It was used in the early centuries to designate the great councils, like the Council of Nicaea, to which representatives came from what was then the whole of Christendom—the section around the Mediterranean where churches had been established. The term began to be used again in modern times after the great missionary conference at Edinburgh in 1910 had inaugurated movements to study the "life and work" and the "faith and order" of the Protestant and Eastern Orthodox churches.

From the standpoint of organization the ecumenical movement of these denominations centers mainly in the World Council of Churches and in the U. S. the National Council of Churches and many regional and local councils. In recent years, the ecumenical Second Vatican Council of the Roman Catholic Church has opened the way to much greater fellowship among all Christians.

In this new fellowship we can all rejoice, for the ecumenical movement, like the holy catholic church from which it derives its authority and function, is not essentially an organization. It is a spirit, expressing itself in fellowship and a sense of the oneness of Christ's followers in a common loyalty to our one Lord.

## 2. The Church at Work in the World

It has become quite customary of late to say that the church has become a barren institution, antiquated in its theology and largely indifferent to great human needs. There is enough truth in these charges to make those who love the church feel that it should become more relevant to changing conditions in the modern world. Hence, we hear a good deal about the "renewal" of the church in Protestant circles, and it was this which led Pope John XXIII to summon the Second Vatican Council.

However, there is a less encouraging side of the picture. A good many people, including many highly trained and effective people, disparage and bypass the church on the ground that it does not do much good and there are other channels into which they might better put their energy and effort. Thus, by withdrawing their moral support from the church because it has points of weakness, they weaken it further by not staying in it to help correct what may be wrong with it.

Some even question that it has ever done much good. But the facts refute these charges. The church is the chief conserver of spiritual values, and it is the institutional embodiment of our Christian heritage. During the Dark Ages it preserved not only religion but civilization; it has founded innumerable schools and colleges and has fostered the spread of education through the centuries. It has nourished the spirit of democracy. It has built moral attitudes into the lives of millions of persons. It has made people more humane in their treatment of the weak and the underprivileged. It has goaded consciences to abolish slavery. It has lifted the position of women and children. We are today the inheritors of this freedom and this spirit of concern for other people, in which the church has not been the sole agent but the principal one in the Western world. To turn our backs on it now is to cast off our cultural heritage.

Nor are these achievements wholly in the past. Overseas today, thousands of devoted missionaries continue not only to impart spiritual help, but in conjunction with Christian nationals they advance education; train native leaders in Christian schools and colleges; combat illiteracy; give vocational skills in agriculture, homemaking, and public health; minister to the sick in Christian hospitals; and in manifold ways help to lift the level of human living. Wherever poverty, hunger, and misery are, the church relief agencies not only give material aid but try to help the people to help themselves. Government agencies like the Peace Corps and the A.I.D. are doing on a larger scale, because of more money, what the churches have long been doing in ministry to human need.

This is paralleled by what is happening at home. In many fields of social welfare, public agencies have taken over what the churches formerly did. This is good, for it was largely the church that spearheaded such services. Similarly, it is now challenged to new forms of ministry to the lonely, the forgotten, the ill-treated, the outcast members of society. At the same time, it must continue to minister to the outwardly more fortunate but often inwardly barren lives of those who make up the greater part of its membership.

In matters of race and of our cultural divisions, the record of the churches is not so good as it should have been. Christians have often followed community patterns instead of the imperatives of the Christian gospel. Yet two things should be said. The first is that the ferment of the gospel is at work to break down barriers and establish a more just society. Real advances in ethical sensitivity have taken place in recent years, among both religious leaders and the rank and file of church people. The second is that today, as in the past but with a more direct focus, the church continues to give incentive to many to work for a better society through other than church-related channels.

I have spoken mainly about the social services of the church, for the critics seem mainly to be concerned at this point. But this is not all. Who can doubt its great services in affording support and comfort in time of trouble, giving goals to live by and imparting meaning to otherwise empty lives, enabling people even in our hurried and harried time to find what Paul called "the peace that passes understanding"? If it did only this, the church would still be of incalculable value.

What all this adds up to is that the church not only needs our support in order to render these services, but it is worthy of it. To withdraw our personal support, whether of "our prayers, our presence, our gifts or our service," is both to weaken the church and to become a parasite, accepting its values but not contributing to them. Furthermore, it is to cut ourselves off from the primary channel which God has ordained for carrying forward the work of Christ. It is to abdicate that without which we cannot expect to have the fruits of disciplined Christian living ourselves or to bring them most vitally to the world around us.

# X. KNOWING CHRIST THROUGH CORPORATE WORSHIP

A story is told of a little old lady, who for the first time was making the grand tour of Europe, eagerly taking in everything she saw and anxious not to miss a thing. As the guide was showing the group through the historical treasure-house of Westminster Abbey, so full of mementoes of the great men and movements of the past, she pulled on his sleeve and asked anxiously, "Say, young man, this is all very well, but has anybody been saved here lately?"

The same question might well be asked about many of our churches. They have beauty and dignity. The symbolism of altar and cross, of pulpit and lectern, of organ and choir and stained glass windows may be ornate or simple. The churches may be old or of quite recent vintage, sometimes with a very modernistic flair. Yet they stand for something that reaches back through the centuries. The same is true of the words of Scripture and liturgy and many of the hymns heard in these sanctuaries. With occasional innovations, they speak the aspiration and the assurances of our great Christian past. Yet does anything of real importance happen in the Sunday morning service of public worship?

If nothing in particular does, we are inclined to blame the minister. That is, we do unless we have become so accustomed to having nothing happen that we think no more about it. The leader of worship has, indeed, the high responsibility of making the service, as far as it is in his power, meaningful, moving, and relevant both to the great foundations of our Christian faith and to the needs of the people.

Some of these needs are perennial, such as the need for companionship in loneliness, comfort in trouble, direction in moral decisions, the need to persevere when life becomes hard and to wait patiently when the fruits of effort are not visible. Other needs, and in particular those which have to do with great social issues within our changing times, have a vital place within the hour of worship when the challenge for meeting them is grounded in great Christian imperatives. Every minister of Christ who is worthy of the name, and that includes a host of them in every land and nation, senses his responsibility and tries with varying degrees of success to measure up to it.

Our concern at this point is not with the minister so much as with the persons in the pews. In almost any enterprise, to secure the desired results there must be both a leader and the co-operation of those who are led. When either side begins to blame the other for the faults in the situation instead of looking within, morale disintegrates. While the form of the activity may continue, the nerve and the verve and the spirit of the enterprise are lost. A service of public worship is no exception.

### 1. What Is Worship?

In the first place, we need as worshipers in the pews to have a clearer idea than many of us have as to what worship really is. It is not a matter of hearing good moral advice, getting the stimulus of new ideas, being entertained by interesting stories, or hearing good music skillfully rendered. Any of these things may be present in a service of worship when they are an adjunct to something deeper. Or they may not. They are out of place when they get in the way of this deeper note.

Worship is centered in God, or it is not worship. The origin of the word is suggestive, for it comes from the old Anglo-Saxon *weorthscipe,* the worth-ship of God. Worship is the act of lifting up our hearts to God in adoration and praise. It is the expression of our gratitude and thanksgiving to God. It is confession of our sin before God, not perfunctorily but with genuine contrition, not with the easy feeling that the words may perhaps apply to somebody else, but with the full certainty of our own guilt before him.

Worship is the release of energy and the new resolve that comes from the assurance of God's forgiveness of the penitent, and in more serious moments we know that this comes only when we are penitent. Worship is petition for the guidance and strengthening and sensitivity to live as God's servants, not in the church only but in our homes, at work, in our world, wherever our lives touch other lives. Worship is intercession for these others in a spirit of deep concern and self-giving, for it is in prayer for others that God enlarges our hearts and widens the scope of our concern both for them and for him, and for them in him. Worship is commitment of our total selves to God for his service and in the assurance of his undergirding, ever-present, and never-failing grace.

Christian worship is the offering of ourselves in these attitudes to the God whom Jesus worshiped, the God whom Jesus came to reveal, and the God through whom in Christ we are brought to new motives, new powers, new life. "Therefore, if any one is in Christ," said Paul, "he is a new creation; the old has passed away, behold, the new has come." This ought to happen not once only, though the overwhelming newness of life that comes with the great decision to be a follower of Christ can come in any Sunday morning service of worship. Yet for those of us who have been Christians for years, any service of corporate worship ought to be a time of renewal, of knowing Christ better, and hence of new life in Christ.

No service of worship will automatically do this for us. What can be hoped for is a fresh grip on the great realities of our faith and a lifting, transforming sense of the Eternal Christ as the Way, the Truth, and the Life. Yet it will cost us much—the willingness not only to learn about but to live in the light of Christ, not only to *do* but to *receive* and to *be*.

## 2. "We Would See Jesus"

In the Gospel of John, directly after the account of our Lord's triumphal entry into Jerusalem, we are told that some Greeks came with a simple but all-important request, "we would see Jesus" (John 12:21, K.J.V.). This prompted Jesus to speak of his own approaching death. The whole meaning of the Cross is compressed into his words of poignant suffering and triumph, "Now is my soul troubled. And what shall I say? 'Father, save me from this hour'? No, for this purpose I have come to this hour. Father, glorify thy name" (John 12:27-28).

In the book of Hebrews, written some fifty years or more after Jesus died, we find some more words about seeing Jesus, and about what his living and dying to bring God to us means to us all. The author first quotes the eighth Psalm, which tells of the greatness and power to control nature which God has given to man. Then he adds:

> Now in putting everything in subjection to man, he left nothing outside his control. As it is, we do not yet see everything in subjection to him. But we see Jesus, who for a little while was made lower than the angels, crowned with glory and honor because of the suffering of death, so that by the grace of God he might taste death for every one (Heb. 2:8-9)

How appropriate these words are for our time! Man has conquered not quite everything in nature, but so much that he often forgets the God who gave him his power. He can split the atom to release tremendous power for human good or his fellowman's destruction; he can ride the heavens in outer space till he is soon to reach the moon. Every day in millions of homes we see and hear what is happening in the most remote places of the earth, a marvel so familiar that we forget to marvel at it. Yet why enumerate them? Anybody can supply his own list of modern miracles.

Yet man has not conquered himself. He still sins; he suffers; he dies. At times the weight of this sinning and suffering and dying makes life seem unendurable. All the time, their weight hangs over the best and most fortunate of us. We can refuse to think about them, or push them into the background by thinking about a million other things. Yet these grim realities are always in the off-stage part of the human drama, ready to step forward when we least expect them to appear.

So, today as always, we need to "see Jesus." He is our only final answer. Elsewhere in Hebrews the author speaks of "Jesus Christ . . . the same yesterday, and today, and for ever" (Heb. 13:8). The times have changed greatly since Jesus lived. Yet man's needs have not changed, or the ministry to them through the love and mercy of God which Jesus came to bring. Whatever other reasons we may have for going to church, the primary and indispensable reason is to worship God through seeing Jesus.

This does not always happen. I am not suggesting we should expect a tremendous inner upheaval each time at church. The hymn writer George Croly had a true insight when he wrote:

I ask no dream, no prophet ecstasies,
No sudden rending of the veil of clay,
No angel visitant, no opening skies;
But take the dimness of my soul away

However, the dimness of soul with which we go to church seems often not to be removed. Why is this so?

### 3. The Barriers

One reason is our *preoccupation with many matters.* Ours is a complex time for Christians as for others, and few of us have long periods of relaxed leisure. The Sunday morning scramble in many homes to get the family up and fed, cleaned up and suitably attired, can itself be a barrier to a worshipful mood. Yet the very fact that the worship costs some effort can make it more meaningful. It would be simpler to stay at home and turn on the radio or the television. This can be a blessing for those who cannot get to church. Yet, if we are honest with ourselves, we know this is no real substitute for worshiping with others at the house of God. If we were to try to worship usually by the air waves because it is easier, before long, like the alleged worship in the groves and on the golf course, it would turn out not to be worship at all.

The physical difficulties are by no means the primary ones. Our deeper barrier is *lack of incentive.* The derivation of the word "liturgy" is suggestive. It comes from *leitourgia,* a public work. This work, this service to God, costs something we are often unready to give—attentiveness of spirit, openness of mind and heart.

Coming as we often do with all our preoccupations, anxieties, hopes, desires, and possibly with our angers and disappointments, we do not find it easy to turn our thoughts to God. The minister, the time-honored words of Scripture and prayer, the music, and the presence of the waiting congregation can help us. Yet it is our own receptivity that determines whether we sense God's presence, know Christ better, and commit our lives more faithfully for having worshiped together.

A third and related major barrier is our *lack of expectancy*. We have attended church many times before and nothing much happened; why should it now? We are not apt to say this outright, and may be only dimly aware of this feeling. It comes to the front in the minds of many nominal Christians who say they "get nothing out of it" and therefore it is a waste of time to go to church. This may go far toward accounting for the disparity between church membership and average attendance in the churches.

The story of the giving of the Holy Spirit at Pentecost can teach us something at this point. We are told, "When the day of Pentecost had come, they were all together in one place." Faithfully observing a Jewish holy day, the disciples had come together as their custom was, and were waiting. Then suddenly "a sound came from heaven like the rush of a mighty wind," and a great glow appeared on their faces. There was a new joy in their hearts, a new speech on their lips, and the church was born. What transformed their lives, quickened their witness, and created the church was from God. They could not have anticipated it or produced it by their own devices. Yet they could not have received it had they not been open to it, waiting before God with fidelity and faith.

What lay back of Pentecost? It was not brilliant preaching, though it stirred the formerly uneloquent Peter to preach a great sermon. It was not the meritorious service of the disciples, for their great deeds were yet to come. It was not the atmosphere of a beautiful sanctuary. It was the mighty act of God that gave Pentecost its outflowing of power, and back of this the mighty acts of God in the life, the ministry, the death and resurrection of Jesus. Not without reason did Peter end his sermon with the words by which we are told his hearers were "cut to the heart": "Let all the house of Israel therefore know assuredly that God has made him both Lord and Christ, this Jesus whom you crucified."

## 4. The Fruits

We can have this kind of expectancy today. Not every service of worship will have world-shaking effects, either in the congregation as a whole or in the individual members. Yet God is present, and he will speak to us if we listen. No tricks are needed to enliven the assembly, though reverent and dedicated skills of leadership are important offerings in his service. What is needed is for our spirits to be open in expectancy of hearing his Word in our hearts as well as in our ears, of feeling a new glow within even if it should not be written on our faces, of going forth from God's house to witness faithfully by our lives if not by eloquent words, of being stirred as were those first Christians to share both our daily bread and our prayers "with glad and generous hearts."

So, it comes about that the ultimate requirement for fruitful worship is our faith in what God has done for us in Christ, what he does today, what we know he will continue to do to the end of time. This is to see Jesus. When we do, whether the service of worship is in Westminster Abbey or in the humblest little church in a far-off land, souls are quickened to new life.

# XI. PRAYER AND LIFE—SOME COMMON OBSTACLES

In the two preceding chapters we have been thinking about the church. This is central to any thought about disciplined Christian living, for while I should not want to be dogmatic enough to say that no person could be a Christian without being affiliated with a church, it happens very rarely. The church through the centuries has been the carrier of the Christian gospel, and directly or indirectly, our whole society is indebted to it for its most cherished values.

In the two chapters after this one, we shall be thinking about the methods and fruits of personal prayer. This chapter stands midway between them. Much that can be said about prayer applies equally to worship in church and in that privacy to which Jesus referred when he said, "But when you pray, go into your room and shut the door and pray to your Father who is in secret . . ." (Matt. 6:6). It is these common elements that we shall now be considering.

Yet the chapter is entitled "Some Common Obstacles." Should we begin thus negatively? I trust the results of this approach will be positive. The reason for looking at the pitfalls is that we may avoid them. Roadside signs that give only arrows pointing to the next town with never a "Caution" or "Danger" or "Detour" sign would not help us much to get there.

Let me first interpose a caution as to how we ought to approach so serious a subject. There is no single clearly marked freeway leading to vital prayer. Presumably some ways in which to think about prayer are more nearly right than others; some ways of praying more effective than others. Yet to maintain that there is only one right way to think about or to practice prayer is antithetical to the spirit of reverent search which is its essence. As there is a diversity of gifts among Christians, so is there a legitimate diversity of opinions about prayer.

Yet openmindedness ought never to drain off conviction. It is a mistake to suppose that one's own way necessarily is the right way; it is a more serious mistake to suppose that it does not matter how one prays, or whether one prays at all. Let us look then, at some of our more common pitfalls.

### 1. Insecure Foundations

The question is often raised whether prayer is not merely self-hypnosis or autosuggestion. The answer depends on the structure of one's belief about God. If there is no God, obviously all that happens in prayer is a rearrangement of one's own thought patterns. If there is a God, he works in us to cause changes which otherwise would not happen. It may be that God's activity in response to prayer is wholly in human minds, and not in the events of physical nature. But if God in response to prayer enhances our peace and poise, our courage and insight, he does the most important thing that could be done.

Not every concept of God is equally conducive to prayer. To believe in God as an impersonal cosmic force or process leaves one with little foundation on which to believe that God can respond to the worshiper. Prayer then has to be limited to an effort to feel one's unity with this power or process, and to work in harmony with it. This is an important aspect of worship and is not to be scorned. If this concept of God is what one believes, it is still something to make the most of.

When one believes—not merely intellectually but vitally— in the God of Jesus, prayer becomes to him, as to Jesus, a natural element of life. One no more speculates about whether he ought to pray than he questions whether to eat, or breathe, or take exercise. There may still be perplexity about how to pray or what to pray for. But in living Christian experience, there is no question of whether it is worth while to pray. Prayer becomes self-validating.

## 2. Formalism

Note that I do not list *form* as an error. To continue the analogy suggested above, as there are definite forms through which to eat and breathe and exercise, so there are useful forms by which to pray. We pray best either through the forms made familiar and beloved by long experience, or through those which have freshness and the appeal of novelty. This is why we need usually to worship in the manner of the church in which we were reared, and sometimes to go reverently to churches or synagogues of a radically different type.

But when form instead of being a useful instrument becomes an end in itself, ritualism has replaced prayer. What we have then is mechanism and motion rather than vital emotion. When one finds himself falling into a parrot-like repetition of any prayer, whether the Lord's Prayer or the great petitions of the Prayer Book, it is time to stop short and do something else. One may use different printed prayers, or express his religious aspirations *extempore,* or put new meaning into old forms. There is no rule here, and often it is valuable to do them all. What one must not do, if he want to *pray,* is to continue to repeat meaningless words.

## 3. Infantilism

This may be either of form or of content. For a person to continue to repeat a juvenile petition when he grows to maturity in other matters is clearly a case of arrested development.

More serious than infantilism of form is infantilism of content. Most children have an anthropomorphic concept of God and they often picture him as a kind-faced elderly gentleman with a beard, sitting on a throne in the sky. This concept, if one's development is normal and one's framework of theology Christian, tends to pass over into a God of spiritual personality, who possesses in infinite degree the highest attributes of goodness, wisdom, and creative power. If one cannot pray without calling up before his mind a visual image, maybe it is better to pray in that way than not at all. But maturity in prayer requires a sense of communion with an invisible, unpicturable deity who is both the ultimate source of our existence and the object of our highest adoration.

### 4. Self-Centeredness

Caution is necessary at this point, for some self-reference in prayer is both legitimate and necessary. Prayer and worship, though related terms, are not synonyms. In worship the center of attention is upon the worth-ship of God. There can be no true worship which is not directed toward the exaltation of God. When a person meditates about his own feelings, such meditation though it may be highly profitable is not worship. In prayer, there is a bringing together of awareness of personal and social need with a sense of the greatness of God's power and its availability for our support. It is not necessary in practice to draw a sharp distinction between prayer and worship. In both there is a lifting up of the soul to God in thanksgiving and dependence. Yet prayer, insofar as it is distinguished from worship, takes the form of petition.

Petition for what? I should not exclude petition for the material necessities of life, provided these are sought with a due sense that they are instruments rather than intrinsic goods, and provided prayer is not made a substitute for honest effort. Petition for spiritual goods, however, ought always to be the primary element. By "spiritual goods" I mean wisdom to discern our shortcomings, cleansing from sin, humility to face our weakness and confidence to face our tasks, insight to discover what is the will of God for our lives, and courage to undertake whatever responsibilities we ought to assume. Such prayer is selfish only when these gifts are sought for selfish ends. When this happens, religion degenerates into a process of bathing oneself in one's own emotions—and prayer is no longer prayer but an instrument for the development of delusions of grandeur.

### 5. Evasion of Responsibility

Clearly, it is not enough to assume that having prayed for wisdom and power to accomplish something, it will get accomplished without further effort! Prayer for clearness of mind and the best use of one's ability is no substitute for action. This seems self-evident. Yet people often pray for the spiritual welfare and sometimes for the physical health of others, assuming that God will do what needs to be done without human agency. This is equally an evasion and leads to an unchristian thwarting of values. It is scarcely defensible to pray for the poor and do nothing toward elimination of the causes of poverty; to pray for peace and go on supporting war.

It is irrational and unchristian to pray for others as an escape from responsibility. But I do not say it is irrational to pray for others. It may well be that God regards our prayer for others as one form of our service to them. To leave others out of our prayers is unduly to limit the scope of religious devotion.

Another dangerous evasion of responsibility is judging prayer to be all that is needful to discern God's will. History is full of deeds of fanaticism wrought by religious persons who have sincerely prayed. To understand either ourselves or the will of God, there is need not only of prayer but of candid self-searching, of the objective judgment of the most trustworthy friends, of a comprehensive, emotionally unbiased survey of the probable consequences of any projected act. Lacking these, prayer degenerates into a hallowing of our own subconscious impulses. But lacking prayer, these other avenues to action miss their most potent incentive and most clarifying source of vision.

## 6. Defeatism

Defeatism is perhaps the most insidious error of all. Many people give up praying because they cannot see that it does any good. The thing to do is to analyze the situation. It may be that one has been praying for things impossible in a world of physical orderliness like ours, or for something psychologically if not physically impossible, or for something one might better not have. It may be one has prayed for *things* when he might better have prayed for sanity and optimism by which to get along without them. It may be that one has strained too hard at the process of prayer, being too voluble and inadequately receptive. It may be that intellectual analysis or criticism has taken the place of the prayer attitude. While one ought both to pray and to think about the nature and foundations of prayer, one cannot do both at the same time. It may be that preoccupation with other interests has robbed prayer of its vitality. It is a prime requisite that while we pray God must have no rival in the foreground of attention.

For many persons what has been termed "the great silence" is the chief barrier not only to prayer but to belief in God. An honest atheism should never be disparaged, or treated lightly. Yet before deciding that there is no answer, one may do well to consider whether any of the pitfalls mentioned may have dimmed our hearing.

Not only does God speak to listening ears, but he speaks before we address him. He speaks first, and prayer is essentially our response to God. His Word comes supremely through him of whom it was written, "The Word became flesh and dwelt among us." It continues to come through the church, the Bible, the lives of faithful Christians, the world of nature, the voice of duty, and all those stirrings of the soul that prompt us to be better men and women.

An immature experience cannot be like one enriched by many years of spiritual fellowship with God. But even a feeble experience, so long as it is growing, gives ground to stand on and hope with which to go forward. We are told, "The prayer of a righteous man has great power in its effects" (James 5:16). So it has proved in the experience of countless numbers of people, and so it can be with us.

# XII. "TEACH US TO PRAY"[1]

There are few, if any, Christians who do not realize that they ought to pray. There is nothing in the Christian life about which there is more agreement. Yet for many, this need and obligation appear to be satisfied by listening as the minister or priest prays in church in their behalf. If one may judge from frank personal testimony, family or personal prayer gets badly neglected today, and there are more than a few who say they would not know how to do it if they were to undertake it.

God does not desire self-righteousness, or a feeling of self-sufficiency, in prayer any more than in action. To have enough awareness of shortcomings to seek improvement is good. Yet to have such a lack of confidence in one's praying as to hesitate timidly before the attempt is to cut the ground from under one's spiritual feet. There is nothing our time needs more than a resurgence of vital, intelligently grounded, deeply motivated prayer, and this is not limited to the prayers spoken in churches. Without such prayer we shall not have those spiritual resources by which to find power to act for a new world.

To analyze the processes of prayer seems to some to mar the sacredness of the experience, like picking a flower apart to discover the secret of its beauty. And even if one has discovered something about it for himself, is it not presumption to try to teach another? Indeed, how can one tell another how to pray? For such reasons as these, instruction in prayer has too often been omitted in the churches. While it is true that no precise chart can

1. "Teach Us to Pray" Copyright 1945 by Whitmore and Stone.

be presented—certainly none that will be a substitute for resolute, patient, personal experience—some suggestions can be given. There are some things to do and others not to do. Since we considered some of the latter in the last chapter, let us look now at the more positive side.

Before saying much about methods it is important to get our minds clear on two basic questions, for without solid foundations the methods are too apt to move either aimlessly or in the wrong directions. These questions are: (1) What is prayer? and (2) What ought we to pray for?

## 1. What Is Prayer?

I know of no better statement of what Christian prayer is than that of the *Westminster Shorter Catechism*: "Prayer is an offering up of our desires unto God, for things agreeable to his will, in the name of Christ, with confession of our sins, and thankful acknowledgment of his mercies." This puts the focus where it belongs—on God and his will and his abundant blessings. But it also suggests that the human side has its place; it is the deep and dominant desires of the soul and the sense of the need of forgiveness that we offer up to him.

Some substitutes for prayer must be ruled out on this basis. The reading or repetition of words, whether those of the Lord's Prayer or a modern devotional manual or the prayers of the ages, is not by itself an act of prayer. Such aids may be very helpful in our praying. But it is the response of the soul, the offering up of our desires and the deep impulses of the heart, that makes such words become prayer rather than muscular exercise.

There are various experiences so closely related to prayer that they tend to become substitutes. There is beauty, particularly the lifting power of great music and the beauty of the outdoor world. God speaks through these channels. Yet the exaltation of spirit beauty gives is not worship unless it is linked with the adoration of God.

There is meditation—honest self-examination or serious reflection on some vital subject. This can be a very fruitful part of prayer, and we do well to engage in it more often than most of us do.

Yet simply to "think things over" is not prayer unless it is related
to God and the doing of his will.

This raises the question of wordless communion, which some
regard as the highest form of prayer. It may be in persons of
great maturity in prayer. Yet with many of us it is apt to pass
over into a kind of aimless day-dreaming. Jesus used words
when he addressed the Father, and we had better follow his
example.

Even labor for God and good causes, essential though this is,
can become a substitute for prayer. Prayer ought to lead to service.
Neither to pray without serving nor to serve without praying is
Christian. Even Christian leaders sometimes fall into such a
feverish round of activities in the service of God that they tend to
forget to what end or by what power such service can most fruit-
fully be offered.

## 2. For What Shall We Pray?

There is a natural movement in both public and private prayer.
Let us look, then, at its constituent elements.

Prayer begins in *worship*—in adoration, praise, and thanksgiving to God. Attention is cast outward from self and upward
toward God. There is a line, but a thin one, between praise and
thanksgiving, for "thankful acknowledgment of his mercies" is part
of the praise we owe to God. To think of God and his goodness
brings (or should bring) both gratitude and a sense of our own
unworthiness.

Thus the second step is *confession*—a vital part of prayer
too often slurred over. Here belongs rigorous, even painful self-
examination, with the stripping off of all rationalizations and alibis
as we try to see ourselves in the light of God's high demands.

Confession should lead on to *petition*—petition for forgiveness
but also for wisdom, strength, courage, and all the good gifts needful for our fullest living.

What we ask for ourselves we should also ask for others,
according to their need. We move to what is usually called *intercession,* though simply prayer for others would be a more
natural designation. We do not need to urge God to change

his mind; we do need to place before him our concern for others.

To ask is a kind of blasphemy unless we intend to act. So, all that goes before should lead on to *dedication,* or to commitment. This is the point for crystallization of the resolution, by the help of God, to go forward in more Christlike living, in greater service to those for whom we pray, in greater obedience to what we believe to be God's will.

With a final word, whether expressed or only felt, of our trust in God and the *ascription* of the prayer "through Jesus Christ our Lord" or "in the name of Christ," our period of prayer is rounded out.

This is not to imply that no prayer is "right" unless it contains all of these elements and in just this order! God demands of us no fixed order. Yet if we habitually lack any of these notes in our praying, something is out of balance. Some such pattern can well be used as a test of whether our praying is many-sided and rightly oriented.

### 3. Some Applications

Let us now run through this pattern again, pausing for a word on some questions that may arise.

About the duty and privilege of praising God there cannot be much question. If we intend to pray at all in any sense that is not simply self-centered demand, the worship of God is central. It is possible to repeat holy words, or feel an emotional lift, or think some good thoughts, or make some fine resolutions without putting God at the center; it is not possible really to *pray* without doing so.

Have we a right to thank God for his bountiful blessings when so many suffer? Not without being sensitive to the agony of the world, penitent for our share in causing it, responsive to what we believe he would have us do about it. "Every one to whom much is given, of him will much be required," says our Lord (Luke 12:48).

What shall we confess? We must not stop with the more overt sins, which most "good people" (by which we generally mean respectable people) are not apt to commit. The grosser sins may be the subtle sins of indifference, evasion, pettiness, compromise, self-seeking, jealousy, irritation, and the like which at times we all

do commit. Sin is epitomized in disobedience to the love commandments, and at this point "None is righteous, no, not one"
(Rom. 3:10).

For what shall we make petition? For a sense of God's presence
and the opportunity to serve him—these above all else. But also
for whatever we need in his service—health of mind and body,
strength of soul, wisdom to act, courage to endure, perseverance
in fidelity when life is hard. Some would stop at this point. But
Jesus taught us to pray, "Give us this day our daily bread." By this
he could hardly have meant spiritual bread alone, for the spirit
is dependent on so many material factors, and these are so vital
to our fullest living, that God must be concerned about these also.

Should one pray for recovery from illness, for safety in battle
or on a journey, for gravely needed economic resources? I see no
good reason for not doing so, with two provisos. The first is that we
must do everything possible to meet these needs ourselves. Prayer
is no excuse for inactivity. The second is that in the kind of
world in which God has placed us, prayer is not the only factor
that determines what takes place. Even Jesus felt constrained
to pray in the Garden, "My Father, if it be possible." We need
equally to recognize that there are some events prayer is not
likely to alter, and at the same time that there is no situation in
which prayer is futile if what we ask of God is the power to meet
victoriously whatever comes.

About prayer for others: many are troubled to understand how
this could be effective except as a means of stirring us to do something for them. If it were *only* that, such prayer would be justified by
its fruits! Yet both the example of Jesus and the experiences of
many who have felt empowered by being prayed for give grounds
for belief that prayer for others means more than that. Jesus
prayed for others as naturally as he prayed for himself, and the
mood of outgoing love prompts one to it. We may not be able to
explain just how God uses our prayers, but it is a true Christian
impulse which bids us do it.

About the prayer of commitment there is no great problem,
except the personal problem of whether we mean it enough to
act costingly in response to our resolves. In the Lord's Prayer we

have prayed countless times, "Thy kingdom come, thy will be done, on earth." But have we always advanced the coming of God's Kingdom by the doing of his will in our corner of the earth? Too often we have not. Likewise we go on speaking great words of assurance such as "thine is the kingdom and the power and the glory, for ever," yet remain snarled up in our petty anxieties as if God did not exist.

The ascription "in Christ's name" is by no means the barren phrase we sometimes make of it. Still less is it a magical incantation as if to ask "what you will" with this formula attached would guarantee fulfillment. To ask in Christ's name is to ask in the spirit of Christ, to ask for what Jesus would pray for if he were in our place, to ask with something of Jesus' insight into the nature of God and his ways with men. If we pray in Christ's name we shall not pray for what is evil, or for selfish gain, or for vengeance on our enemies, or for the upsetting of the orderly ways of God's world in our private interest. To pray in Christ's name is to seek to be more Christlike both in our devotional life and in our active serving of God and neighbor in obedience to the love commandments.

About a century and a half ago the poet Coleridge wrote in *The Rime of the Ancient Mariner* some words which are equally appropriate for the nuclear-space age:

> He prayeth best, who loveth best
> All things both great and small;
> For the dear God who loveth us,
> He made and loveth all.

It is as the heart overflows with love for God and man that our praying is most fully vital, for "out of the abundance of the heart the mouth speaks."

# XIII. THE MECHANICS OF PRAYER[1]

At first glance this title may seem a contradiction in terms. Have we not warned that prayer must not be a mechanical repetition of words? Is it not the very essence of prayer that it must not be a mechanical procedure, but a spiritual experience—the upward lift of the soul toward God? Certainly. Yet still the questions arise. How can I find time to pray? When is the best time? For how long? Where? With what manuals or other helps? Must I kneel and shut my eyes? Do I say "You" or "Thou"? Then perhaps the most searching question of all, "If I pray and nothing happens, what is the matter?"

This chapter is an attempt to give some answers to such questions as these. Since prayer is living experience, another person's experience may differ. Yet every experience rests on some kind of framework, or it is shaky and insecure. It is this framework we shall now be considering.

## 1. *"Take Time To Be Holy"*

These words of an old hymn give an injunction not easy to carry out in our complex world. In fact, failure to take time to pray and to be resolute in keeping it is a major reason for the disappearance of the practice. Due allowance must be made for emergencies and for the fact that there are times when God may be requiring something else of us. Yet to ensure that we do pray instead of letting it slide in the pressure of things, a regular and definite time is necessary.

---

1. "The Mechanics of Prayer" Copyright 1945 Whitmore and Stone.

Such a time does not have to be long-drawn-out, and there is no merit in praying an hour by the clock. It ought never to be so long as to become mechanical or tedious. Fretfulness over pressing duties left untended dispels its value. Yet however brief, it does need to be an unhurried time, carefully guarded against all rivals. It needs to be long enough for serious thought about God and for listening as he speaks to us. For most persons in our high-pressured existence, I believe the best time is a relatively brief period in the morning and a longer time at night. Circumstances, however, may reverse this sequence.

It is a very helpful orientation if, when we awake in the morning, our first thought is of God with gratitude for the new day and its opportunities. This will take only a few seconds but it helps to set the tone of the day. Either then or before the day has progressed very far, we ought to pray what the devotional writers of the past have sometimes called "the prayer of intention." This means placing ourselves and our work in the hands of God, seeking his help, and offering to him whatever gifts he has placed in our hands.

While the "morning watch" is the traditional time for an extended period of private devotions, there are certain advantages in evening prayer. At night one can look back over the hours and think gratefully how God has shown himself in the events of the day, in the splendid souls that have touched ours, in the beauty around us, in new ideas that have challenged us, in suffering and needful humanity that has called to us for service. At night, too, we can search our souls in penitence and lay our shortcomings before God *to leave them there.*

If any problem disturbs us, we are far more likely to sleep restfully and find its solution in the morning if we leave it with God, saying mentally such familiar words as:

> Drop Thy still dews of quietness,
> Till all our strivings cease;

or

> O Love that wilt not let me go,
> I rest my weary soul in Thee.

Brother Lawrence, the monk in a monastery kitchen three centuries ago who authored the immortal little classic "The Practice of the Presence of God," had probably never studied psychology. Yet with a true psychological insight he wrote, "Those whose spirits are stirred by the breath of the Holy Spirit go forward even in sleep."

Morning and evening are for most persons the best times for extended prayer. But what of Paul's injunction to "pray without ceasing"? This can hardly mean continuous spoken or mental prayer, for our full attention is demanded for many things. It means, I think, being in such an attitude of responsiveness to God that the whole of life is offered up to him, and within this orientation prayer can be spoken at any time. To Brother Lawrence, practicing God's presence meant being attentive to God's "inward drawings"; little shafts of prayer spoken silently to God in the midst of work, a petition for help in time of special need, a prayer for forgiveness if sin gets the better of us, an inward song of rejoicing for God's great goodness. This can take place inwardly without any change of posture or interruption of other duties— and who among us would not be the better for such practicing of God's presence?

## 2. Family Prayer

The problem of family prayer is not an easy one, for families today are inclined to scatter in many directions, and without an undesirable dictatorship, no one can fully control the activities of the other members. Yet families need to be knit together in prayer as in other common interests and pursuits.

If we cannot maintain the oldtime "family altar," may we not at least maintain the practice of grace at meals? This has very great value. Its basic purpose is to give thanks to God for his provision for our need. Yet it does something also of great worth to the family. It makes overt the recognition that this is a Christian family. In a sense it makes a sacrament out of a common meal, imparting to it a touch of divine dignity in the recognition of God's presence. It cements the family together through the gratitude expressed for the procuring and the preparation of the food. It turns the thoughts of those partaking outward in compassion toward those less fortunate. Insofar as the children participate in the saying of grace, it gives them experience and growth in Christian fellowship and self-expression. In short, we surrender this practice only at great loss.

I doubt that any statistics are available as to how many children today are taught or encouraged to say bedtime prayers. Probably the practice is less common than formerly. Yet when this is surrendered, children are denied their Christian birthright. Children, in words and thoughts appropriate to their own stage of maturity, can lift up to God their own deepest desires, their feelings of thankfulness, their concern for those they love. Such rootage can be of incalculable worth as the years unroll before them.

### 3. Some Open Options

Some other matters can be canvassed more rapidly. The place for one's private devotions should be as quiet and as worshipful as possible. Yet there is still the possibility of vital inward communion with God in the midst of noise or with other people around. If we waited for all of the distractions to be removed, many of us would never pray!

As to posture, God does not withhold his blessing until we pray in some particular position. Yet it is natural and wise to assume the position which best connotes reverence and the mood of prayer.

The same can be said about diction. Though our words ought to be reverent and appropriate to the nature of God, to be too fussy about words makes one self-conscious and interrupts the vitality of the praying. Traditionally God has been addressed as "Thou"; the more informal "You" is coming into vogue even in some pulpit prayers and this is the usual form in the English Mass of the Roman Catholic Church. In one's private prayers either form may be used, depending on what seems most natural and at the same time reverent. Should we use time-honored prayers of the past, it is best to keep to the form in which they were written instead of altering them.

There are many helpful aids to private devotions, and most of us do better with something to direct our thoughts along particular channels. The one indispensable foundation is the Bible, to which an earlier chapter has been devoted. There are priceless collections of prayers of the ages; there are compilations in the modern mood; there are various devotional aids appearing serially. Temperaments differ, and one must find out by experience what helps him most in his listening to God.

### 4. What If Nothing Happens?

In Chapter Eleven, some common obstacles to fruitfulness in prayer were cited. A review of this chapter might be useful at this point. Yet there are other hindrances which seem to call for further presentation. We shall take a look at these in the remainder of this chapter.

Who of us has not tried to pray and found his thoughts wandering? John Donne, the Dean of St. Paul's three centuries ago, thus graphically describes his experience:

> I throw myself down in my chamber, and I call in and invite God and his angels thither; and when they are there, I neglect God and his angels, for the noise of a fly, for the rattling of a coach, for the whining of a door; I talk on in the same posture of praying, eyes lifted up, knees bowed down, as if I prayed to God; and if God or his angels should ask me when I last thought of God in that prayer, I cannot tell. Sometimes I find that I had forgot what I was about, but when I began to forget it, I cannot tell.[2]

There are several things to do about this situation. One is to realize that everybody's thoughts sometimes wander, and not be too much worried about it. But if it happens habitually there is a reason, and we ought to find the cause and correct it. We may be too tired, or too tense, or too distracted by the things about us or things waiting to be done. Outward distractions are often less subtle barriers than the plethora of extraneous thoughts that clamor for attention. The best corrective is to *care enough* to "rest in the Lord" and let God capture and direct our thinking.

A more baffling problem, particularly in the serious-minded and devout Christian who may have been praying vitally for years,

2. *Works,* Vol. III, p. 476.

is the disturbing discovery that our spirits, seeking spiritual refreshment, are as dry and feeble as before. It seems that we are getting nowhere and that our prayers do not rise any further than our own lips. This is something quite different from sheer laziness or indifference. The saints and mystics of the past knew this experience well, and their writings are full of allusions to such "dry times." Sometimes they called it "the dark night of the soul."[3]

What these devotional writers always counsel is patience, trust in God even when one cannot feel his presence near, and the knowledge that if one waits in faith and patience before God, the dryness will pass. It is not unusual for them to speak from the far side of this hard experience of what God has taught them through it.

Usually, such a wrench in one's prayer life is an aspect of a larger disturbance of one's personality, often accompanied by deep depression. In such instances the help of the physician or the psychiatrist may be needed to get at the cause of it and correct it. Yet almost always there are some things, apart from professional help, that we can do about it. It is essential to avoid both indifference and nervous fretting. The best procedure is to keep one's attention outward as far as possible, do what one can for other people, avoid undue strain but keep profitably busy, avoid making crucial decisions unless one has to, and all the time trust God and wait.

A final hindrance to be spoken of is again one to which earnest Christians are more subject than the careless ones. This is the discouragement and self-condemnation that may arise from unfulfilled expectations. It is possible to become too introspective and get a sense of thwarted ego if one does not make out as well in his praying as he thought he was going to. Prayer ought to lead to soul-searching and induce humility; it ought not to put us in a dither from a sense of failure.

The most subtle of all sins is pride in our spiritual achievements. It is not Christian to be careless about prayer. But neither is it Christian to be self-centered in our earnestness. The backswing

---

3. See my book by this title (Abingdon, 1945) in which I have dealt with this experience at much greater length.

of discouragement when we think *we* ought to be more powerful in prayer than we are savors both of egotism and of lack of faith. Since God hears and answers prayer, though the answer may come in his ways rather than in ours, we can trustfully leave our discouragements like our sins with him *and go forward*.

So, if our praying is rightly centered in God, we do not need to worry overmuch about its effects in us. Dom Chapman, a Roman Catholic devotional writer, said the most important thing that can be said about method when he wrote, "The only way to pray is to pray, and the way to pray well is to pray much. The less I pray, the worse it goes."

# XIV. VOCATION AND WORK IN PROTESTANT PERSPECTIVE

For several chapters we have been discussing the foundations and procedures for disciplined Christian living. Most of what has been said could apply equally to Roman Catholic and Eastern Orthodox Christians, though if written from these viewpoints in personal experience one would certainly have placed a larger emphasis on the Mass and the sacred liturgy. Much of what is said in this chapter is no exclusive prerogative of Protestants, and a number of these matters have been actively discussed and furthered by the Second Vatican Council. However, to avoid misunderstanding it seems best to keep to the above title.

It has been made clear, I trust, that both public and private worship must eventuate in application to the whole of life. Prayer is by no means all that our Lord requires of us. Indeed, it can become a substitute for disciplined Christian living if attention is centered wholly in church attendance and the securing of personal peace of mind and other good feelings. It is such substitution that today brings the strongest charges against the churches. Yet beyond the criticisms, which might be disregarded if based on misinformation, lies the fact that it is a betrayal of the spirit and commands of our Lord. The words spoken by Jesus remain eternally true: "Not every one who says to me, 'Lord, Lord,' shall enter the kingdom of heaven, but he who does the will of my Father who is in heaven" (Matt. 7:21).

There are many great social issues in which the will of the

Father needs to be done that all may have the more abundant life. In the fields of racial equality, peace and world order, the conquest of poverty, illiteracy, hunger, disease, ignorance, alcoholism, narcotics addiction, and a host of other matters Christians ought to be concerned and active. It would not be possible to speak specifically of each of these fields without writing another book— or many of them. We shall instead speak in this chapter of one area which branches out in many directions, the Christian's work and sense of calling within it.

As a setting for what I wish to say I will quote from the report of the section on "The Laity—The Christian in His Vocation" at the Evanston Assembly of the World Council of Churches.

> The time has come to make the ministry of the laity explicit, visible and active in the world. The real battles of the faith today are being fought in factories, shops, offices, and farms, in political parties and government agencies, in countless homes, in the press, radio and television, in the relationship of nations. Very often it is said that the church should "go into these spheres"; but the fact is, that the church *is* already in these spheres in the persons of its laity.[1]

Let us ask first to what extent it is true that the church is already in these spheres; then examine the grounds on which Protestantism rests its convictions in this matter.

## 1. Various Points of View

Consistent with the principle of individual freedom of judgment, Protestants hold various views about the relations of vocation and work to the Christian faith. I believe there are at least six, although they overlap.

1. Perhaps the most prevalent in practice, though seldom defended in principle, is the great divorce. Religion is something that happens on Sunday. To be a good Christian is to attend church faithfully and to serve in some of its many agencies for maintaining the institutional life of one's church and denomination. What happens on Monday through Friday, with its stiff competition, its cutting of corners to make money, its alignment of group against group, its rat-race existence in which good wages are blended

---

1. Report of Section VI, 4.

with a deep insecurity, lies in another world and a different dimension of being.

2. A second understanding of being a Christian on the job is to be honest, cheating nobody in money, time, representation of goods, or the keeping of agreements. In part this stems from an important biblical emphasis on integrity of character; in part from a Puritan, and hence Calvinistic, emphasis on honesty and law observance embedded in our culture. It converges easily with the adage "Honesty is the best policy."

3. A third contemporary approach is an attempt to inject the devotional life into business, industry, and politics. This is illustrated by the gathering of businessmen or Congressmen for prayer breakfasts; the providing of meditation chapels in large plants, sometimes with an industrial chaplain employed to conduct services and do counseling; the lending of well-known business, professional, or political names to evangelistic campaigns and to "religion in American life" emphases. It is related to, though not identical with, the issues raised by prayer and Bible reading in the public schools.

4. In reaction from what has been termed this "job-related piety," the emphasis has fallen on technical competence. It is contended that to be a Christian on the job is simply to do the best work possible within one's chosen field, even though there may be within it moral ambiguities, and in the case of compromise of conscience to trust to the Reformation doctrine of justification by faith for the penitent sinner.

5. In recent years there has been a great ground swell of interest in the ministry of the laity, spearheaded by the World Council and National Council of Churches but taken up by many of the denominations. This movement attempts to recover Martin Luther's insight into the sacredness of the common life and the priesthood of all believers, and to put it into contemporary life. It centers in the idea that the *laos,* the people of God, are not second-class churchmen whose calling it is to pay the minister and help him run the church, but that they themselves are ministers witnessing to their faith in factories and offices, on farms and in legislative halls.

This new impact has taken numerous forms, among which are the evangelical academies of Europe and their American counterparts, the initiation of retreat groups to consider these issues, the starting of local church classes and community schools of religion to help laymen to understand their faith better and thus its bearing on their daily work. Numerous books have been written on this theme, inaugurated by Hendrik Kraemer's *A Theology of the Laity*. The World Council has a full-fledged Department on the Laity, as well as another with the long title "The Department on the Co-operation of Men and Women in Church, Family and Society." Together they publish the periodical entitled *The Laity*.

So significant is this emphasis on the ministry of the laity that it might have been singled out as *the* Protestant approach to vocation and work. I have not done so because there are still many laymen who have not heard of it. Among those who have, it is still an open question how much it has affected their actual attitudes toward their work.

6. An even newer movement seems to have emerged, partly from the preceding but centered more in Dietrich Bonhoeffer's words from prison about "religionless Christianity" in a world "come of age." It forms the setting of Bishop Robinson's chapter on "Worldly Holiness" in his much-discussed *Honest to God*. The main purpose of both men, if I understand them, is to protest a withdrawal from the world and its needs to cultivate an aura of personal holiness. However, it seems to have been seized upon to laud what is called "the fullness of the secular life," and thus to diminish if not obliterate the distinctions between "the world" and biblical faith.

What shall we do with these various points of view? In my judgment, we do well to reject both the divorce of Christian faith and ethics from the claims of the job and the near-identification. Honesty and integrity in business, the devotional life within the whole life, and good work done to the best of one's powers, certainly belong to the Christian's vocation. Yet each of these is a fragmentary approach which becomes false when substituted for a larger vista. The movement to accent the ministry of the laity is more inclusive, and should be extended. Yet it too has its pitfalls, for it ought not to take the place either of professional ministerial leadership or of the layman's faithful support of his own church.

## 2. Key Words in Biblical Faith

Christian vocation within daily work must be grounded in biblical faith. This requires reinterpretation of four key words: vocation, stewardship, witness, and mission.

*Vocation* means far more than a job. It means God's call to serve him by serving other persons with all the gifts of mind or hand, talent and training, time and strength, with which God has endowed us. It calls into the foreground such basic questions as the choice of a vocation, its bearing on family life, both vocational and population mobility, what constitutes adequate income, creativity and the possibility of drudgery, group congeniality versus conflict, the creation of right working conditions. The scope of vocation is the whole of life.

*Stewardship* is a basic note in the Christian doctrine of creation. It centers in the conviction that the "earth is the Lord's and the fulness thereof," and that all we have—whether of material, mental, or spiritual treasure—is the gift of God to be used in trust. Thus it means far more than contributing to church expenses or tithing. In the Genesis story of creation, man is commissioned to "fill the earth and subdue it; and have dominion" over the lesser creatures. Today it is not "the birds of the air" and "the fish of the sea" that make the primary demands on our stewardship, but our participation in great social structures and technological enterprises.

*Witness* to one's faith is a basic requirement of the Christian. In the past this has often been conceived as verbal proclamation by preaching or personal testimony. Its meaning must be greatly enlarged but without the loss of these notes. The report of the New Delhi Assembly of the World Council of Churches has these significant words:

> Those who are enslaved to the gods of this age, race, wealth, power and privilege, are likely to be deaf to the preaching; and also those who are oppressed by the burdens of poverty and drudgery and racial discrimination will be like the Israelites who "hearkened

not for anguish of soul and cruel bondage." Witness to the Gospel must therefore be prepared to engage in the struggle for social justice and for peace; it will have to take the form of humble service and of a practical ministry of reconciliation amidst the actual conflicts of our times.[2]

*Mission* in its most inclusive and authentic meaning converges with vocation, stewardship, and witness. The church in the past has done great things through the witnessing and serving of those designated as its missionaries. There is still need of them, and need of vocational guidance toward the high opportunities of such service. Yet the most basic note in the new emphasis on the ministry of the laity is that every Christian has a mission, a call to witness and service which may take the form of words under appropriate conditions but is always a witness of life in obedience to God and in service to neighbor.

*Callings* must differ greatly in the complexity of modern life and the vast variety of types of work that are open and that need to be done. Yet the Christian's *calling* is always the same—to be the church in obedient discipleship within his church, in his home, in his social relations, in his civic and political duties, and in his daily work. Only so can one live in a full sense the disciplined Christian life that God requires of us.

I trust it has become evident throughout this book that the disciplined Christian life cannot rightly be given the narrow meaning too often attached to it. Spiritual disciplines involve far more than saying prayers and engaging in devotional exercises, though worship and prayer are the energizing center of a life lived as God would have it. The disciplined life means simply the Christian life, lived with serious concern and dedicated commitment in every aspect of human relations.

Inevitably the disciplined life is a costing life, whether in the fulfillment of one's calling in the place of employment, in the family, in the immediate community, or in the larger field of the world. It could not be otherwise, for authentic Christian living has a cross at its center. In the cross we see the perfect union of

---

2. The Report of the Section on Witness, "Reshaping the Witnessing Community," I.

suffering with love, and of utter self-giving with the victory of God over sin and evil. It is to such living that we are called by him who has borne it before us.

Yet it need not, and should not, be a dreary life. It can be a life of joy, even in the midst of the most forbidding outward circumstances. It ought to be a life of continuous thanksgiving. At this side of it we shall look in our concluding chapter.

# XV. "GIVE THANKS UNTO THE LORD"[1]

Running through the book of Psalms like a great refrain is the thought:

O give thanks to the LORD, for he is good;
    for his steadfast love endures for ever!

This upsurge of rejoicing is so deeply embedded in our Christian heritage that these words might well be expected to be the under-girding mood of our lives. On the contrary, we are apt to take them too much for granted, singing them more often with the lips than with the heart and mind. If we say or hear them in church on Sunday, then go out from church to be vexed or upset over small matters, it may be a sign that our disciplined living does not go very deep. There are, to be sure, serious matters over which we ought to be disturbed; yet the gift of joy even in trouble and pain lies close to the center of Christian faith.

## 1. Joy in a Time of Troubles

Though the Psalms were written over a long period, most of them probably date either from the time of the exile or of the return to a barren and desolate land. In any case they do not come out of light-hearted days. Nor do the rejoicings of the early Christians. One of the most significant verses in the book of Acts ends an account of opposition, strife, and beating with the words: "Then they left the presence of the council, rejoicing that they were counted worthy to suffer dishonor for the name"(Acts 5:41).

---

1. "Give Thanks Unto the Lord" Copyright 1948 by Stone and Pierce.

The key to this resolute rejoicing is in the next verse: "And every day in the temple and at home they did not cease teaching and preaching Jesus as the Christ." As for Paul, who did more teaching and preaching and probably also more suffering than any of the others, his attitude is epitomized in words written from a Roman dungeon: "Rejoice in the Lord always; again I will say, Rejoice."

So it has continued to be among the Christians of many times and places. At Thanksgiving time, when we especially honor our debt to the Pilgrim fathers, it will not do to let a sumptuous family dinner blot out the recollection of how they wrestled with death and destiny in a strange new land, yet could gather at the end of the first harvest season to give thanks to God for his goodness. When the odds are most against him the Christian can still praise God with a glad heart, for he has something that no earthly peril or distress can take away.

No thoughtful person has a right to be superficially light-hearted in our time. A good many things are wrong with our world, some of which we looked at in Chapter Two in thinking about the insecurity of these days. When hosts of people die before they should, whether the cause be hunger, neglect, and preventable sickness in great sections of the world or violence, crime, and death on the highways around us; when war brings not only loss of life but great disruption to a society; and when racial and economic injustice combine to produce slums and ghettos, complacency becomes sin. Our country is an oasis of prosperity in a desert of human misery, but within it there are also great pockets of human misery before which God cannot be complacent, nor does he expect us to be.

Nor is this all. Tensions without are reflected in neuroses and conflicts within the inner life. These appear in all sorts of outward conditions, and are often more conspicuous at the higher economic levels because an abundance of possessions can breed restlessness rather than inner security. With all our opulence in America and the many fruits of technology which our Pilgrim fathers neither possessed nor dreamed of, our age is probably more joyless than Puritan days. If we are to rejoice, we must find our grounds of rejoicing in "the God of our salvation" and his good gifts.

## 2. In What Shall We Rejoice?

In what follows I shall speak not only of spiritual blessings in the usual meaning of this term, but of certain great sources of joy which God spreads lavishly in his world and which we may well believe he desires all to have. If some do not possess them, it may be because of constricting circumstances for which others are responsible. Yet often, it is because we have not opened our eyes to see and our hearts to receive them. From both angles, there is a Christian duty.

In what then may we rejoice? First, let us rejoice in the beauty and bounty of the earth and in its nourishing sustenance. About its beauty there is no doubt; it lies strewn about in blue skies, green grass, growing things, flashing waters, bird songs, and all that gives loveliness to nature. As for its sustenance, God has provided enough for all if we will use it right. The great epic of creation in the first chapter of Genesis has as its refrain: "And God saw that it was good." It always has been and still is true that the earth on which God has placed us with its recurrent seasons, its seedtime and harvest, its provision through sun, soil, air, and moisture for the daily bread of humanity, is "the good earth."

Not all are so situated that they can enjoy these blessings to the degree that others can. Christians must be concerned that they are more freely open to all. "Every one to whom much is given, of him will much be required." Furthermore, God's good gifts can be misused, but they need not be. The world of physical nature with its orderly processes can yield atomic bombs for the destruction of life and property in great masses, but it can also yield a constructive release of energy for economic development. God has placed us here as stewards of his creation: let us rejoice in this high calling and use in his service these goods entrusted to us.

Let us rejoice also in the ties of fellowship that God has endowed us with—families, friends, communities of every kind within every sort of human relationship. Here the enjoyment of these blessings is less dependent on economic goods, more upon ourselves. There are, certainly, external conditions that tend to increase loneliness.

Yet loneliness at all levels is often self-induced through failure to respond to those about us. It is a simple, but a very true, saying that "to have friends one must be a friend."

Family ties can be supportive and close-knit, or loose and even disruptive, in any situation. One of the great verses of the Psalms, in the King James Version, reads, "God setteth the solitary in families" (Ps. 68:6). The Revised Standard gives a somewhat different turn, but a very meaningful one, to this passage:

> God gives the desolate a home to dwell in;
> he leads out the prisoners to prosperity;
> but the rebellious dwell in a parched land.

It is appropriate that the great days of the Christian year— Christmas, Easter, and Thanksgiving—should so often be family festivals with home-comings and joyous reunions. It is inappropriate that they should be simply feast days with limited vision. On such occasions in the Christian outlook our eyes see beyond our immediate family and friends to the desolate and the prisoners. Not then only, but certainly then, we must see that the lonely are not left out; that the undernourished, the homeless, and the cold in other lands share in our abundance; that ties of fellowship the world around are brought into firmer, more enduring bonds; that racial barriers of every kind are broken down in the awareness that we are all one family in the great household of God.

One family though we are, each of us is also a citizen of a nation. Let us rejoice in our nation, and in its great potentialities for moral leadership among the nations of the world. Over the hall of humanities in the university I attended was carved in stone the inscription "Above all nations is humanity." We may well believe this to be true without having less of patriotic devotion to our own nation. This does not mean automatic approval of all one's nation does; the best service may lie in constructive criticism and the expression of one's dissenting judgment to legislators and others in authority. In any case, it calls for responsible participation. Christians who love America can best show their devotion by putting the weight of their voices, votes, and acts on the side of racial justice, the elimination of poverty, and the human ills that accompany it here and around the world, on the support of the United Nations and the increase of international vision and service.

To the present, war has cursed the earth. Two world wars in one generation, followed by two more wars less extensive but nevertheless horribly destructive, should prevent any complacency. Yet war is not inevitable. It has been affirmed many times by church bodies and by informed students of world affairs that the best way to avert war is through economic advancement, improved conditions of social welfare which will counteract the deceptive promises of Communism, and the spread of a democratic respect for human rights and fundamental freedoms. Let us rejoice that these channels are still open, and act in that faith.

Finally, and throughout all our other rejoicing, let us give thanks to God for his greatest of all gifts to men—the gift of himself in Jesus Christ, our Lord. Through him our fears are overcome, our sins are forgiven, in weakness we find strength, our broken lives are made whole. "For it is the God who said, 'Let light shine out of darkness,' who has shone in our hearts to give the light of the knowledge of the glory of God in the face of Christ." Because we have this light to guide us we can say, even in the darkest times, that we are "afflicted in every way, but not crushed; perplexed, but not driven to despair; persecuted, but not forsaken; struck down, but not destroyed" (2 Cor. 4:6, 8). Many of our fellow Christians, not only in times past but in our own day, have passed through such deep waters with their faith undimmed and souls victorious. Shall we be less faithful?

This time in which we live may well be a time of soul-searching, of sober concern for the welfare of humanity here and abroad, of realistic endeavor to further the peace of the world through firmer bonds of fellowship and the meeting of basic human needs. These tasks not only call for disciplined Christian living, but they are themselves exacting enough to put iron in our souls if we fulfill our calling faithfully.

These are serious days, but it is no time for faintheartedness or despair. Instead of surrender to inaction either through the deploring of evil days or the self-satisfied enjoyment of good

fortune, let us live like Christians! Then every day can be a day
in which to say with the psalmist of old,

> Praise the LORD!
> O give thanks to the LORD, for he is good;
>     for his steadfast love endures for ever!